THE SOCIAL WORK GENERAL PRACTITIONER:

A Book of Readings for the Undergraduate Social Work Major

Edited by
Donald F. Fausel
Arizona State University

With the assistance of
Ross A. Klein

MSS Information Corporation
655 Madison Avenue, New York, N.Y. 10021

This is a custom-made book of readings prepared for the courses taught by the editor, as well as for related courses and for college and university libraries. For information about our program, please write to:

MSS INFORMATION CORPORATION
655 Madison Avenue
New York, New York 10021

MSS wishes to express its appreciation to the authors of the articles in this collection for their cooperation in making their work available in this format.

Library of Congress Cataloging in Publication Data

Fausel, Donald F comp.
The social work practitioner.

1. Social service--Addresses, essays, lectures.
I. Title.
[HV37.F37] 361'.008 73-7996
ISBN 0-8422-0276-5

CONTENTS

PREFACE

After twenty years of struggling, baccalaureate programs in social work finally achieved legitimacy when the National Association of Social Workers admitted in 1970, as full members, individuals who had bachelor degrees from undergraduate programs that are approved by the Council on Social Work Education (CSWE).[1] Reinforced by CSWE, an increasing number of undergraduate programs are giving priority to the preparation of students for practice.[2] In pursuing this primary goal of preparation for entry level positions in social work a choice of practice approaches is possible. This reader provides material to support the model of the generalist or general practitioner, an approach which seems appropriate for training on the undergraduate level.

Traditionally, distinctions among casework, group work, and community organization have been made in social work practice. In recent years, these boundaries have been strained. Although many graduate programs are taking a more integrated approach to practice, they still seem at least in the second year of training, to focus on these specializations.[3] A particular graduate school may well opt to train clinicians to provide needed services in the more traditional agencies, but it would be completely unrealistic to expect a B.A. social worker to offer such specialized services. Although not a clinician, his contacts with consumers in a multi-purpose-service center or as a service worker in a welfare department are in a broad sense "therapeutic." Although not a group therapist, he might be called upon to work with a group of tenants in a housing project to help facilitate their airing grievances against the management. Although not a policy-planner, he might be in a position to work with welfare mothers as they organized to effect some change in the welfare system.

The old adages of "a little knowledge being a dangerous thing" and "jack of all trades and master of none" are certainly appropriate to bear in mind. It is incumbent upon the undergraduate social work educator to equip students with not only knowledge of what he can

1. *NASW News*, (National Association of Social Workers), Vol. 15, No. 2, January, 1970.

2. Pins, Arnulf. "The 'New Look' in Social Work Education," *The Current Scene in Social Work Education*, N.Y., Council on Social Work Education, 1971, p. 4.

3. See *Concentrations and Special Learning Opportunities in the Masters of Social Work Curricula of Graduate Schools of Social Work, 1971-1972*, Mimeographed, N.Y., Council on Social Work Education.

do, but of what he cannot do; of skills for what he can do as a beginning practitioner and not to water-down skills more appropriate for a MSW; and of knowledge and skills in how and when to make appropriate referrals.

This reader will attempt to present the basic values, knowledge, and skills that a B.A. social worker needs to practice as a generalist. A number of books and readers in recent years have purported to adapt the general practitioner model. However, in essence, they seem merely to have changed the traditional terms of casework, group work, and community organization to social work with individuals, groups, and communities and proceeded to talk about the three traditional methods. In order to avoid this pitfall we have adapted the model presented by Allen Pincus and Anne Minahan.[4] Although primarily directed at first year students in graduate school, it seems most appropriate for the undergraduate general practitioner. Their conceptualization of the types of systems (change-agent system, client system, target system, and action system) and the skills required by the social worker (data collection, data analysis, and intervention) cut across all three traditional boundaries as well as the practitioner's level of skill. The articles chosen for the reader will often use the terms casework, group work, and community organization, but we will be using the articles as they relate to collecting or analyzing data as it applies to individuals, groups, or communities and selecting the appropriate interventive techniques. In other words, we are suggesting that we do not first study how to be caseworkers or group workers, but that we first learn how to collect data for work with individuals, groups, and communities, then how to analyze it for each of these client systems, and how to choose the interventive strategy and role for the change-agent.

This task is indeed presumptuous and makes no claim to offer anything more than a tentative framework for the general practitioner at the baccalaureate level. The reader has been prepared out of necessity. Complaints from students about several popular texts and the problems with access to journal references, especially the realities of students attending evening classes have prompted us to put under one cover those articles which we consider basic and a bare minimum for stimulating directed discussion and understanding of the social work process as practiced by the general practitioner.

It is hoped that the selected bibliography at the end of each section will stimulate students to do further readings. The "Group Discussion and Activities" are intended just as suggestions for helping the

4. Pincus, Allen and Anne Minahan. "Toward a Model for Teaching a Basic First-Year Course in Methods of Social Work Practice," *Innovations in Teaching Social Work Practice;* ed. Lilian Ripple, N.Y., CSWE, 1970, pp. 34-57.

student to develop skills in social intervention. The group itself should be an experience the instructor can use to integrate the materials, to apply his knowledge, and to develop skills in social intervention.

We are particularly grateful for the encouragement and assistance given in the preparation of this reader by our colleagues in the undergraduate program at Arizona State University, Dr. E. Elizabeth Guillot and Mrs. Naomi Harward.

THE VALUES AND PRINCIPLES OF THE PROFESSION OF SOCIAL WORK

The philosophical concepts which are basic to the practice of social work have remained constant despite differences of opinion as to how they are operationalized. The primary value of belief in the dignity and worth of the individual has been a hallmark of the social work profession. It is from this cardinal value that all the other values and principles of the profession flow. It is well established that these values are common to all methods and levels of practice. The MSW worker who communicates to a client a fundamental lack of a sense of his worth, is less a professional than a para-professional who demonstrates an intuitive sensitivity for the client's dignity as a human being.

The following articles are suggested to stimulate class discussion about the profession of social work and its values and principles. In-put from consumers of the service indicates that the values which are so ably articulated by social workers are often not put into practice. It is just as essential for the B.A. social worker to have incorporated these values as it is for the MSW social worker.

To put these values in the framework of the profession of social work it is first necessary to have a firm grasp on the attributes of a profession and what the term professionalization means in the 1970's. Donald Feldstein's article "Do We Need Professions In Our Society? Professionalism Versus Consumerism," challenges the conventional wisdom that has leaned heavily on Greenwood's formulation, traces the evolution and nature of the concepts of profession and professionalization, and offers his suggestions for making social work more responsive to the needs of the consumers of the service.

Bernard Coughlin defines values, discusses their importance to the individual and society and analyzes the major values of the profession: 1) The person's dignity and worth; 2) Brotherhood of man; 3) Human rights; 4) Responsibility to others; 5) Self-realization.

It also is suggested that at this point those principles that flow from the primary values be discussed. The principles that Felix Bistex has outlined, although directed at the casework relationship, are generic to social work with any size system, and essential for any activity that the social worker is involved with.[1] Individualization, self-determination, controlled emotional involvement,

1. Bistex, Felix. THE CASEWORK RELATIONSHIP, Chicago Loyola Press, 1957.

purposeful expression of feelings, acceptance and a non-judgmental attitude, and confidentiality are necessary ingredients for forming meaningful helping relationships with individuals, groups, or communities. Again the student will have to do more than just memorize these principles. Hopefully through discussions and interaction with his peers he will begin to internalize them.

The Younghusband article reports the results of a two week seminar on intercultural perspectives in social work education related to values, function, and method. Although it does not specifically address itself to the major ethnic minority cultures in this country, its approach is universal and can be used to stimulate discussion about similar cultural differences in the Black, Chicano, and Indian communities. The seminar did not confine itself to values. It took a generic approach to social work function, systems, and methods.

In spite of the fact that the profession still adheres to the basic values, social work practice reflects changes in social values, family life, urban life, bureaucratic and economic structures. Dr. Meyer's article illustrates material which indicates that social values expressed nearly a centruy ago presented a markedly different social philosophy from that of today. It also supports our basic thesis that the traditional separation of social work methods is no longer justified and the inevitable fusion will alter the boundary lines between fields of practice.

BY DONALD FELDSTEIN

Do We Need Professions in Our Society? Professionalization versus Consumerism

■ ***Professionalization versus consumerism is one of the basic conflicts in society. In this article the author discusses the evolution and nature of the concepts of profession and professionalization and offers suggestions for reforming social work that will make the profession more responsive to the consumers of service.*** ■

ONE OF SOCIETY'S contemporary conflicts is the struggle between those striving to maintain professional standards and those new constituencies that are challenging the professional in the name of consumerism or new careers. Two rather dichotomous trends exist side by side in contemporary society: (1) the trend toward a greater technocracy, a dependence on scientific skills and expertise, and power exercised over larger occupational groups in professional territories as well as over consumers of the professional's services and (2) the trend toward consumerism, plebiscitary politics, participatory democracy, and open entry into all previously closed groups. The second trend is based on the claim that masses of people have the right to increased decision-making power regarding the kinds of services that are offered and they receive from society.

DONALD FELDSTEIN, MSW, *is Director, Center for Social Work and Applied Social Research, Fairleigh Dickinson University, Teaneck, New Jersey.*

EFFECT ON SOCIAL WORK

This conflict affects social work because of social work's concern for open opportunity and democracy generally, but also because the profession itself has been the target of attack as a closed, restrictive system. Social work is particularly exposed for a number of reasons. Its professional expertise is less shrouded in mystery, magic, and special languages than some of the physical sciences. It operates in the very arenas where the confrontations are taking place. Social work is, therefore, more susceptible to demands for entry by paraprofessional groups and for decision-making and power by consumer groups.

Should one conclude from this confrontation that either professionalism or democracy must go? Is it possible to achieve an accommodation that will protect the rights of the public and maintain the concept of profession? Is this even desirable? How should the insecure social work profession

Reprinted with permission of the National Association of Social Workers, from SOCIAL WORK, Vol. 16, No. 4 (October 1971) pp. 5-11.

respond to this challenge? In this article the author discusses the evolving concepts of a profession and professionalization and some of the implications of the present understanding of professionalization for society and for social work.

ATTRIBUTES OF A PROFESSION

In 1957 Greenwood published an article on the attributes of a profession.[1] Since then, conceptions of profession and professionalization have evolved and changed considerably, but in the social work literature writers continue to lean on the Greenwood formulation, as though it were the last word on the subject.

Greenwood specifies five attributes by which one might recognize whether an occupational group is a profession: (1) possession of systematic theory, (2) authority recognized by the clientele, (3) sanction of the community to operate, (4) a code of ethics in client-colleague regulations, and (5) a professional culture (e.g., associations). In this formulation, Greenwood does not stray far from A. M. Carr-Saunders's classic formulation of a profession's five attributes, although the latter conceived of the categories in slightly narrower and more specific terms. Carr-Saunders's attributes of a profession are as follows: (1) the acquisition of special skills and training, (2) setting of minimum fees, (3) professional association, (4) code of ethics, and (5) enforcing minimum qualifications for entering and thus achieving professional status.[2]

Goode tries to condense the basic characteristics of a profession to two: (1) prolonged special training in a body of abstract knowledge and (2) a service orientation or collectivity. This second characteristic is in a context of authority recognized by the clientele. For instance, in his address to librarians, Goode suggests that they cannot truly be a profession because, unlike doctors who can prescribe medicine to their clients whether those clients like it or not, librarians are not in a position to prescribe reading materials for their clients.[3]

Barber's formulation also belongs in this grouping.[4] It lists four attributes along the same lines: (1) a community orientation, (2) self-control and autonomy over work, (3) generalized and systematic knowledge, and (4) a reward structure based on more than money.

These formulations have one thing in common: they all assume that it is possible to examine some occupational group and decide on the basis of a checklist of attributes whether that occupation is in fact a profession. They assume that one can give a definite answer, based on specific characteristics, to the question of whether a specific occupational group is a profession.

SEQUENTIAL STEPS

Caplow moves in another direction in the analysis of professions or what is now called the process of professionalization.[5] He is less concerned with the knowledge and skills a group must possess to define itself professionally and more interested in the sequential development of certain characteristics that mark the steps in the professionalization process. Caplow identifies four sequential steps: (1) establishment of a professional association, (2) assertion of a monopoly over some area of service, (3) development of a code of ethics, and (4)

[1] Ernest Greenwood, "Attributes of a Profession," *Social Work,* Vol. 2, No. 3 (July 1957), pp. 45–55.

[2] A. M. Carr-Saunders, *Professions: Their Organization and Place in Society* (Oxford, England: Clarendon Press, 1928).

[3] William Goode, "The Librarian: From Occupation to Profession?" *Library Quarterly,* Vol. 31, No. 4 (October 1961), pp. 306–318.

[4] Bernard Barber, "Some Problems in the Sociology of the Professions," *Daedalus,* Vol. 92, No. 4 (Fall 1963), pp. 669–688.

[5] Theodore Caplow, *The Sociology of Work* (Minneapolis: University of Minnesota Press, 1954).

political agitation for certification and licensing. There are two other steps that are concurrent: (1) control of training facilities and (2) the development of working relationships with other groups. Wilensky goes even further.[6] He develops historical studies to determine the sequence of the characteristics mentioned by Caplow. He finds that most commonly the training school was the first, professional association was the second, and other characteristics followed.

RITES OF PASSAGE

Fine makes explicit what some of the previously mentioned sociologists are implying in their definitions.[7] While Greenwood went so far as to say that a body of knowledge rather than skills was characteristic of a profession, Fine says that neither skill nor knowledge is the criterion of a profession—rites of passage and their acceptance by the public are the key to the professionalization process.

This change in approach is fundamental. As Hughes states:

> I passed from the false question, "Is this occupation a profession?" to the more fundamental one, "What are the circumstances in which people in an occupation attempt to turn it into a profession and themselves into professional people?" [8]

In terms of discrete attributes, there may not be any such entity as a profession—only steps in the development of professionalization. One group may be more professionalized than another, but the argument about whether a group has the necessary attributes of a profession is somewhat meaningless.

Does this mean that there is no such thing as a profession? No. But the definition of a profession or a professional is not based on a strict rule of logic or the possession of given attributes. There is a progression of steps in professionalization. At some point in the process a group is called a profession. Professional groups make a professional of whomever they say is one (if society accepts their definition). Professional associations develop rules and codes of ethics. Whoever falls within their definition and is subject to their code is a professional. When their definitions are too restrictive, they are attacked from without; if their definitions become ridiculously loose, they fall apart from within. Thus some reasonable balance is maintained. But there is certainly an element of arbitrariness in deciding who is a professional.

Thus there are various ingredients that contribute to the professionalization of occupational groups—a body of knowledge, training, schools, a code of ethics, and so forth. Professional associations decide how much of the various ingredients are necessary for acceptance into given professions. If the definition is demanding enough, the occupation will achieve public acceptance as a profession; if not (barbering, for instance), it will simply be licensed without professional status—no matter what the group calls itself.

MEANS VERSUS ENDS

The presence of a long period of study or of calling should not obscure the fact that the goal of professionalization is a kind of license—the right granted by society to limit and define practice. But even now most of the definitions seem to ignore the crucial difference between means toward and the end of professionalization. They

---

6 Harold L. Wilensky, "The Professionalization of Everyone?" *American Journal of Sociology*, Vol. 70, No. 2 (September 1964), pp. 137–158.

7 Sidney Fine, *Guidelines to the Design of New Careers* (Kalamazoo, Mich.: W. E. Upjohn Institute, 1967).

8 Everett C. Hughes, as quoted in Howard M. Vollmer and Donald L. Mills, eds., *Professionalization* (Englewood Cliffs, N.J.: Prentice-Hall, 1966), p. v.

include both together as if they were the same.[9]

The means are the various rites of passage—training schools, bodies of knowledge, professional associations, codes of ethics, and so forth. The end is autonomous expertise, the community's acceptance of the profession's right to set its own rules for practice and not to be governed by the consumer. There is a fundamental difference between this goal and the various steps that professions use to achieve that goal. Autonomous expertise is the goal of professionalization. Professions succeed to the extent that society permits them to operate autonomously.

Autonomous expertise used to consist of the right to do something directly to or with clients. But the autonomous expertise that professions are claiming today tends to be related more to territory (e.g., the right to decide who may administer what drugs to whom) than to specific practice (e.g., the right to administer drugs). Thus the surgeon-general of the U.S. Public Health Service could describe himself as "a member of that rather small group which administers the enormous health industry—in short, a physician."[10]

If a profession is to function with any kind of power, it must control not only the activity of its members, but the activity of the other workers in the territory or industry over which it claims expertise. Professionals increasingly are working in and through organizations and group practices so that this aspect of the professional's role becomes increased. In fact, one of the emerging differences between professionals and licensed technicians may be the profession's control over other parts of the system.

FOUR CRITICISMS

Given the nature of professions and current social trends, it is not difficult to understand the present conflicts. As a technocratic society becomes increasingly dependent on expertise, the complaints against the professions take four forms:

Professions have excluded too many from entry. Since professional definitions are somewhat arbitrary, since new careerist and other groups see this, professions come under attack for refusing membership to specific groups.

Autonomous expertise is antidemocratic. Because of the growth of a planned society, consumers cannot depend on the laws of the marketplace—supply and demand—to dictate the quality of services. In a laissez-faire capitalist system, one could argue that consumers were free to accept or reject a given service and that the laws of the marketplace would dictate that they would eventually receive the services they wanted and for which they were willing to pay. However, services are increasingly government sponsored and offered by right; standards are centrally set and become similar. Therefore, consumers argue that they must exert power at the source. Consumers who wish to affect the quality of the services they receive feel they must exert some control over the standards set by and operations of expert groups.

Professions make public policy through their control of larger territories. Attorneys may represent clients, physicians may treat patients. But when bar associations set the rules for certain legal procedures or medical groups affect decisions on forms of medical insurance, they are using their expertise to make public policy, when policy should be made "by the people."

[9] Even the recent *The Semi-Professions and Their Organization,* Amitai Etzioni, ed. (New York: Free Press, 1969), uses a definition of profession that includes length of time in training, body of specialized knowledge, and so forth along with degree of freedom from societal control, as though all were on the same plane. Only Goode continues to stress the centrality of self-control. *See* William Goode, "The Theoretical Limits of Professionalization," in Etzioni, pp. 266–313.

[10] As quoted in *Training Health Service Workers: The Critical Challenge* (Washington, D.C.: U.S. Government Printing Office, 1966), p. 61.

The professions have not "delivered." The medical profession has not brought about health, the legal profession has not brought about justice.

SHOULD PROFESSIONS EXIST?

If professions have not been functional—keeping the unfit from practice, permitting the fit to practice, serving the needs of society—then perhaps they should not exist. But what would take their place? "Freedom" for any individual to hang out his shingle and practice in any field? Although laissez-faire economists and radical critics approach such a position, neither seems prepared to pursue it seriously.[11] If professions were abolished, new groups would arise to set rules for responsible entry into practice. Entry requirements into a given area of practice should exist; hence professions should exist, whatever name a restructured society might give them.[12]

If professionalism in society is needed and at least some of the criticisms of professions have a basis in fact, then the challenge to society is to reform the professions. If society moves quickly and substantively, reform (rather than revolution) is still possible. Professions have enough to give so that protesters can be co-opted. That is, power can be shared and entry opened to a degree that will dissipate the demand for destruction of institutions. Such reform should take several directions.

REFORM

The improvement of professional services, vital for its own sake, is probably *not* the key to the dissipation of conflict between professionals and consumers. When students seek legitimate power, their bill of particulars always includes the failures of the educational establishment. But there is no evidence that protests are greatest at the worst universities, nor is there evidence that the greatest protests are directed at those professions that are furthest from fulfilling their promises. The very idea that medicine could or should be expected to bring about health, that law could or should be expected to bring about justice is a new one. The demand is a function of the affluent, immediate, "satisfaction-now" society in which we live. Professions have always been imperfect and probably always will be. Improved services should be the first priority, but not in the expectation that this will stop protest.

Rational, sensible rules. What is crucial is that rules, limits, and the bases for credentials must become more rational and sensible. One can point to the value of magic, mystery, and ritual, but a profession under attack must be able to justify its restrictions in terms of client and consumer benefit. Traditions simply cannot be maintained for their own sake.

Access to the professions must be made easier. Although one may be committed to formal educational institutions, it is still possible to acknowledge that such institutions are not the only vehicles for achieving levels of competence. At present they are the best that society has developed for formalizing a system under which large

---

11 Milton Friedman, in *Capitalism and Freedom* (Chicago: University of Chicago Press, 1962), pp. 137–160, builds a case for a free market in place of occupational licensure. He pictures medical "department stores" and entrepreneurs operating freely and the public being protected by the reputation of the various sellers of service. He catalogues professional abuses, but does not deal with the right of free people to create mechanisms to help them make selections in a complex society, nor does he seem to be aware of the abuses of department stores and entrepreneurs. Matthew P. Dumont, "The Changing Face of Professionalism," *Social Policy*, Vol. 1, No. 1 (May/June 1970), pp. 26–31, talks of a "new professionalism" that has "indifference to credentials." But what the romantic rhetoric does not make clear is whether this means the end of professionalism. In any event there is no coherent intellectual movement calling for an end to occupational licensure or professions.

12 For a discussion of this theme, *see* Charles Frankel, "Social Values and Professional Values," *Journal of Education for Social Work*, Vol. 5, No. 1 (Spring 1969), pp. 29–36.

numbers of people can be brought to given levels of knowledge or skill. Of course, individuals may reach these same levels through life experiences, independent study, and the like. The problem is to join those individuals who have achieved levels of competence through maturity and experience to a formal credential system that may be necessary for maintaining services in this society. Professional groups will need to take the initiative in developing various alternatives to the traditional routes toward professional competence. This need not mean the breakdown of standards. When a strong commitment exists, such alternative methods can usually be found, so that large numbers of the poor and disadvantaged can be brought into professions from which they have been excluded.

Social policy decisions, which are the right of the body politic, will need to be made by the people and not by professional groups or associations. The dividing line between decisions that must be made on the basis of professional expertise and those that are social policy decisions, properly made by the consumer, is at best hazy. However difficult it may be, professions will need to draw that line. Many professions are less accustomed than is social work to such policy-making bodies as boards of directors and advisory committees. This inability of professionals to be responsible to the community was one of the several factors that aggravated the educational crisis during the 1968 schoolteachers' strike in New York City.

SOCIAL WORK'S INSECURITY

If the professions—including social work—move in these directions quickly and substantively, the desire of most people to have access to power will probably overwhelm the desire of the few to destroy institutions. Social work is faced with another problem as well—professionalism. That is, social work has been insecure as a profession almost from its inception. It established itself by confirming graduate education as the basic professional prerequisite in a long and sometimes bitter struggle with proponents of baccalaureate social work. All the available stratagems of mystery and magic were used. Still most practice was performed by individuals with bachelor's degrees.

Now the situation has shifted dramatically. The National Association of Social Workers' policy-making body—the Delegate Assembly—has decreed and the membership has confirmed by referendum that graduates of baccalaureate programs in social welfare are to be accepted as professional members of the association, subject to the same code of ethics and discipline and listed in the same professional directory. Not all professionals or all segments of the profession comprehend or are ready to act on the significance of this major change. They talk of the bachelor's degree social worker as being the "first practitioner" but not the "first professional." They talk of the need for better task differentiation among different levels. However, the baccalaureate social worker has more than enough of the basic characteristics of a professional so that the public will recognize the professional status that the professional association, which is the arbiter of such matters, has granted him. Baccalaureate and master's degree social workers represent two levels of professional practice, as is true with other fields as well —e.g., education or engineering.

TASK DIFFERENTIATION

The problem of task differentiation is not so lightly dismissed. It is not clear which level of practitioner can perform specific tasks most effectively. But this lack of definition need not become a major barrier to the full acceptance and utilization of baccalaureate social workers. Here, too, there is something to be learned from the nature of professionalism.

The difference between professional and nonprofessional groups, such as paraprofessionals and technicians, in the same field is that the professional has permission to perform certain functions that nonprofessionals do not. Therefore, it is necessary to differentiate tasks formally so that appropriate divisions can be set. However, once a person is accepted as a professional, he has license to act within the profession. For example, the three levels of engineers are all engineers. It is assumed that the master's- and doctoral-degree engineers can do some things that some baccalaureates cannot, but that is demonstrated in the market. There are variations and no one gets too concerned about formal task differentiations. Even in medicine the various specialties for advanced competence in certain fields are simply aids to the consumer or institution, but any physician with an MD has the ethical and legal right to practice medicine in its fullest sense.

If we believe that the higher levels of education do in fact produce more skills, we need not be frightened by having several levels, all defined as professional. Although more work must be done on task differentiation in social work (as is now being done), the acceptance of the baccalaureate social worker into full social work practice must be adjusted to fully and quickly to provide a strong and rational professional base for leadership in the social welfare arena. If this problem is resolved, social work will then be able to address itself to the technical, paraprofessional, and indigenous workers whose appropriate tasks do need more careful definition.

If social work can finally come to peace with the old baccalaureate-graduate problem that has bedeviled it for so long, it may not only survive as a profession, but may be strengthened and unified enough to provide leadership in meeting its own problems with consumer and paraprofessional groups in a world that needs both better standards and more freedom.

Value Orientation in Social Welfare

by BERNARD J. COUGHLIN, S.J.

VALUE IS A SUBJECT that is much discussed but perhaps too vaguely understood and variously defined. Most of the literature on value is by philosophers and anthropologists and, more recently, by psychologists and sociologists. Social workers recognize the need to clarify the concept and its function in social welfare; but we are aware of a gap in the development of the theory of value and its application to practice. The task of bridging that gap is one for many minds and many years. My more modest purpose is to explore one facet of value, namely, the contribution that church-related social welfare makes to the value orientation of the American social welfare system.

Value pertains to, and is part of, the broader concept of culture. Definitions of culture vary according to one's bent and view. In general, it refers to a design for living or to the patterns of behavior that are distinctive of a group. Culture, therefore, includes the traditional ideas of a people and their ways of doing things. Kluckhohn and Kelly, for example, define culture as "a historically derived system of explicit and implicit designs for living, which tends to be shared by all or specially designated members of a group." [1]

Now a group's design for living is the result of a complex of conscious and unconscious ideas and beliefs; and these ideas and beliefs which guide the group in choosing its style of life are called "values." There are three general types of beliefs or convictions, and a brief analysis of them conveys additional insight into the concept of value. First, the group possesses and shares certain

[1] Clyde Kluckhohn and William H. Kelly, "The Concept of Culture," in Ralph Linton, ed., *The Science of Man in the World Crisis* (New York: Columbia University Press, 1945), p. 98.

SOCIAL WELFARE FORUM, 1967, pp. 115-126.

kinds of knowledge, beliefs, or theories about nature and man, society, time and space; and these beliefs are expressed in a certain way and through certain symbols. These are the "cognitive values" of the culture. Second, the group has a common idea of beauty as it is expressed in certain forms and styles that to the group are thought to be pleasing to sight and sound and sense. There exists, as it were, an aesthetic group sense. These are called the "aesthetic values." Finally, the group shares a certain conception of good and bad behavior, of what is right and wrong. This is expressed in the mores and the laws of a society and in the codes of ethics of business and professional groups. These are called the society's "moral values."

Value, therefore, pertains to the true, the beautiful, and the good; but more than this, the society develops norms with regard to them. Every society holds some things to be false and other things to be true, and these it values. Every society has its idea of what is ugly and what is beautiful, and this it values. And every society has its idea, on the one hand, of what is bad, what is wrong and "ought not to be done," and on the other hand, of what is good, what is right and "ought to be done," and this it values. Every culture, therefore, develops not only values but value standards according to which it differentiates the true from the false, the beautiful from the ugly, and the good from the bad.[2] A value standard means, as Tolman states, not only that a culture encourages cognitive, aesthetic, and moral values, but that it tends "to impose its rules or *standards* about just what is 'so' or true, what is beautiful, and what is good." [3]

There are several corollaries to this that are important to the understanding of value. First, it is clear that value is more than preference. Preference merely assigns priority or at most indicates like and dislike. Value conveys obligation and responsibility with respect to a standard of the true, the beautiful, and the good. Value, then, is more than merely what one desires. Clyde Kluck-

[2] Talcott Parsons and Edward A. Shils, "Systems of Value-Orientation," in Parsons and Shils, eds., *Toward a General Theory of Action* (Cambridge, Mass.: Harvard University Press, 1959), pp. 159 ff.

[3] Edward C. Tolman, "Value Standards, Pattern Variables, Social Roles, Personality," *ibid.*, p. 344.

hohn defines value as "a conception, explicit or implicit, distinctive of an individual or characteristic of a group, of the desirable which influences the selection from available modes, means, and ends of action." [4] The *desirable* in this definition influences action because it is true, or because it is beautiful, or because it is good. Again in Kluckhohn's words: "A value is not just a preference but is a preference which is felt and/or considered to be justified—'morally' or by reasoning or by aesthetic judgments, usually by two or all three of these." [5]

Secondly, value as such does not exist in reality. Value is not a goal, but it influences and directs individuals and groups in the selection of goals. Value is a conception and therefore not observable in reality. Value is the desirable as conceived by the individual and group and as influencing individual and group choices. The desirable influences choice because its concept has cognitive and affective content which conveys what must be believed and admired and done.

This is not to say, however, that value is unrelated to reality. On the contrary, value is based on nature as understood by man. There is an ontological relationship between what is and what ought to be. Thus Maslow says: "Do you want to find out what you ought to be? Then find out what you are! . . . The description of what one ought to be is almost the same as the description of what one deeply is." [6] What nature ought to be is nature's self-realization. Man is fulfilled by being what man should be. Obviously, this is a dynamic conception of nature. Nature contains within itself the seeds of the flower, for life is a process of self-realization. Again, in Maslow's words, "the facts themselves carry, within their own nature, suggestions of what *ought* to be done with them" [7]; "the more clearly something is seen or known, and

[4] Clyde Kluckhohn *et al.*, "Values and Value-Orientations in the Theory of Action," *ibid.*, p. 395.

[5] *Ibid.*, p. 396.

[6] Abraham H. Maslow, "Fusion of Facts and Values," *American Journal of Psychoanalysis*, XXIII (1963), 121.

[7] *Ibid.*, p. 130. This, of course, is a rejection of certain assumptions of nineteenth-century positivistic science which sought to extricate itself from values. The world of facts was thought to be totally different from the world of values; and science had everything to do with facts, but nothing to do with values. Values were "unscientific" and so relegated to the nonscientists, to philosophers, poets, and re-

the more true and unmistakeable something becomes, the more ought-quality it acquires." [8]

Value statements, therefore, are existential statements. Clyde Kluckhohn is explicit: "There can be no doubt that an individual's or a group's conceptions of what is and of what ought to be are intimately connected." [9] They are related to reality as known and as the individual or group think reality should be. " 'This is a value for me' is an existential proposition about me." [10] "This is a value to me" means "this to me is the good." As Thorndike says, "judgements of value are simply one sort of judgements of fact." [11] Value, then, is not fully given by nature but presupposes nature and is limited by it. Existential propositions describe nature, and then value propositions say, in effect:

> This appears to be naturally possible. It does not exist or does not fully exist, but we want to move toward it, or, it already exists but we want to preserve and maintain it. Moreover, we aver that this is a proper or appropriate or justified want.[12]

The importance of values to the individual is well recognized; less well recognized is their importance to the society. Three critical areas or phases in the society's endeavor today especially call for a common value-orientation and ideal among individuals and social institutions.

First, a value-orientation gives stability to the society. Individuals in the group and institutions in the social system need mutual trust and confidence. Social stability requires both that an individual can rely on the action of other individuals and that an institution can rely on the actions of other institutions. Reliance comes from the reasonable assurance of what others in given circumstances will do. Action is difficult where one is not sure of the response of others. Therefore, a group is unified and can act as a group

ligionists, who, because their concerns reached beyond positivistic science, were thought to be unconcerned with the world of fact. Of course, such a conception of science casts values out of the realm of human knowledge.

[8] *Ibid.*, p. 127.

[9] Kluckhohn *et al.*, *op. cit.*, p. 391.

[10] *Ibid.*

[11] E. L. Thorndike, "Science and Values," *Science*, LXXXIII, No. 2140 (1936), 2.

[12] Kluckhohn *et al.*, *op. cit.*, pp. 393–94.

only if certain basic values are recognized and accepted.[13] It is from a shared philosophy of life and a common value orientation that group security, unity, and solidarity are born. This means that a people must answer for itself these questions: What is the society's value ideal? What is the ideal personality system? What is the ideal social system? If values are significant determinants of individuals and institutions, then every society needs to have a clear conception of the value orientation that it would wish to see internalized in the personality and institutionalized in the social system. Every stable society has, to use Florence Kluckhohn's phrase, a "personality configuration which is shared by the bulk of the society's members." [14] But in the opinion of at least one perceptive critic of the society, modern democracy has no clear conception of that configuration.[15]

When a society loses its ideal, when it no longer has an identifiable value orientation, then it no longer has a consistent guide for selecting political, economic, educational, and social welfare policies. Then the danger is that any dream or whim, any fad or ideology, of one who has the public ear—be he educated statesman or demagogue—will become the basis of decision. As Socrates is supposed to have said, "for the ship that does not know toward which port it is sailing, no wind is favorable."

The second reason for a shared value orientation is long-range policy-making. Cultural values should look not merely to the past, but to the future as well. Since one purpose of value is to link the past with the future, certain values must be universal enough to span time and space. We tend to identify the cultural with the traditional and the past. But, as we have just seen, value propositions relate to, and build upon, existential propositions about man and nature; therefore, while they tie a society to the richness of the past they propose a world of existential possibility not yet realized. Values spring from charisma as well as from tradition,

[13] Karl Mannheim, *Freedom, Power, and Democratic Planning* (London: Routledge & Kegan Paul Ltd., 1965), p. 231.

[14] Florence Rockwood Kluckhohn, "Dominant and Variant Value Orientations," in Clyde Kluckhohn, Henry A. Murray, and David M. Schneider, eds., *Personality in Nature, Society, and Culture* (2d ed.; New York: Knopf, 1954), p. 344.

[15] Mannheim, *op. cit.*, p. 199.

and society needs both. "No society is healthy or creative or strong unless that society has a set of common values . . . that fit with the situation of the time as well as being linked to the historic past." [16]

A value orientation is required, therefore, that will weather the economic and social change and the political upheaval that our times witness. One wonders whether we have a social philosophy and value stance that we can trust for long-range planning. In 1952 Clyde Kluckhohn, at least, questioned that we do:

> The mistakes that we make on the international scene and have made in the past decade and more are primarily political mistakes. This is in part because the ideas that our leaders do have are largely *ad hoc* ideas . . . that do not add up to a long-term postive policy.[17]

A third social imperative for a common value orientation has international dimensions. This is not the occasion to take up the dispute that centers on the relativity and universality of human values, and yet the issue cannot be entirely passed over. The most recent and reliable research in anthropology seems so ably to substantiate the universality of at least certain human values that Kluckhohn states: "No anthropologist . . . doubts that the theory of ethical relativity is in some sense forced by the facts." [18] Among sociologists, the evidence is no less convincing. In treating the theory of absolute cultural relativity Parsons and Shils write:

> In its extreme form, the proponents of this view have even asserted that every moral standard is necessarily unique. There is much aesthetic sensibility underlying and justifying this contention, but it is neither convincing logically nor fruitful scientifically. If carried to its logical conclusions, it denies the possibility of systematic analysis of cultural values.[19]

The matter comes to this: if there is not recognized a common human nature as the ontological ground for human values, and if there is not at least a cluster of values shared by the entire human

[16] Clyde Kluckhohn, *Culture and Behavior: Collected Essays of Clyde Kluckhohn*, Richard Kluckhohn, ed. (Glencoe, Ill.: Free Press, 1962), pp. 297–98. The quality of values whereby they span time is related to their universality.

[17] *Ibid.*, p. 297.

[18] *Ibid.*, p. 273.

[19] Parsons and Shils, *op. cit.*, p. 171.

family, what existential basis is there on which to rest the hope of peace among nations? Of course, cultural relativity is in fact amply verified and documented. But diverse as he is, at the heart of his being man is the same the world over. And it is highly important, especially at this period in international relations, that the nations of the world and the cultures of East and West come to see the cultural differences that exist among the nations as "so many variations on themes supplied by raw human nature." [20] There would seem to be little hope for peace until men recognize the ontological human root from which variations grow. And there would seem to be little hope for this recognition until we in this one nation achieve greater clarity about what we value, what we hold to be right or wrong in our private and official duties, and in the responsibilities of our nation in its dealings with other nations.[21] Only when this goal has been achieved, can we approach with confidence the family of man that lives beyond the borders of our culture.

The distinction between the personality system and the social system is familiar. Perhaps less familiar are references to a "cultural system." This term is useful in that it distinguishes the former as actor systems from the cultural system which has its effect by being internalized into the personality and institutionalized into the social system.[22]

The personality and social systems are empirical systems. They are the actors in the society. The cultural system as such is not an actor because it is an abstract pattern of ideas and values, symbols and norms; yet it is highly significant for action since it greatly influences both actor systems. Cultural values as internalized and institutionalized in the personality and social systems direct and guide both systems in their choice of goals and their orientation toward goals and means.[23] It is from the culture that the actors adopt standards of the true, the beautiful, and the good.[24] Both

[20] Kluckhohn, *Culture and Behavior,* p 297.

[21] *Ibid.,* p. 286.

[22] Parsons and Shils, *op. cit.,* p. 174.

[23] Parsons and Shils, "Categories of the Orientation and Organization of Action," in Parsons and Shils, eds., *op. cit.,* pp. 54–56.

[24] Tolman, *op. cit.,* p. 343.

actor systems become committed to a particular value system. This does not mean that either is incapable of tolerating conflicting values and of accommodating to values that are at variance with its own.[25] The significant point is, however, that neither system can intelligently and consistently direct itself in the choice of goals and means without an internalized and institutionalized value system. Moreover, it is through the institutionalization of values that a particular value system is transmitted from one generation to another. Hence the importance of social institutions: as value carriers they at once image to the personality a value ideal, and they transmit to other institutions the value standards of the society.

From these considerations there seem to flow three highly relevant conclusions. First, those who have responsibility for developing the social welfare system and for determining social welfare policy should have a clear conception of the value system on the basis of which choices are made. Second, the developing and strengthening of the value ideal of the social welfare system should not be haphazard or left to chance. And third, those institutions that transmit a value orientation which strengthens the society's social welfare value system should be reinforced.

Now, I submit that the value ideal of the social welfare system grows out of certain truths and principles of the Judaeo-Christian tradition, and that the values of that ideal are transmitted, among other ways, through the social welfare institutions of the churches. These institutions are part of the social welfare system. Surely, the values that they transmit span other fields than social welfare, because the values are part of the total culture. These values enjoy a place of prominence in this society; and they are values both of the churches and of social work. The churches, however, give them a depth of knowledge that they seem not otherwise to attain; and the churches elicit a commitment to them that few social institutions seem to elicit.

A brief analysis of five values of the social welfare system will point out the depth of knowledge and commitment that these values receive from the welfare institutions of the churches.

[25] Parsons and Shils, "Systems of Value-Orientation," p. 179.

First, consider the dignity and worth of the human person. Why is man of worth and dignity? One may regard him as of dignity and worth because he is biologically productive or an economic asset, or because of his contribution to the educational, scientific, political, or social development of the society. Or one may regard man of dignity because he ranks high in the hierarchy of beings on earth. Or one may merely assert man's dignity for no reason at all, not assigning an ontological ground to it. Within the Judaeo-Christian tradition the concept of human dignity transcends these reasons for dignity, all of which are based on purely extrinsic references to man. There are reasons intrinsic to man that account for his dignity. The cognitive content of the value is that the human person is an intellectual and free being, endowed with the capacity for, and so destined to, union with God. Since this is his very being, his very being is the ground for his dignity whether he is a contributor to the social order or not, and regardless of his relationship to other creatures. And it is important that the designers of the social welfare system understand this fuller conception of human dignity and be committed to the consequences that it implies for social policy formation.

A second value on which the society places high priority is sometimes referred to as the "brotherhood of men." Philosophically, the concept is that of the natural unity of men. The intellectual content of this value is that all human beings possess generically the same human nature. Whatever the variances among cultures and societies, just as whatever the ethnic, economic, educational, religious, and racial differences among any group of people, there is underlying everything the "raw human nature" which all men share. Within both the Jewish and the Christian traditions this unity of mankind is intensified through the concept of creation by a personal God who is toward men as a father toward his children. In the Christian tradition this concept of unity is further intensified by the supernatural unity of men in God through grace. The moral content of the value is the responsibility that men have to design a social order based on social justice and motivated by the love of one's fellow men. Surely church-related welfare institutions rank high in internalizing and institutionalizing this value that is also so endemic to social work.

A third value that is central to social welfare is human right. Among us it is a commonplace that all men have a right to a certain level of food, shelter, clothing, education. But why does man have this right? What is the basis of human rights? Though we protest for them, perhaps we do not always clearly understand them or know why we demand them. Ultimately, human rights rest on the spiritual nature of the human person. I would define "right" as a moral power in virtue of which human beings may make just claims to certain things. It is a power that pertains not to the physical but to the intellectual and volitional order. The founding document of our government says that right is inalienable; that is, it belongs to man by reason of his very existence as a human person, and therefore is not conferred upon him by parents, or church, or state, or any individual or community of men. It is inalienable because it flows from the very nature of the human person and therefore can neither be withheld nor taken away. It may be ignored or violated; but unlike my purse, which may be robbed, human right is as indestructible as the human person.

Like human dignity, right is not a claim which a person earns as a result of his contribution to the economy or to the social order. Human right is based on the fact that the person is master of himself and his own actions, and that therefore he is not a means to an end but rather an end unto himself. Created by God with a purpose, man is a free moral being with reference to that purpose. Integral to his being, therefore, are obligation and responsibility. Therefore, the human being may justly claim those things that are necessary for the attainment of his purpose and the fulfillment of his responsibility. If human right is such a rich concept it is largely because the philosophical and religious traditions of the West have developed it in theory and insisted upon it in fact. Here, again, the social welfare system and the churches coalesce and reinforce a common value.

These three values contain the seed of a related value that is a cornerstone of social welfare, social responsibility. *Responsibility* comes from *respondere,* to respond. Responsibility implies relationship, communication, and sharing between persons. The cognitive content of the value is the existential unity and brotherhood of all men, and the right that every man has to those things that are necessary to fulfill his purpose. The moral content of the value is that man is obliged to respond to the rights of his brother. And where the individual man cannot carry the burden of a brother, then men in community, the society, must respond to a brother's need for the body's bread and the mind's bread and the bread of the human spirit. The conviction that man is his brother's keeper inspired the earliest programs of a social welfare nature: recall God's command that the Jews not go back through the fields to glean the harvest a second time since the remnants were to go to the resident alien, the orphan, and the widow; and recall, primitive as they were, the welfare programs in the monasteries of early Christendom.

Finally, there is one other universal value which is central both to social welfare and to the churches, because it is central to man. This value I might call "self-realization." It is the master value and key concept: the highest possible level of self-fulfillment and completion of the human being. Although societies variously interpret human self-realization, by every culture it is highly valued. The intellectual content of the value is that the human person is in a state of both being and becoming, of perfecting himself, of striving to achieve the ideal of the good life.

The moral implications are that man not only has responsibility and the obligation to become what deep within his being he calls "his better self," but also he wants to achieve that ideal. Within the human person there is both the will and the potential to pursue the ideal of self-realization. This is a theme that cuts into many values and principles of social work. The goal of the profession is the maximum well-being of personality and social systems; and the achieving of this goal is based on this principle that man wants self-fulfillment and under suitable conditions will motivate himself and actively pursue it. It is likewise a value that religion both presupposes and fosters. One moral imperative that informs religion is that man can stretch the fiber of his life even unto God; and all psychic and social programs of treatment and prevention are in order to free man, at every level, for maximum functioning: physical soundness for the sake of emotional maturity; emotional maturity for the sake of intellectual development; intellectual development for the sake of spiritual freedom. And the maximum functioning of the parts that make up human life is for the self-fulfillment of the whole man.

I hope that I have not implied that only church-related institutions contribute to the value orientation of American social welfare. This was not my intention. Neither was it my intention to evaluate the relative contributions of various welfare institutions to that value orientation. Obviously, many institutions feed into it: politics, economics, education, the family, business and industry, as well as the churches; and there is an interdependence among them all. No one institution has its effect in isolation from others.

Nevertheless, it would seem to be highly important that church-related institutions by positive design and public policy be strengthened and encouraged to embellish and build up the value orientation of American social welfare. This value orientation is our welfare heritage. It is the rich earth in which this nation was nourished.

Intercultural Aspects of Social Work

by EILEEN YOUNGHUSBAND, D.B.E.

A SEMINAR on intercultural perspectives in social work education was held at the East-West Center, University of Hawaii, from February 21st to March 4th, 1966, sponsored by the Council on Social Work Education and the East-West Center and financed by a grant from the Vocational Rehabilitation Administration of the United States Federal Department of Health, Education, and Welfare with assistance from the East-West Center. The Director was Dr. Mildred Sikkema, and the discussions were led by the Chairman, Dr. Herman Stein, Dean of the School of Applied Social Sciences, Western Reserve University. Among the twenty-two participants were social work educators, sociologists, psychologists, and anthropologists from the U.S.A., Canada, India, Japan, Pakistan, the Philippines, Singapore, and Thailand, including the presidents of the International Conference of Social Work and the International Association of Schools of Social Work from Yugoslavia and the United Kingdom, respectively.

The mixture of cultures and disciplines resulted in very lively discussions in which no holds were barred. The usual danger in such intercultural gatherings is that because they take place between people who have all been educated in the West, they lead either to over-denial of difference or to over-assertion of difference as a matter of national pride. The members of this seminar were too varied and experienced to let either happen.

The agenda for the discussions was made up of the intercultural aspects of social work—values, function, and method. Because nothing was taken for granted, but everything was meant to be analysed and questioned, it looked at times as though nothing would be left but a few vague generalizations. The group went through the normal group processes of analyzing, discarding, and going around in circles. Fi-

JOURNAL OF EDUCATION FOR WOCIAL WORK, 1966, Vol. 2, No. I, pp. 59-65.

nally, in the last few days, it found it was clear about a good many questions with regard to social work values, the relation between social work and the social sciences, and the nature of social work and its desirable course of professional development, together with the uses and limitations of its present three methods: casework, group work, and work with communities.

SOCIAL WORK VALUES

Social work values were a constantly recurrent theme all through the discussions, with much pressure exerted by the North Americans on the Asians to examine whether and to what extent the traditional social work values were truly universal or were instead derived from a particular Western culture at a given point in its historical evolution. In essence, the conflict was recognized as being between values regarded as inherent in the individual and values deriving from status, kinship, religious affiliation, and ethnic group membership.

The term "values" itself tended to be rather loosely used to include ethical values or "oughts," people's actual preferences and choices, and cultural attitudes: for example, past or future orientations to time.

The Asians, whether anthropologists or social work educators, took the view that what are often described as Western values, like the worth and dignity of the individual, are not specifically Western, but first emerged in the West in the processes of historical evolution associated with industrialization. They pointed out that previously Western and Eastern values were much the same, and that the values of the educated elite in Asia are closer to those of the West than to peasant population in their own countries. They also pointed out the similarities shown in attitudes and values by studies of groups that are grossly deprived—economically, emotionally, and socially—in any part of the world, in both urban and rural conditions.

The Asians were much less troubled about the imposition of values than the Westerners and said that if social work values (which derive largely from Greek philosophy, some aspects of the Judeo-Christian tradition, and the Age of Enlightenment) are good values, then it is a desirable social work function to act as a change agent in the spread of these values. In any event, historical evolution everywhere is producing a convergence of values.

There was a good deal of discussion as to how social workers could base their practice upon the principles of individual freedom and choice in situations where decisions are customarily made by authority figures: the head of the family, the wise elders, the head man. Instances were cited of the use for change that can be made of the slack that exists in any social system.

It was agreed that any professional practice must rest upon some degree of common perception of purpose and function between the practitioner and the client and be demanded by the wider community. This creates problems for social work in those situations where people expect authoritarian solutions, expect to be told what the problem is and what they ought to do. This is true especially in community work where people often expect the worker to get things for them or to side with them against some other group rather than that they themselves should be involved in working to meet their needs.

It was agreed that the ultimate aim in social work is the well-being of the individual human being, that nothing should be done to diminish his humanity and everything possible done in the given circumstances to enhance it. As one member put it: "It isn't possible to analyze this value further; it is a value at the end of the line, and one can only assent with a grunt."

There are obviously various derivative or instrumental values related to this. There was much discussion about the derivative value of self-determination and some feeling that this had ceased to be a useful concept, particularly in work with groups and communities where it is not at all obvious who or what is the "self" which determines. Various alternative terms like personality growth, self-reliance, self-enhancement, self-realization, self-fulfillment, and increased capacity for choice were explored. Also, the idea that behind these various terms lay a real experience, a sense of the desirability of bringing more elements in the personality within the central organizing system, of promoting the growth of the self, of a sense of self-worth, of the self as cause, and of enhancing the capacity for responsibility and choice. This of course raised the question of whether personality development was synonymous with self-determination, or whether there are different ways in which the self develops, and thus whether the extended family or other group might be a means to self-development rather than a hindrance. In any event, the whole concept of self-determination may be culture bound; and it is not clear whether it is a goal or a process or both.

Quite early in the seminar it was agreed that social work is committed to social change. This was defined as "change for the better" but although participants kept on coming back to it, they never came to grips with what was meant by "better." The Indian member suggested that it included concepts of individual freedom, of material well-being, of mastery of self, of better opportunities for all, and of better social adjustment.

There were various attempts to list values, in the sense of human needs, like a rising standard of living, or desires like liberty or equality, but with recognition of problems that arise from the clash between values and the dilemma of "what trumps what." This dilemma included the clash between professional and culturally held values. Such a clash occurs, for example, in circumstances where it is assumed that one should get jobs for one's relatives or where one's professional values conflict with the tenets of one's religion.

There was much stress on the increase of rationality (as against prejudice, superstition, ignorance, and traditional procedures) as a value and therefore the commitment of the professions to the increase of rationality, even including, as one member put it: "the rational use of the irrational." At the same time it was clear that the growth and application of scientific knowledge, particularly in the social and behavioral sciences, the greater the need for professional value commitments in order to protect the individual, group, or community from manipulation and exploitation.

This same essential problem of values, kept on cropping up in various forms. It was expressed in such questions as should the social worker give expression to his values or only encourage the client to express his, in the hope that sooner or later he will arrive at those of the social worker? This specter of skillful manipulation, of forcing men to be free, of "Daddy knows best" kept floating across all the discussions.

SOCIAL WORK FUNCTION

The function of social work gave the group quite as much trouble as values. Here, too, more questions were arrived at than answers. It became clear that the social work function differs in different parts of the world according to major needs, resources, and priorities in the culture, but the similarities seemed sufficient for the same profession to be recognizable everywhere. At the same time, it was clear that social work is a fluid and emerging profession, and like many other professions, it is not stable either at its center or its circumference.

The social scientist chided the social workers with picking up bits of knowledge from the social sciences and psychology but not developing any "hard" knowledge of their own. Nonetheless, an American sociologist in the seminar suggested that social work has a cluster of activities and values that are not exclusive in content but in configuration; while its aims and methods are not identical with those of any other profession.

Historically speaking, social work began as a social movement but is now developing more clear professional functions and methods. Because of its heavy commitment to certain social values and to social betterment, it is desirable that it should continue to have this social reform element in it. For various reasons, much of the responsibility for this devolves on social work educators. This is because they are expected to be in the vanguard of professional progress, and also because university or other schools of social work are often powerful—partly because they are more neutral than social agencies or professional associations.

The social work function was variously defined as follows: an endeavor to do something rational in the field of social living; to enable people to be able to function more adequately on their own behalf in relation to social problems; to promote socially constructive and personally gratifying transactions between individuals, groups, and communities, including an improvement in their circumstances; and to generate in individuals a capacity to meet multiple role demands.

There was a good deal of discussion about the relation between social role and social work. The concept of social role clarifies the way in which social systems, which consist of enduring patterns of social interaction, are embodied in individual behavior. In other words, social roles are the bridge between the individual and the social system. A key function of social work is, therefore, to help increase opportunities for individuals to fulfill multiple role requirements with satisfaction to themselves and others. This includes helping individuals to achieve adequate role performance and also helping to change any given social system that makes it hard for the individual to perform roles adequately. Social work also comes into action where breakdown of role performance occurs in crucial or deviant or crisis situations. There is a value element in the concept of social role. It is important to emphasize this because this formulation of the social work function could be used in the interests of bringing about social conformity. In any event, role theory does not necessarily cover all dimensions of human motivations, aspirations, and values.

It was fairly easy to agree that social work is committed to facilitate the meeting of unmet need; to help the underprivileged of any kind, the deprived, and the deviant; to aid in dysfunctional situations, in crisis situations, whether individual or group, and in conditions of violent social change, such as disaster, urbanization, mass migration, or drastic innovation (for example, the social consequences of building a dam).

These all imply direct service of an individual or social therapy type: indeed, the therapy function of social work is the most highly developed so far. But if this is its sole function, then it becomes essentially a peripheral profession, dealing with the deprived, malfunctioning, and deviant, and acting as an adjunct to the professions of medicine and education. Social work is also not as socially useful in this form, particularly in developing countries where mass change is the first necessity, as it would be if it could develop further basic knowledge and practice skills in social administration, social planning, and policy formulation, in working with communities. The task which faces social work—and the most pressing demand upon it—is to develop abilities to act as a regulator of social change. It is not yet clear whether therapeutic treatment skills and social planning and policy formulation can both be accommodated within the same profession, nor whether, as knowledge grows, there will be increasing divergence so that the present common base will be lost in the growth of specialist knowledge.

The analogy of the range of skill and knowledge comprised within the medical profession was often used. The public health model also served to stimulate exploration of the need for an epidemiology of social problems, including the assessment of need and determination of priorities; of strategies of intervention; of identification of "at risk" groups and crisis situations; and of the deployment and use of social workers for preventive as well as treatment purposes. It was agreed that social workers should be located where people came most easily: in well-baby clinics, in schools, in doctors' surgeries, or at other natural points. This should not preclude the setting up of a comprehensive social welfare service.

SOCIAL SYSTEM MAINTENANCE, CONTROL, AND CHANGE

The term "client" took some hard knocks. This was partly because in community work, frequently it is not possible to decide who *is* the client, and partly because the term implies a contract to serve a particular individual or group, whereas it is becoming increasingly clear that the appropriate function of social work lies in intervention in a system rather than commitment to a given client. The relevant question may be not "Who is the client?" but "What is the storm center of this particular problem situation, and what method of intervention would be the most effective and at which points?" "For what purpose?" "What kind of change is desirable and possible?" The "client" is thus not a person but a variable in a process.

Within the threefold division of social system maintenance, control, and change, the social work function is primarily concerned with system maintenance and control where large social systems are concerned, but it may also be able to bring about system change (which implies radical discontinuities) in smaller social systems. The concept of dynamic equilibrium suggests that system maintenance includes considerable possibilities for change and adaptation, in which social work should be able to play a useful role in predicting consequences, in planning, and as a regulator and shock absorber, as well as being sensitive always to social welfare needs and resources. For this purpose, it is also necessary for social workers to be aware of the directions in which major structural change is taking place and of its consequences: the consequences, for example, of demographic change or changes in work patterns or in standard of living. Changes in the opportunity, power, and income structures must also be taken into account for their effects on the strategy of social welfare and the practice of social work.

METHOD AND PRACTICE

Trying to clarify emerging or agreed upon social work functions led into discussion of practice and method. After some preliminary struggles with such problems as the role of social workers on planning committees and so forth, it became clear that there was a range of necessary activities which might or might not be an integral part of the social work function as such. It also became clear that social work practice goes well beyond social work methods, though it must be in harmony with the social work commitment to meet need from within a certain value system: for example a committee should *not* be manipulated on the basis of a hidden agenda.

All three social work methods—casework, group work, and community work—are evolving and changing; all take account of the individual in his family and social setting as the ultimate source of reference. Needed are new methods and reformulation of existing methods, as, for example in bringing about and regulating large scale organizational change.

The essence of the casework method is a way of dealing with certain human problems on a case by case basis—the "case" being an individual or family unit. Although the diagnosis is on an individual basis, the treatment may include the use of group work. The cliché that casework is a luxury was examined. It was obvious that it can be afforded to only a limited extent and in developing countries only in particular places, and that there are many higher priorities and more appropriate services in such countries. For example, it is absurd to use trained caseworkers to interview public assistance applicants in dire poverty and primarily in need of food, clothing, and shelter. In other circumstances, it may not be the casework method but the service that is inappropriate, as in starting a child guidance clinic before basic child welfare services exist.

The Asian participants from schools of social work contended that all students should have some experience of casework because this is the analysis in depth of individual human situations and thus the best way to study under the microscope how people and their families react under stress. In casework, all dimensions of an individual's life are seen more effectively than they are in work with groups or communities.

There was almost no discussion of group work, except a brief reference to the value for the individual of group experience as a means of learning how to function better socially. It was regretted that group work had progressed from recreational activities to group therapy without developing a wider range of methods and skills in working with a variety of normal groups, a development that might have provided some of the much-needed practice skills in various segments of work with communities.

So far as community organization and community development are concerned, it is probable that these are not really separate methods, but represent a range of different processes in community work. They have been thought of as different, because community organization developed in urban centers in the United States in work with a diversity of organizations, while community development evolved in other countries in rural conditions where there was little organizational structure. The various senses in which the term "community" may be used were not examined; throughout the discussions, it was used with reference to geographical communities.

Community work may either be task oriented—that is to say the purpose may be a literacy campaign or a campaign to start a clinic or to absorb immigrants—or it may be process oriented, the purpose being to help community leaders to identify the community's most pressing needs. In the first type, outside agents or some group in the community will have decided on a specific priority and be using various methods to persuade the community to accept the service, to undertake the enterprise, or to change the attitudes of the members of the community. In the second, or process oriented type, the emphasis is on helping people to work together to determine their own priorities and to find the resources from within or outside the community to meet them. The process itself, with the resultant growth in people's capacity for decision making and implementation, is the primary aim. A third form consists in enabling groups of people to adjust to the stress of change, as for example, when tenants move to a new housing project.

In developing countries' community development, largely of the process orientation type, is used to increase the country's resources by inciting people to do things for themselves—dig wells or build roads, with some technical help. Thus, they increase resources far more quickly than if they waited until the state had the means to provide these services. This type of community development is usually based on persuading people to become involved in a nationally determined program of priorities.

Unlike casework, community work is not normally concerned with pathology or deviance. On the other hand, it does not always operate in situations where there is agreement about the nature of a given social need or the aims and methods to be employed in meeting it. In conflict situations, the aim is to bring about resolution or compromise without open aggression or ostracism or withdrawal. No matter what the circumstances, the aim is always better allocation of resources, community cohesion, ability to identify and meet needs, and ability to cope with conflict without disruption.

Community workers must constantly guard against having a hidden agenda that they are trying to maneuver the community into accepting; being drawn into taking sides with one group against others; lacking clarity about what processes are at work in the community and what their own aims are in often diffuse situations; or relinquishing their professional role and becoming simply "a good sort" in the community.

It seemed fairly clear in the discussions that the American term *community organization* had much the same meaning as *social administration* has in some other contexts if it is accepted that this latter includes working with different administrative or other groups in a community in order to facilitate a process which results in a better use of resources and improved social relationships.

Though the present three social work methods—casework, group work, and community work—are distinct, they are not necessarily separate. They have a common base; and any or all of them should be used flexibly in any given situation in whatever would be the most effective form of intervention. This raised the difficult question of whether students could be adequately trained in all three methods, and what range of training, including knowledge and practice skills, they could absorb and use effectively. Too wide a range could result in shallow knowledge and performance; too much emphasis on one method might result in over-training but not for the real task. It is quite likely that casework is being over-emphasized in training at the expense of community work. This is partly because casework is very much better developed as a method by comparison with community work in which the clarification of practice skill and understanding of process is still weak. It would also be all too easy to broaden the base of practice at the expense of depth of penetration in social problem intervention.

All through the seminar, participants were conscious of the effects of historical evolution, changing cultural values, the level of economic development, the increase of knowledge and complexity, and the nature and direction of social change as they played upon and molded the values, function, and methods of social work. They were also fully aware of the need for much more social research, including cross-cultural studies. They did not think that in ten days of discussion they added to knowledge, but they did, to their own satisfaction, clarify some issues, shake up and jolt some sacred cows, raise many questions, and see gigantic fresh tasks ahead.

The Changing Concept of Individualized Services

CAROL H. MEYER

THE CONCEPT of individualized services has been accepted by the social work profession and by leaders in the field of social welfare for almost a century, but throughout this period the concept has undergone many radical changes. These changes must always be viewed against the backdrop of the prevailing social and economic conditions and the preoccupations of the particular era in which they occurred, for it is the broad societal influences in each era that have shaped social legislation, agency programs, and professional methods and techniques. In this article, I shall present an examination of the concept of individualized services as it has been altered and reshaped by four kinds of change that have continually had an impact on the social welfare field—specifically, on social work practice. It is my thesis that the concept of individualized services has been influenced by changes in social values, changes in the structure and functions of family life, change in the concept of the unit of social work attention, and new developments in knowledge. Moreover, additional changes will inevitably take place, and the result will be further transformations in the practice of social work.

A prediction about the nature and place of individualized services in the social welfare programs of the immediate future must rest on a concept of the ultimate purpose of these programs. It is my conviction that this purpose can be summed up by this phrase: service to human beings. All our knowledge, including the knowledge that is increasingly being validated by research, and all our agency programs and professional commitments must be directed toward the primary goal of giving service. The acquisition of knowledge should not be an end in itself, and there is no social justification for an administratively tidy, but self-protective and nonserving, agency program. The hallmark of the profession of social work must be its readiness to commit itself to meeting human need before expending its energies on intraprofessional strivings that might compete for attention with its fundamental service aims. Agreement on this essential value will enable us to consider more profitably the changing concept of individualized services in social welfare programs.

Changing Social Values

How have changing social values affected the concept of individualized services? In the nineteenth century, in both England and the United States, individualized services were provided for the wanton, the helpless, and the poverty-stricken by the charitable and benevolent souls of the period. Even before the western nations experienced the full impact of the industrial revolution and the subsequent increase in urban development and social isolation, individualized services existed to help or uplift those "deserving" unfortunates who lacked the capacity to be self-supporting and who failed because they were not strong enough or wellborn enough to cope with the surrounding social and economic pressures. Perhaps the particular concern for the individual that characterized the nineteenth century was the result of a universal hopelessness that social reforms could be effected. Working in the shadow of the Poor Law, the social worker of that day —the minister, the public agent, or the vol-

SOCIAL CASEWORK, May 1966, Vol. 47, No. 5, pp. 279-285.

unteer—provided food, shelter, and comfort to the impoverished out of religious or humane motives.

A paper presented at the fifth annual meeting of the National Conference of Charities, held in Cincinnati, Ohio, in 1878, put forward the view that if pauperism was to be eliminated, "the history and character of paupers as individuals must be carefully studied; the precise causes and influences that made them such must be ascertained. . . ." [1] Indeed, individualized services were accepted in this country at that time, but the social workers of the day seemed unaware of their social significance. That was before the robber barons were recognized for what they were and when people denied the existence of a class-ridden society. That was when Negroes could still remember their recent bondage, and civil rights legislation was more than two generations away. That was before two world wars and a great depression; before the emergence of new nations and the demise of colonialism. Today, in this era of space flights, atomic energy, and automation, it can be fairly stated that 1878 was centuries, not merely eighty-eight years, ago.

In the latter part of the nineteenth century, the concept of individualized services had the conservative flavor of the times. Notwithstanding the social action programs of the community organization society and the settlement house movement, this was the prevailing dictum: Caring for the individual will improve society—society cannot be changed, and it is the individual who must learn to adjust to society. According to this point of view, impoverished families were an insult to society; it was they who were at fault, never society itself, which seemed to be impervious to change. Perhaps it is a derivative of this view of the relation between the individual and society that has given casework the reputation of being a reactionary, narrowly defined method of service. Even today it is not unusual to hear that social casework is an antiquated, albeit technically effective, method of service designed to keep the poor in their place, to represent the establishment, and to keep out the social reformer. It should give us pause that social casework is so often viewed as a nineteenth-century anachronism when, in fact, tides of change in the twentieth century have swept casework along quite as quickly as they have the scientific quest in medicine, the space probes, and atomic research.

The changing role, substance, and characteristics of individualized services in the modern world may be accounted for to a large extent by changes in social values. Despite the fact that our nation has not yet dealt adequately with the surging problems of the day—poverty, unemployment, inadequate housing, the deterioration of the inner city, family breakdown, and so forth—our social values have changed drastically, and the intent of individualized services is quite different from what it was a century ago. For example, we no longer hold the individual totally responsible for his condition. Services are now viewed as the individual's right, not only because he makes a contribution to society but also because—unless he bands together with others—he is practically helpless to affect the social, political, and economic forces that govern his life. Today individualized health and welfare services are viewed not as an aid to those persons who are inadequate, but as a requirement for survival in a complex industrial society.

Whereas family members and residents of close-knit communities once provided each other with the supports that were lacking in their lives, today public and voluntary social services have to be organized to meet a variety of human needs. We have moved even beyond the point of providing services to alleviate problems that already exist and have begun to pursue the idea of establishing services to prevent the emergence of problems. Alfred Kahn's concept, "social utilities," suggests that individualized social services should become as much a part of the fabric of life in our highly automated and bureaucratized civilization as are the services of the police department, the fire department, and the parks department.[2] Social services should be available to all persons because of the "normal" conditions of their lives, not merely for those who are failures. The social values that have changed from those represented by the Poor Law to those that underlie social insurance and now social planning have swept us along with them. Social workers face the necessity of providing more, not fewer, individualized services. The character and premises of these services are changing and will continue to do so.

Changes in the Structure and Functions of Family Life

The structure of family life has undergone such drastic changes in recent years that it is becoming increasingly difficult to find agreement even on the definition of *family*. Our concepts of family life and the nature of institutional responses to the family's functions have been revolutionized by the increase in the number of fatherless families; of families in which the mother is employed; and of nuclear, rather than extended, family units. Since 1900 there has been a 50 per cent increase in the proportion of manless households.[3] In 1962, over 60 per cent of all working women were married and living with their husbands.[4] In 1964, there were about 9 million children less than twelve years of age whose mothers were employed outside the home.[5] Of all divorcing couples in 1960, 57 per cent had children under eighteen years of age.[6] The divorce rate was 2.2 per cent per thousand population in 1960.[7] Per 1,000 total live births in 1962, 58.8 were illegitimate.[8]

We are all familiar with the assumed causes of the disruption in family life reflected in these startling figures: movement from the farm to the city, movement from the comfortable familiarity of the small community to the social isolation of the urban complex, increase in the population, and automation. Whatever the view of causation, the *effect* of the present social chaos has been felt by families who have, in turn, made dysfunctional accommodations to the severe impact of these conditions on the structure and requirements of family life. On the one hand, urban mobility and convenience have lessened the reliance of family members on each other to have their needs met. On the other hand, the highly organized, bureaucratized way of life that exists in the modern megalopolis has placed special demands on the family unit as the last resort for its members.

What is the significance of these seemingly conflicting statements? Today it is less necessary for marital life to be dependent upon the traditional (or rural) division of labor between men and women, and the resultant confusion of roles has placed the burden of marital adjustment almost totally on the emotional tie between the partners rather than on their separate but complementary functions as wage earner and homemaker. None of the previously defined marital functions is now clearly the responsibility of the man as husband and father or of the woman as wife and mother. Not only have these roles and functions become interchangeable within families, but many of them have been usurped by social institutions other than the family.

Surely the vast increase in programs, such as day care of children and Operation Head Start, and the new roles assumed by schools, hospitals, courts, and social agencies in the daily lives of all individuals are social responses to the changes occurring in family life and in the functions of family members. Day care centers for children have proliferated because mothers have become breadwinners. Operation Head Start, a program of uncommon significance, has come into being because the very poor and the culturally deprived family cannot give its children adequate care and education. Reliance on job-training programs, on public welfare, or on unemployment insurance has become a way of life for increasing numbers of men who once were wage earners but cannot now find continuity or dignity in employment because they lack appropriate skills or have been displaced by automation.

The social service of fifty years ago has become the institutionalized necessity of today. The client-recipient of the welfare programs of the 1930s has now become the citizen-participant of the poverty program and the social insurance program. And, indeed, he will be the citizen-participant of the public welfare program. For every aspect of family life that becomes dysfunctional in our complex and demanding civilization, some public or voluntary social service program arises to ease the problem.

Vast shifts in family roles and functions

have indeed occurred. Accompanying these shifts have been the social phenomena of increasing behavior problems in children, divorce, unmarried parenthood, delinquency, crime, narcotics addiction, and so on. To compensate in a rehabilitative, if not preventive, fashion for the weakening of family ties that underlies these social maladies, the court and the social agency have had to assume additional roles and responsibilities.

What, then, is left for family members to do for themselves? It would appear that the singular purpose of the family today is to provide a last stronghold of intimacy, love, and companionship in an impersonalized, mechanized, and merchandized society. This is a great burden for many persons to bear, for it casts the individual into the arena of close human relationships without his being able to receive the gratification provided by the opportunity to rear his children successfully, to work at a job he likes and can do well, or to be depended upon to carry out the essential tasks of family life. The countless material conveniences of life today may be welcome, but they also have forced family members to make an attempt to relate to each other emotionally and to try to sustain a family structure that is fast becoming obsolete.

Change in the Unit of Social Work Attention

Few would disagree with the assertion that the primary concern of social welfare is the well-being of man. This is indeed a global concern, and one that the social work profession shares with the disciplines of health and education. In fact, health, education, and welfare are looked upon as three distinct expressions of the concern for man because the concern is expressed through the functioning of separate programs, not because there can be such a separation in man himself. In other words, if it were feasible to integrate health, education, and welfare programs into a unified whole, the result would more nearly approximate the way in which a person visualizes or experiences his needs. Each of these fields of endeavor, however, has its own history, personnel, professional requirements, and expertise. Therefore, the division of labor is likely to be perpetuated, despite the fact that the services provided by each field ultimately result in the same benefit to an individual: his increasing intellectual, physical, emotional, and social well-being.

What does the social welfare field mean when it speaks of individualized services? Does it mean service to man as an individual, or does it mean individualized concern for a unit of attention, the definition of which will vary according to the kind of knowledge available and the prevalent social philosophy? I believe that it *should* mean the latter. For example, under the Poor Law, concern for the individual was just that. In that era man was not perceived as a *social* animal. Had social interaction been the overriding concept then, as it is today, man and society would have been viewed as having a mutual responsibility for the condition of each, and the separation of efforts in pursuit of social reform and efforts in pursuit of the modification of individual behavior would not have occurred.

Moreover, the concept of individualized services has been modified by the changing conditions in society that have been characterized by a growing interdependence. Obviously, the more complex a society, the more an individual must rely on significant others in his social sphere, on his government, and on other organized programs that enable him to survive. Today, the unit of attention can no longer be an isolated man, woman, or child; such individuation is no longer a reality. Human beings cling to one another in family units and in formal and informal social organizations of all kinds, because relationships with others are essential to the physical and emotional health of everyone. Moreover, the clusters of relationships that find their expression in family life, in neighborhoods, and in various kinds of groups are not separable from the society that surrounds them, with which they must interact.

Today's concept of individualized services, then, must embrace the unit of attention that is currently valid. This unit is not the individual man—who will nevertheless be the ultimate beneficiary of such services—but man in his family, in his group, and in his neighborhood; each unit continually acts upon society at large and is, in turn, being acted upon by it. This is not a statement of values; it is a description of the urbanized, mechanized, bureaucratized world of today, in which individual man's only chance to find expression and fulfillment for himself is in the company of others.

New Developments in Knowledge

In the past fifty years, social work has moved from the social sciences to the psychological sciences and back again in its search for reliable knowledge that would explain the psychosocial phenomena that are the objects of its concern. A characteristic of the social work profession, and one I view with fondness, is that it continues to act in a pragmatic fashion while it is seeking knowledge and building theory. Thus, in the periods of its history when it was seeking knowledge from the disciplines of sociology and economics, it was also going about the business of helping individuals with whatever tools were at hand. Even while caseworkers were going through the psychoanalytic phase of refining those tools, the cry for social reform was raised. Somehow, as we sought the correct ingredients of knowledge, those of us concerned with social action and those concerned with clinical mastery continued to practice despite the rough edges in all areas of work.

Not much more time should have to pass before the issues concerning the clinical emphasis *versus* the social emphasis, pathology *versus* normality, or the residual view *versus* the institutional view of social work's place in society are relegated to the same niche in history that the heredity-*versus*-environment issue occupies. Surely we now acknowledge that social work is basing its performance on knowledge gleaned from a variety of sources. We do not yet have an integrated theoretical understanding of human behavior in a society, but we are on the brink of capturing the essence of that knowledge. At least we know that the-person-in-society is the concept that forms the framework within which knowledge must be sought.

In truth, social workers have accumulated a respectable amount of knowledge about human behavior. In the practice of social casework, especially, this knowledge was accumulated at the risk of our being drawn into a form of psychoanalytic practice. We managed to avoid that pitfall and finally achieved a balance between clinical knowledge and social work activity. Now, pure Freudian psychoanalytic theory has given way to a new ego psychology that may yet bridge the gap between theories of human behavior and theories of social functioning.

What about social science theories? They have not, as an integrated whole, served us so well as have the theories of individual growth and development. Each of us selects a particular concept or theory from the social sciences and applies it where it appears to be most useful or relevant. Some caseworkers prefer the concepts of social role; some, the theories of class structure; some, the theories of reference groups; and so on. There is not yet a unified theory that offers a cohesive explanation of society and its adaptations. Social workers use what they can of the knowledge available, but there is not yet as high a level of theoretical development in the societal sphere as there is in the arena of individual behavior.

Nevertheless, theoretical knowledge that can support practice is growing rapidly, and practice, in turn, is contributing to the development of theory. The most useful meeting place of practice and knowledge today is in the realm of social interaction. The processes of family life, of group interaction, and of community interaction are being studied at the same time that they are being acted upon. In fact, all social workers, in the course of their daily practice, must both call upon and contribute to the existing knowledge of social interaction in order to do their work. Social interaction, therefore, is the unit of attention of almost all social work practitioners; it is the concern of almost all social agencies.

At last, all of us—the theoretician, the caseworker, the group worker, the community organization worker, the agency administrator, the board member, the taxpayer, the student, and the teacher—have converged on the same focus of concern. We have but one question: How can we explain and do something about the circumstances that support or hinder the interaction of man with his fellow man and with the institutions and provisions of society at large?

What Does Individualized Service Mean?

As a result of all the changes that I have reviewed, new modes of social work practice must be devised. The traditional separation of casework, group work, and community organization is no longer tenable. Even now there is no clear answer to the question whether the caseworker who works with a family group is doing casework or group work, whether a community organization worker who talks with a neighborhood leader is assuming a casework role, or whether a group worker who makes a home visit is doing casework. We cannot much longer justify the separateness of methods in social work.

The concept of social interaction discussed previously encompasses concern with human personality and concern with social functioning. Neither of these concerns is the prerogative of any one method in social work practice; both are the concerns of all methods. To offer individualized services means that a community organization worker may direct his attention to a particular neighborhood composed of people with singular characteristics and problems. Similarly, the group worker and the caseworker both select the particular units to which they will give attention. In each instance, the individualizing process is identical; only the unit of attention varies from one worker to another. Assuming a measure of agreement that the three methods of social work practice use the same knowledge base (perhaps with different emphases) and the same concepts and principles, one can speculate that eventually they will fuse. Currently, the dividing lines seem to be contrived on the basis of professional commitments rather than the needs of people to be viewed separately as individuals, groups, or communities.

Earlier I touched upon the changing values and commitments that have transformed the older concept of the client-recipient into the modern concept of the citizen-participant. It is, therefore, no longer appropriate for us to view the caseworker as acting *upon* the client and the community organization worker as acting *with* the citizen. Nor is it valid to view the work of the caseworker as the handling of clinical pathology alone and the work of the community organization worker as the handling of social problems. In present-day terms, the client and the citizen are one and the same. Consequently, since the individual's well-being is dependent on the nature of his interaction with society, clinical pathology and social problems are also inextricably intertwined.

Before considering some of the implications of this concept for social agency functioning, I think it important to affirm that the suggestion that practice be broadened in scope does not imply a dilution in professional competence. I am not suggesting that the social worker of tomorrow become a Jack-of-all-trades. Far from it. Rather, I am saying that a social worker who has integrated within himself a piece of casework, a piece of group work, and a piece of community organization will view the people whom he serves through a transactional lens; he will use his special knowledge of a variety of human behaviors interacting with a variety of social forces. Moreover, the social worker who adheres to the true concept of individualization will treat each person-in-situation differentially, thus calling upon relevant theory and classification schemes. He will need to be equally skillful in determining the presence of individual pathology, in assessing the degree of family breakdown, and in comprehending the cultural conflicts in a neighborhood.

In the light of the inevitable fusion of social work methods, we may question whether there will be the same boundary lines between fields of practice. I think it is doubtful that they will remain if we are to be concerned with social interaction wherever it appears. One can cite as an example the field of psychiatric social work practice. Community psychiatry is here at last. The role of the social worker in a preventive mental health program based in a neighborhood unit is a far cry from the role of the psychiatric social worker in the state hospital of the past who took the anamnesis for the psychiatrist. Case finding, marital counseling, treatment of parent-child problems, group education, and group therapy, as well as the mobilization of resources in the community, will be the practice concerns of the future social worker in a community mental health center.

The person-in-situation or persons-in-situation should be the unit of attention in all social agencies, albeit each agency will have a distinct emphasis. The boundary lines now separating fields of practice and social work methods must inevitably disappear as the significant issues are joined. Our concerns are not different. The well-being of man in his interaction with society and the necessity of individualizing a case—whether it is a person, a patient, a family, a group, or a neighborhood—are the goals we have in common. Logic dictates that we use our knowledge and skills earlier in the process of social breakdown, that we turn our collective energies to prevention even as we treat people who have problems. Our communities require the most judicious and disciplined use of the many talents of social workers in all social agencies. Only to the extent that we are effective in increasing the well-being of man will we meet the standards to which we have committed ourselves.

In summary, the concept of individualized services in social work practice reflects changes in social values, changes in family life, change in the unit of attention, and developments in knowledge. A new use of this concept must be accompanied by modifications in methodology and the disappearance of practice boundaries. We have the tools available; all we now require is a readiness to set in operation dynamic and effective programs to be carried out by our community of social agencies. The profession, the schools of social work, and the agencies themselves must get on with the task.

REFERENCES

1 Nathan Allen, "Prevention of Crime and Pauperism," in *Proceedings of the Fifth Annual Conference of Charities,* A. Williams & Co., Boston, 1878, p. 117.

2 Alfred J. Kahn, "The Societal Context of Social Work Practice," *Social Work,* Vol. X, October 1965, pp. 145–55.

3 *Converging Social Trends: Emerging Social Problems,* Division of Research, Welfare Administration, U.S. Department of Health, Education, and Welfare, Washington, D.C., 1964, p. 55.

4 *Ibid.*

5 *Ibid.,* p. 60.

6 Hugh Carter and Alexander Plateris, "Trends in Divorce and Family Disruption," in *Health, Education, and Welfare Indicators,* September 1963, p. x.

7 *Ibid.*

8 *Ibid.,* p. xvii.

GROUP ACTIVITIES AND ASSIGNMENTS

1. Establishment of class groups

Use part of the time to get acquainted with each other; decide how the group will be structured and identify the resources which each person brings from his background (job experiences, volunteer work, ethnicity, positive and negative contacts with social workers, etc.).

Discuss why each person wants to be a social worker, or any area of common interest which the group feels will provide an opportunity for getting to know each other.

Write up your initial reactions towards everyone in the group and your feelings about participating in the group.

2. Individual values

How do we operationalize the major social work values? Do we really believe in the inherent worth and dignity of the individual? In practice do we really allow the consumer the right of self-determination, etc.?

Discuss possible ways an individual's value system might vary from the majority value system because of cultural, ethnic, or socio-economic background? Be Specific! How might the social worker's own values interfere with the helping relationship?

Write a brief account of an instance from your own life when you had to ask someone for help. Describe the feelings you had.

SELECTED BIBLIOGRAPHY

Bell, Winifred, "The Rights of the Poor: Welfare Witch Hunts in the District of Columbia," Social Work, 13 (1), 1968, pp. 60-67.

Bernstein, Saul, "Self Determination: King or Citizen In the Realm of Values," Social Work, 5 (3), 1960, pp. 3-8.

Boehm, W.W., "Social Work: Science and Art," Social Service Review, 35 (2), 1961, pp. 144-152.

Coser, Lewis A., "The Sociology of Poverty," Social Problems, 13 (2), 1965, pp. 140-148.

Frankel, Charles, "Social Values and Professional Values" Journal of Education for Social Work, 5 (1), 1969, pp. 29 to 35.

Gordon, W. E., "A Critique of the Working Definition," Social Work, 7 (3), 1962, pp. 3-13.

Gordon, W. E., "Knowledge and Value: Their Distinction and Relationship In Clarifying Social Work Practice," Social Work, 10 (3), 1965, pp. 32-39.

Kahn, A. J., "The Societal Context of Social Work Practice," Social Work, 10 (4), 1965, pp. 145-155.

Keith-Lucas, Alan, "A Critique of the Principle of Client Self-Determination," Social Work, 8 (3), 1963, pp. 66-71.

McCormick, M.J., "The Role of Values in Social Functioning," Social Casework, 42 (2), 1961, pp. 70-78.

Perlman, Helen Harris, "Self Determination: Reality or Illusion," Social Service Review, 39 (4), 1965, pp. 410-421.

Pumphrey, M. W., "Transmitting Values and Ethics Through Social Wor Practice," Social Work, 6 (3), 1961, pp.68-75.

Rein, Martin, "Social Work In Search of a Radical Profession," Social Work, 15 (2), 1970, pp. 13-28.

Stretch, J. J., "Existentialism: A Proposed Philosophical Orientation for Social Work," Social Work, 12 (4), 1967, pp. 97-102.

Thursz, Daniel, "Social Action As A Professional Responsibility," Social Work, 11 (3), 1966, pp. 12-21.

SKILLS IN COMMUNICATION

The most basic skill needed by the general practitioner is the ability to communicate meaningfully. It is impossible not to communicate. The student must become more aware of what verbal and non-verbal messages are being communicated in every interaction. The "helping interaction" should assist individuals, groups, and communities to express thoughts and feelings so that needs can be identified and met. The interaction between the change agent and the client-system, the target system, and action system, is the medium through which the helping process flows or is impeded.[1] The change-agent will not be able to effectively collect the data necessary for analysis and intervention if he has not learned how to interact with the various systems in a purposeful way. Techniques for facilitating communication with individuals are just as applicable with other size systems. For example, the technique of reflecting all or part of the person's statement can be used to facilitate communication, as can an individual's sharing more of his feelings about being out of work; members of a group "opening-up" in a group session; or a community group's reaction to a service delivery system that is not responsive to the needs of the neighborhood. Conversely, the change-agent can block communication of any client-system by using stereotyped comments, social cliches, or trite phrases, etc.

Interviewing is essentially a structured form of communication. It is a major tool of the helping process, which cuts across all the systems in and with which the social worker functions. A good interviewer is a person who has good skills in communication. He is aware of the interaction between himself and the system he is addressing. He purposefully uses techniques that will facilitate communication and avoids intentional blocks to communication. The article by Alpine et al., "Interview Techniques for Social Work Student Training," although it was intended for caseworkers and speaks of treatment, identifies nine specific techniques that can be used generically to "turn-on" client systems.

"The Racial Factor in the Interview" by Alfred Kadushin, acknowledges cultural differences in client-systems and discusses the findings of a number of studies that have been conducted on this complex subject.

1. For a definition of client-system, target system, action-system, and change-agent system, see *op. cit.* Pincus and Minahan, pp. 38-41.

Albertina Mabley's article demonstrates how the group interview can be used to communicate feelings and thoughts rather than just as an expediency for long waiting lists for individual interviews.

Since written communication, along with verbal and non-verbal communication, is an important part of the learning process, the Dwyer and Urbanowski article, "Student Process Recording: A Plea for Structure" is included in this chapter.

GEORGE C. ALPINE, M.S.S.S.
ROBERT CHESTER, M.S.S.W.
NATHAN H. KAUFMAN, M.S.W.
JOHN K. MATSUMURO, M.S.S.S.
MURRY K. CUNNINGHAM, M.S.

Interviewing techniques for social work student training

A review of the literature concerning casework interviewing techniques reveals a paucity of material. What is available is not interwoven into the over-all casework process. In addition, each student for years has become familiar only with those interviewing techniques which his supervisor has "highlighted."

This is realistic since it is impossible to become acquainted with all the numerous techniques available during the training period. It is even more unrealistic to expect the student to master more than a few techniques, since this is accomplished only through additional professional experience.

The authors, through their years of supervising students and attending supervisory seminars and professional meetings, became aware that nowhere were techniques written down in a meaningful manner. There were no explanations that could be understood and defined outside of the ongoing casework process itself. They further realized that the interviewing techniques with which each student became familiar varied from supervisor to supervisor. After months of attempting to separate techniques from process, they felt that the time had arrived to put into writing their progress to date. They realize this is not an exhaustive listing of techniques, but from their viewpoint these techniques are the ones most commonly used. They realize there is a danger that the student may use these techniques inappropriately. However, they are offered as a basis for a "take-off" discussion with the supervisor.

MENTAL HYGIENE, Jan. 1965, Vol. 49, No. 1, 126-131

The authors think that the basic task of the student caseworker is to learn the techniques which help him to create that unique relationship experience wherein the client is enabled to participate in an ongoing, self-helping process. The casework interview is a basic tool of this helping process, and in the following pages varied techniques of interviewing are offered for the student's consideration in his learning process.

Casework interviews may be conducted on several levels, dependent upon the student's focus, the client's need and ability or desire to give of himself, and the purpose of the agency. Interviews serve to give necessary factual information to clients. With this information the clients are then able to follow through on treatment plans or to accept referrals to the proper agency or service. Interviews also serve as a means of gathering data for future diagnostic interpretation and treatment planning. Clients are often fearful of revealing information. They may also be forgetful or unaware that certain information is important. In such interviews the student's skill and sensitivity in probing and exploring increases the knowledge gained about the over-all case situation.

Interviews are dynamic, one-to-one, therapeutic climes wherein the client, through the relationship with the student, is helped to view and modify those aspects of personal behavior that have helped create his problem. Many techniques will be unfamiliar to the student, but he should make an effort to learn as many as possible. He is cautioned not to use unfamiliar techniques indiscriminately. He is further cautioned that it is important that the beginning of an interview be a positive one or the client will not keep subsequent appointments and treatment never begins.

TECHNIQUES TO BE USED IN THE BEGINNING

Setting the client at ease: One of the most helpful techniques to remember is to be a human being. Be relaxed. Any tenseness on your part will be sensed by the client. Be sure to introduce yourself. If it is a nice, bright day, say so. If the weather is terrible, say so. If the client has come to you, request that he explain in his own words what he sees as his problem or situation, or how and what services he expects. If you have requested the appointment, explain to him why the interview is being held. Thus, in the beginning the client knows he is a participant in the treatment process and that his thinking and feelings are important.

Exploring in a meaningful manner: Let the client know you want to help by asking pertinent questions. To relieve his anxiety, share with him the purpose of the interview. Have a purpose for each question you ask. Clarify where there is doubt as to the meaning of what the client says.

Listening: Listen to the tone of voice and note the manner of speaking, as well as noting the exact words said. By listening, you are less apt to draw erroneous conclusions or cut off the client so that meaningful material does not come out.

Silence: Although this appears an easy technique to master, it is not. It can be used to give the client enough time to muster his own thoughts. It can be helpful to the student, preventing his speaking too soon or jumping to a conclusion. It can lead to empathy. It can be agonizing to both the client and the student.

Summarizing: Periodically summarize what

is said to help crystallize your own thinking, as well as the client's.

Structure the interview: Once treatment starts, the use of time can be an important technique in the casework process. Any attempt by the client to leave early or to prolong the session may be meaningful behavior. If so, it can be dealt with. The student should feel free to accept this fact and not be bound to keep the client longer than necessary and thus create undue anxiety for the client himself.

Convey interest: The student can do this by the tone of voice he uses, his facial expression, gesture, posture, attentiveness. Remember that the client is human and that you should treat him as such. Neglecting to get across your warmth, acceptance and understanding makes the caseworker's job more difficult because of the resistance it usually creates.

The above-mentioned techniques are means of letting clients know that you are trying to help. These also help the student in setting goals and formulating treatment plans for the client. Summarizing the interview focuses on the progress made and helps the client to see where he is. Whether to focus on immediate or long-range goals is a decision which varies with agency purpose, expectations of the client, the student's techniques and the client's level of functioning.

However, it is important to have a common goal on which the worker and client can focus and attempt to attain. This results in the client's being willing to accept treatment through an ongoing casework relationship. How successful ongoing casework treatment is depends upon the student, the interviewing techniques used and the client's ability to accept help. In order to secure meaningful, workable information about the client's social and emotional life, the student needs a method of having the client reveal specific information in order to diagnose and treat.

It should be kept in mind that the casework process is in a constant state of flux, and that we always need to know areas of anxiety and difficulties, as well as the patient's resourcefulness and strength. This helps to set the casework treatment as a two-way process of effecting the client's ability to handle and verbalize about his problems, and allowing ourselves to be affected by the impact of his difficulties so that we can think with empathy.

TECHNIQUES TO USE DURING TREATMENT

The group of techniques in this area of interviewing activity can be defined as helping the patient to concentrate on the relevant aspects of his conflict (internal) and problems (external). Also, the complement of this process is to help the client let go of the irrelevant (symptoms) misdirection, confusion, etc., in order to grasp the full meaning of this difficulties.

Allow the client to tell his own story: Try to structure the interview so that you can find out from the client why he is seeing you and what the circumstances are which led to his request or need for help. This is of diagnostic value in terms of telling you how a client views people and problems, and also what his perceptual distortions and blank spots are. If you requested to see the client, after you have explained your reason, let him relate in his own words his thinking and guilt.

Reinterpret what the client says: Reinterpret what the client says so that you can gauge his capacity to view the problem with a different slant. This will tell you about the client's flexibility of ego and help you to determine a mutually agreed upon area of concentration. Otherwise, uncalled confusion and resistance may crop up.

Avoid generalization and particularize the problem with the client: Ask for a specific example of what the client means. You can thus get a better idea of the client's feelings as he relates the story and what part he or others play in the difficulties. Generalization can often serve to avoid problems and portray a fatalistic attitude. People usually have specific feelings about a problem in spite of their denial. For instance, you can ask, "At whom were you angry, and about what?"

Universalize or use analogy: When necessary and appropriately used, this is a way of adding humor to a situation or taking the onus out of the client's catastrophies. For example, one might tell the client an incident or story about other people.

Repeating the last word of the sentence: Do this with an inflection of a question. This is a way of avoiding a cross-examination kind of tone in the interview.

"Oh!"

This can be uttered in such a way as to indicate to a client that he should talk more or explain more fully.

Use a puzzled or questioning facial expression: This is used to indicate to the client that what he has said is not understood and that further clarification is needed.

Never agree with or attack a client's distortion: A client's prejudice or distorted perception usually serves a purpose for his mental equilibrium. The student should inquire into the background history of the prejudice or distortion so as to understand why the client is the way he is. Generally, the student never directly attacks or agrees with a client's prejudice or distortions.

Say words the client has been hinting at but needs license to use: This will help to break down resistance the client may have in discussing difficulties.

Avoid stereotyped responses: Such responses usually lead up a blind alley. They do not help the patient to think more flexibly. They may also be a sign of your own anxiety prejudice. Repeatedly asking "How do you feel about it," "think about it" and "Aha" can be frustrating to the client and create the feeling that the student is avoiding the issue or problem with the client.

Avoid being stingy about advice: Give advice and information if the client is specifically asking for it. However, try to get him to talk about what he really may be wanting to say or know. He may be knowingly or unknowingly requesting something more than advice, and the student should be aware of it.

Be alert to one-word answers: When the client uses the word "upset" or "nervous" what emotional significance does this have for him. Does he mean he is losing control of himself? Is he fearful of being harmed by his fellow man? Is he indicating incoherence and helplessness, or is he blocking? He may not be clear himself as to what he does mean. The student should help him clarify.

Set the stage for a dialogue: Explore with the client what he reports. For example, "What did she say" and "What did you say," until the event in its entirety is clarified.

Be careful when asking for explanations of behavior: Such statements as "Why did you do that" may put the client on the defensive.

Avoid moralizing or overidentifying: Avoid moralizing or overidentifying with the hospital administrative procedure or the agency structure. When hearing about an injustice done to a fellow patient or client, don't jump to the defense or explain why this is done. Open the door for further communication by saying "I feel that you don't like the way it was handled; Can you tell me more about the way it affects you?" The client may be expressing significant feelings or attitudes about authority or dependency needs.

Motivating: These interviewing techniques are used to try to help the client to increase his desire for helping himself.

Explaining: This technique is the use of the student's professional awareness of person situation configuration and his use of this knowledge to help the client gain understanding and control of his total situation.

Clarifying: This is helping the client to see his distortions and destructive use of self which operate on a conscious or preconscious level and to see his responsibilities for functioning in relation to his social problems. This of course has to be done partially with one attitude at a time and repeatedly done as it crops up in different situations. For example, when the client states that he always gives in to his wife or father, he may have previously stated in relation to others that unless you give in to people or help them, then they don't do anything for you. It becomes a student's job to help him see what reaction he has to it, such as later taking a drink or "blowing his top."

TECHNIQUES TO USE DURING TERMINATION

The following interviewing techniques are suggested for use in ending an interview and/or termination of treatment which has encompassed many interviews:

Summarize: Try to end interviews by summarizing the material covered, particularly when concrete material is covered. For example: referral, things to do, action to take. The emotionally charged material need not be summarized. Ask the client to think about new material until the next interview. If new material does not penetrate (for example, denial of feelings of hostility and aggravating situations), ask the client to keep it in mind when the situation arises again, and to discuss it again in the next interview.

Ask the client if he has any questions: This is a culturally developed means of termination, as we all know that questions come last.

Walk toward the door after the summary: This is generally considered rude. Do not do this unless all else fails. Walking to the door is a strong indication of ending the interview, and may be resorted to only with the most stubborn client who refuses to leave.

Prepare client for termination: Long treatment interviews are not fruitful. There is a limit on how much emotional material can be covered in an hour, and extended interviews are largely a waste of time. Watch the time and start preparing the client for termination 10 minutes earlier. Start going over previous material as a means of summary and do not go into new material.

Separation anxiety: Usually this is best handled by preparing the client well in advance for separation. Bring up the subject of termination four to six interviews before actual termination. Thus, the client has a chance to work through the anxiety of termination.

Leave the door open for future contacts: Try to handle termination so the client does not feel abandoned or that termination is final. You might terminate on a positive note of progress and competency, that he can function alone, but also assuring him that he may come back to the agency or that the agency will be ready to accept him again.

The varied methods and techniques of interviewing offered in this article were not meant to be all-inclusive. However, it is hoped that the student's learning process will be more meaningful when he sees these techniques and explanations. This is our attempt to catalogue interviewing techniques commonly used in daily practice. It is hoped that this article will stimulate others to compile further techniques.

The racial factor in the interview

by Alfred Kadushin

Ethnicity, broadly speaking, means membership in a group that is differentiated on the basis of some distinctive characteristic, which may be cultural, religious, linguistic, or racial. The nonwhite experience in America is sufficiently differentiated so that race can be regarded as a specific kind of ethnicity. Although the term nonwhite includes Mexican-Americans, American Indians, orientals, and blacks, this article on the racial factor in the interview is almost exclusively concerned with black-white differences, not only because blacks are the largest single nonwhite minority, but because most of the descriptive, clinical, and experimental literature concerned with this problem focuses on blacks.

The black client often presents the interterviewer with the problem of socioeconomic background as well as differences in racial experience. Although the largest number of poor people are white, a disproportionate percentage of the black population is poor. Hence the racial barrier between the white worker and black client is frequently complicated further by the class barrier—white middle-class worker and black lower-class client. However, the exclusive concern here is with the racial factor, i.e., the differences that stem from the experiences in living white and living black.

THE PROBLEM

Racial difference between worker and client is an ethnic factor that creates problems in the relationship and the interview. Understanding and empathy are crucial ingredients for an effective interview. But how can the white worker imagine what it is like for the black client to live day after day in a society that grudgingly, halfheartedly, and belatedly accords him the self-respect, dignity, and acceptance that are his right as a person or, more often, refuses outright to grant them to him? How can the worker know what it is like to live on intimate terms with early rejection, discrimination, harassment, and exploitation?

A relaxed atmosphere and comfortable

Reprinted with permission of the National Association of Social Workers, from SOCIAL WORK, Vol. 17, No. 3, (May 1972), pp. 88-98.

interaction are required for a good interview. But how can this be achieved when the black client feels accusatory and hostile as the oppressed and the white worker feels anxious and guilty about his complicity with the oppressor? In such a situation the black client would tend to resort to concealment and disguise and respond with discretion or "accommodation" behavior.[1] Concealment and "putting the white man on" have been institutionalized as a way of life—they are necessary weapons for survival, but antithetical to the requirements of an effective interview. Often the black client openly refuses to share, as expressed in the following poem, "Impasse," by Langston Hughes:

I could tell you,
If I wanted to,
What makes me
What I am.

But I don't
Really want to—
And you don't
Give a damn.[2]

The attitude toward permeability of the racial barrier for the social work interview has changed over the last twenty years. In 1950 Brown attempted to assess the importance of the racial factor in the casework relationship by distributing questionnaires to social agencies in Seattle, Washington.[3] Eighty percent of the practitioners responded that the racial factor did intrude in the relationship, but it was not much of a problem for the experienced worker with some self-awareness.

By 1970 blacks' disillusionment with the integrationist stance and a greater accentuation on their special separate identity from the white culture and the unique effects of their historical experience resulted in frequently repeated assertions that no white could understand what it meant to be black. Consequently, it is said, an effective interview with a black client requires a black interviewer. Many who have studied this problem, although not ready to go this far, generally concede that currently the racial barrier in the interview makes rapport and understanding much more difficult than was previously imagined.[4]

Obviously people who share similar backgrounds, values, experiences, and problems are more likely to feel comfortable with and understand each other. In sociology the principles of homophyly (people who are alike like each other) and homogamy (like marries like) express these feelings. Synanon, Alcoholics Anonymous, and denominational agencies are organizational expressions of this idea.

Social workers tend to follow the same principles by selecting for continuing service those clients who are most like themselves and subtly discouraging or overtly rejecting those "who cannot effectively use the service." The rich research literature about differential access to mental health services by different class groups tends to

---

[1] Thelma Duvinage, "Accommodation Attitudes of Negroes to White Caseworkers and Their Influence on Casework," *Smith College Studies in Social Work,* Vol. 9. No. 3 (March 1939), p. 264.

[2] Copyright © 1967 by Arna Bontemps and George Huston Bass from/*The Panther and the Lash.* Reprinted by permission of Alfred A. Knopf, Inc.

[3] Luna B. Brown, "Race as a Factor in Establishing a Casework Relationship," *Social Casework,* Vol. 31, No. 3 (March 1950), pp. 91–97.

[4] *See,* for example, George P. Banks, "The Effects of Race on One-to-One Helping Interviews," *Social Science Review,* Vol. 45, No. 2 (June 1971), pp. 137–146; Dorcas Bowles, "Making Casework Relevant to Black People: Approaches, Techniques, Theoretical Implications," *Child Welfare,* Vol. 48, No. 8 (October 1969), pp. 468–475; Marylou Kincaid, "Identity and Therapy in the Black Community," *Personnel and Guidance Journal,* Vol. 47, No. 9 (May 1969), pp. 884–890; Jean Gochros, "Recognition and Use of Anger in Negro Clients," *Social Work,* Vol. 11, No. 1 (January 1966), pp. 28–38; Clemmont Vontross, "Counseling Blacks," *Personnel and Guidance Journal,* Vol. 48, No. 9 (May 1970), pp. 713–719; Vontross, "Cultural Barriers in Counseling Relationships," *Personnel and Guidance Journal,* Vol. 48, No. 1 (September 1969), pp. 11–16; and Vontross, "Racial Differences—Impediments to Rapport," *Journal of Counseling Psychology,* Vol. 18, No. 1 (January 1971), pp. 7–13.

confirm that this is a euphemism for people who are different from "us."

There is similar research with regard to agency selectivity relating to race. For example, a study of patients seen for ten or more individual psychotherapy interviews at a metropolitan psychiatric outpatient clinic found that "Caucasian women were seen proportionally longest, followed by Caucasian men.[5] Racial minority group patients had proportionately fewer contacts—black males had the lowest number of interviews. Nonwhites not only had fewer contacts, but their attrition rate was higher. All therapists, including psychiatric social workers, were Caucasian. Therapist ethnocentricity was measured with the Bogardus Social Distance Scale. Those who scored low in ethnocentrism were more likely to see black patients for six or more interviews; those who scored high treated black patients for this length of time much less often. (Differences were statistically significant.) Worker ethnocentrism may help account for the higher attrition rate of black clients who apply for social services. It is certainly true for black clients in family service agencies and black applicants for adoption.[6]

But the following statement by a black mental health worker, retrospectively analyzing her own personal experience, indicates that a therapeutic relationship with a white person, although difficult, is possible:

> In answering the question of whether a white middle-class psychiatrist can treat a black family, I cannot help but think back over my own experiences. When I first came to New York and decided to go into psychotherapy I had two main thoughts: (1) that my problems were culturally determined, and (2) that they were related to my Catholic upbringing. I had grown up in an environment in which the Catholic Church had tremendous influence. With these factors in mind, I began to think in terms of the kind of therapist I could best relate to. In addition to being warm and sensitive, he had to be black and Catholic. Needless to say, that was like looking for a needle in a haystack. But after inquiring around, I was finally referred to a black Catholic psychiatrist.
>
> . . . he turned out to be not so sensitive and not so warm. I terminated my treatment with him and began to see another therapist who was warm, friendly, sensitive, understanding, and very much involved with me. Interestingly enough, he was neither black nor Catholic. As a result of that personal experience, I have come to believe that it is not so much a question of whether the therapist is black or white but whether he is competent, warm, and understanding. Feelings, after all, are neither black nor white.[7]

Thus the question of whether a white worker can establish contact with a black client is more correctly stated as "How can such contact be established?"

WHITE WORKER–BLACK CLIENT

What can be done to ease the real difficulties inherent in white worker–black client cross-racial integration? Because the white worker is initially regarded as a potential enemy, he should carefully observe all the formalities that are overt indications of respect—e.g., start the interview

[5] Joe Yamamoto et al., "Factors in Patient Selection," *American Journal of Psychiatry,* Vol. 124, No. 5 (November 1967), pp. 630–636.

[6] *See* "Non-White Families Are Frequent Applicants for Family Service," *Family Service Highlights,* Vol. 25, No. 5 (May 1964), pp. 140–144; and Trudy Bradley, *An Exploration of Caseworkers' Perceptions of Adoptive Applicants* (New York: Child Welfare League of America, 1966).

[7] As quoted in Clifford J. Sager, Thomas L. Brayboy, and Barbara R. Waxenberg, *Black Ghetto Family in Therapy—A Laboratory Experience* (New York: Grove Press, 1970), pp. 210–211.

promptly, use Mr. and Mrs. rather than the client's surname or first name, shake hands and introduce himself, listen seriously and sincerely. Rituals and forms are not empty gestures to people who have consistently been denied the elementary symbols of civility and courtesy.

Discussions about racism have left every white with the uneasy suspicion that as a child of his culture he has imbibed prejudices in a thousand different subtle ways in repeated small doses and that the symptoms of his racism, although masked to himself, are readily apparent to a black person. These suspicions may be true. Thus a worker must frankly acknowledge to himself that he may have racist attitudes and make the effort to change. To paraphrase a Chinese maxim: The prospective white interviewer who says, "Other white interviewers are fools for being prejudiced, and when I am an interviewer I will not be such a fool," is already a fool.

To conduct a good interview, the worker must be relatively confident that he knows his subject matter. But how can he feel confident if he is aware that there is much about the black experience he does not and cannot know? Certainly he can dispel some of his ignorance by reading about and becoming familiar with black history, black culture, and black thinking and feeling. This is his professional responsibility. When a worker lacks knowledge about the client's situation, he appears "innocent." Thus he is less respected, more likely to be "conned," and less likely to be a source of influence.

The white worker may find it helpful to be explicitly aware of his reactions to racial differences. In making restitution for his felt or suspected racism, he may be overindulgent. He may oversimplify the client's problems and attribute certain behavior to racial differences that should be ascribed to personal malfunctioning. When color is exploited as a defensive rationalization, race is a weapon. Burns points out that black children

> . . . have learned how to manipulate the guilt feelings of their white workers for their own ends. They have also learned to exploit the conceptions most white workers have about the anger of black people.[8]

In interracial casework interviews the participants are keenly aware of the difference between them. Yet they rarely discuss the racial factor openly.[9] It is not clear whether this is because race is considered irrelevant to the work that needs to be done or because both participants agree to a conspiracy of silence about a potentially touchy issue. Nevertheless, race—like any other significant factor that contaminates interaction—must be at least tentatively discussed because to be "colorblind" is to deny real differences.[10]

The presumption of ignorance, necessary in all interviews, is more necessary when interviewing a black client because the worker is more likely to be ignorant of the client's situation. Therefore, he must listen more carefully, be less ready to come to conclusions, and be more open to having

[8] Crawford E. Burns, "White Staff, Black Children: Is There a Problem?" *Child Welfare*, Vol. 50, No. 2 (February 1971), p. 93.

[9] *See* Roger Miller, "Student Research Perspectives on Race," *Smith College Studies in Social Work*, Vol. 41, No. 1 (November 1970), pp. 1–23; and Michele Seligman, "The Interracial Casework Relationship," *Smith College Studies in Social Work*, Vol. 39, No. 1 (November 1968), p. 84.

[10] Julia Bloch, "The White Worker and the Negro Client in Psychotherapy," *Social Work*, Vol. 13, No. 2 (April 1968), pp. 36–42.

his presuppositions corrected by the client, i.e., he must want to know what the situation is and be receptive to being taught.

It is frequently asserted that lower-class black clients lack the fluency and facility with language that are required for a good interview. Yet studies of speech behavior in the ghetto suggest that blacks show great imaginativeness and skill with language.[11] Thus the worker has the obligation to learn the special language of the ghetto. The agency can help by hiring black clerical and professional staff. If the black client sees members of his own group working at the agency, he has a greater sense of assurance that he will be accepted and understood.

BLACK WORKER–BLACK CLIENT

If both worker and client are black, different problems may arise. The pervasiveness of the cultural definition of blackness does affect the black client. Thus he may feel that being assigned to a black worker is less desirable than being assigned to a white worker because the latter may have more influence and thus be in a better position to help him.

The fact that the black social worker has achieved middle-class professional status suggests that he has accepted some of the principal mores of the dominant culture—e.g., motivation to achieve, denial of gratification, the work ethic, punctuality. To get where he is, he probably was educated in white schools, read the white literature, and associated with white classmates —as he now associates with white colleagues.

The black middle-class worker may feel estranged not only from whites but from his own blackness. The problem of establishing a clearly defined identification is more difficult for "oreos"—those who are black on the outside, but white on the inside because of their experiences while achieving middle-class status.

The black worker who returns to the ghetto after professonal training may be viewed with suspicion.[12] An alien returning from the outside world, where he has been "worked over" by the educational enterprise to accept white assumptions, values, and language, he has supposedly lost contact with the fast-changing ghetto subculture in the interim.

If the black client sees the white worker as representing the enemy, he may see the black social worker as a traitor to his race, a collaborator with the establishment. Therefore, barriers to self-disclosure and openness may be as great between the black worker and black client as between the white worker and black client.

The black client is also a source of anxiety to the black worker in other ways. A black psychiatrist stated it as follows: "For the therapist who has fought his way out of the ghetto [the black patient] may awaken memories and fears he would prefer to leave undisturbed." [13] Thus Brown's findings that black workers were less sympathetic to black clients than to white clients is not surprising.[14] They were made anxious by black clients' failure to live up to the standards of the dominant culture and felt that such deviations reflected on the race as a whole—thus decreasing the acceptability of all blacks, including themselves.

Calnek aptly defines overidentification in

---

[11] *See,* for example, Thomas Kochman, "Rapping in the Black Ghetto," *Transaction,* Vol. 6, No. 4 (February 1969), pp. 26–34.

[12] Orville Townsend, "Vocational Rehabilitation and the Black Counselor: The Conventional Training Situation and the Battleground Across Town," *Journal of Rehabilitation,* Vol. 36, No. 6 (November–December 1970), pp. 26–31.

[13] As quoted in Sager, Brayboy, and Waxenberg, op. cit., p. 228.

[14] Brown, op. cit.

this context as a "felt bond with another black person who is seen as an extension of oneself because of a common racial experience." [15] A black AFDC client described it as follows:

> Sometimes the ones that have had hard times don't make you feel good. They're always telling you how hard *they* had to work—making you feel low and bad because you haven't done what they done.[16]

The black worker also may be the target of displacement, i.e., the black client's hostility toward whites is expressed toward the black worker because he is less dangerous.

One clear advantage in the black worker–black client situation, however, is that the black professional provides the client with a positive image he can identify with. Kincaid states that

> a Black counselor who has not rejected his own personal history may be most able to inspire a feeling of confidence and a sense of hope in his Black client.[17]

When the worker is black and the client is white, other problems may arise. The client may be reluctant to concede that the black worker is competent and may feel he has been assigned second best. If the client is from the South, he may be especially sensitive to the reversal in usual status positions.[18]

If the client sees himself as lacking prejudice, he may welcome being assigned to a black worker because it gives him a chance to parade his atypical feelings. He may be gratified to have a black worker since only an unusually accomplished black could, in his view, achieve professional standing. On the other hand, because the white who turns to a social agency for help often feels inadequate and inferior, he may more easily establish a positive identification with the "exploited" and "oppressed" black worker.[19]

MATCHING

Any discussion of the problems inherent in cross-cultural interviewing inevitably leads to the question of matching. On the whole, would it not be desirable to select a worker of the same race as the client? Would this not reduce social distance and the resistance and constraints in interactions that derive from differences in group affiliation, experiences, and life-style? If empathic understanding is a necessary prerequisite for establishing a good relationship, would this not be enhanced by matching people who are culturally at home with each other?

Obviously, empathic understanding is most easily achieved if the worker shares the client's world. However, the difficulties of empathic understanding across subcultural barriers can be exaggerated and the disadvantages of matching worker and client can be underestimated.

The world's literature is a testimonial to the fact that people can understand and empathize with those whose backgrounds and living situations are different from their own. For example, an American

---

15 Maynard Calnek, "Racial Factors in the Counter-Transference: The Black Therapist and the Black Client," *American Journal of Orthopsychiatry*, Vol. 40, No. 1 (January 1970), p. 42.

16 As quoted in Hugh McIsaac and Harold Wilkinson, "Clients Talk About Their Caseworkers," *Public Welfare*, Vol. 23, No. 2 (July 1965), p. 153.

17 Kincaid, op. cit., p. 888.

18 Andrew D. Curry, "Negro Worker and White Client: A Commentary on the Treatment Relationship," *Social Casework*, Vol. 45, No. 3 (March 1964), pp. 131–136.

19 William Grier, "When the Therapist is Negro: Some Effects on the Treatment Process," *American Journal of Psychiatry*, Vol. 123, No. 12 (June 1967), pp. 1587–1592.

Christian, John Hersey, demonstrated empathic understanding of a Polish Jew in *The Wall;* an American Jew, Elliot Liebow, demonstrated his ability to understand ghetto blacks in *Tally's Corner;* and a white South African psychiatrist, Wulf Sachs, showed his sensitive understanding of a Zulu in *Black Hamlet.*[20]

If the worker's professional training enhances his ability to empathize with and understand different groups and provides the knowledge base for such understanding, the social and psychological distance between worker and client can be reduced. If the gap is sufficiently reduced, the client perceives the worker as being capable of understanding him, even though he is a product of a different life experience.

Some of the relative merits and disadvantages of close matching and distant matching are succinctly summarized in the following statement by Carson and Heine:

> With very high similarity the therapist may be unable to maintain suitable distance and objectivity, whereas in the case of great dissimilarity he would not be able to empathize with, or understand, the patient's problems.[21]

Thus it is not surprising that relevant research suggests effective interviewing is not linearly related to rapport, i.e., it is not true that the more rapport, the better. The relationship appears to be curvilinear, i.e., little rapport is undesirable, but so is maximum rapport. The best combination is moderate closeness or moderate distance between participants. Weiss, in a study of the validity of responses of a group of welfare mothers, found that socially desirable rather than valid responses were more likely to result under conditions of high similarity and high rapport.[22]

Clinical evidence also suggests that racial matching is not always a crucial variable in the interview. A study that tested the degree of distortion in responses to black and white psychiatrists by patients in a county psychiatric ward concluded that "the factor of race did not significantly affect the behavior of the subjects in the interview situation." [23] The patients perceived and responded to black psychiatrists as psychiatrists rather than as members of a different race. In a California study AFDC recipients were asked to assess the help they received from their caseworkers. The study group was large enough so that black and white caseworkers were able to contact both black and white recipients. The general conclusion was that the "race of the worker, per se, did not make a significant contribution to the amount of 'help' recipients received from the social service." [24]

---

[20] New York: Alfred A. Knopf, 1950; and Boston: Little, Brown & Co., 1967 and 1947, respectively.

[21] R. C. Carson and R. W. Heine, "Similarity and Success in Therapeutic Dyads," *Journal of Consulting Psychology*, Vol. 26, No. 1 (February 1962), p. 38.

[22] Carol H. Weiss, *Validity of Interview Responses of Welfare Mothers—Final Report* (New York: Bureau of Applied Social Research, Columbia University, February 1968). *See also* Herbert H. Hyman, *Interviewing in Social Research* (Chicago, Ill.: University of Chicago Press, 1954); Barbara S. Dohrenwend, J. A. Williams, and Carol H. Weiss, "Interviewer Biasing Effects, Toward a Reconciliation of Findings," *Public Opinion Quarterly*, Vol. 33, No. 1 (Spring 1969), pp. 121–129; and Dohrenwend, John Colombotos, and B. P. Dohrenwend, "Social Distance and Interviewer Effects," *Public Opinion Quarterly*, Vol. 32, No. 3 (Fall 1968), pp. 410–422.

[23] William M. Womack, "Negro Interviewers and White Patients: The Question of Confidentiality and Trust," *Archives of General Psychiatry*, Vol. 16, No. 6 (June 1967), p. 690.

[24] *California Welfare: A Legislative Program for Reform* (Sacramento: Assembly Office of Research, California Legislature, February 1969), p. 10.

PARAPROFESSIONALS

The shortcomings of matching have become more apparent as a result of experience with indigenous paraprofessionals in the human services. In efforts to find new careers for the poor during the last few years, many social agencies have hired case aides from the area they serve. These indigenous case aides live in the same neighborhood as the client group, generally have the same racial background, and often struggle with the same kinds of problems. Therefore, they are in an excellent position to empathize with and understand the problems of the poor, blacks, and poor blacks—and in fact they often do.

In a study of agency executives' and supervisors' evaluations of paraprofessional performance, it was found that these workers were rated high on their ability to establish rapport with clients. One agency administrator described this ability as follows:

> In intake interviewing, paraprofessionals are very good at picking up clues and cues from the clients. They have a good ear for false leads and "put-ons." Their maturity and accumulated life experience, combined with firsthand knowledge of the client population, assists the agency in establishing communication with clients rapidly. . . . The new client is more comfortable with a paraprofessional because he or she is someone like himself.[25]

Riessman, however, notes the following difficulties:

> Frequently professionals assume that NP's [nonprofessionals] identify with the poor and possess great warmth and feeling for the neighborhood of their origin. While many NP's exhibit some of these characteristics, they simultaneously possess a number of other characteristics. Often, they see themselves as quite different from the other members of the poor community, whom they may view with pity, annoyance, or anger. Moreover, there are many different "types" of nonprofessionals; some are earthy, some are tough, some are angry, some are surprisingly articulate, some are slick, clever wheeler-dealers, and nearly all are greatly concerned about their new roles and their relationship to professionals.[26]

Much of the research on nonprofessionals confirms the fact that with close matching, the problems of overidentification and activation or reactivation of problems faced by the worker are similar to those that concern the client. The client, feeling a deep rapport with the worker and anxious to maintain his friendship, may give responses that he thinks will make him more acceptable. He has an investment in the relationship and does not want to risk it by saying or doing anything that would alienate the worker.

If the effects of matching are not invariably advantageous, the effects of difference in cultural background between worker and client are not always disadvantageous. The problem that is created when a worker is identified with one subculture (e.g., sex, race, age, color, or class) and the client is affiliated with another is one specific aspect

---

[25] Karolyn Gould, *Where Do We Go From Here?—A Study of the Roads and Roadblocks to Career Mobility for Paraprofessionals Working in Human Service Agencies* (New York: National Committee on Employment of Youth, 1969), pp. 5–6.

[26] Frank Riessman, "Strategies and Suggestions for Training Nonprofessionals," in Bernard Guerney, ed., *Psychotherapeutic Agents—New Roles for Nonprofessionals, Parents and Teachers* (New York: Holt, Rinehart & Winston, 1969), p. 154. *See also* Charles Grosser, "Manpower Development Programs," and Gertrude Goldberg, "Nonprofessionals in the Human Services," in Grosser, William Henry, and James Kelly, eds., *Nonprofessionals in the Human Services* (San Francisco, Calif.: Jossey-Bass, 1969): and Francine Sobey, *The Nonprofessional Revolution in Mental Health* (New York: Columbia University Press, 1970).

of in-group–out-group relations generally. The worker, because of his higher status, may encourage communication from the client. In addition, because he is an outsider, he does not reflect in-group judgments. If the client has violated or disagrees with in-group values, this is an advantage. Currently, for instance, a middle-class white-oriented accommodative black client might find it more difficult to talk to a black worker than a white worker.

If the client with upwardly mobile aspirations is looking for sources of identification outside his own group, contact with a nonmatched worker is desirable. Thus the lower-class client, anxious to learn middle-class ways, would seek such a worker. The fact that the worker does not initially understand him may be helpful. In trying to make his situation clear, the client may be forced to look at it more explicitly than before—i.e., in explaining it to an outsider, he may explain it better to himself. Further, the client may feel that the white worker has more influence in the community. Thus he may feel more hopeful.

In contrast, however, numerous studies indicate that in most instances some disadvantages derive from racial difference between interviewer and interviewee.[27] With white interviewers blacks are more likely to make acceptable public responses; with black interviewers they give more private answers. For example, blacks are less ready to share their feelings about discrimination with white interviewers. Carkhuff, in a study in which black and white therapists from middle- and lower-class backgrounds interviewed white and black patients from various class backgrounds, found that both class background and race affected the readiness with which patients shared intimate material. They were most open to therapists of similar race and class.[28]

CLIENT PREFERENCE

Research on client preference does not uniformly support the contention that clients invariably select professionals from their own group. Dubey, for example, offers empirical support for the contention that blacks do not overwhelmingly prefer black workers.[29] Using black interviewers, he asked some five hundred ghetto residents questions such as "Would you rather talk with a Negro social worker or with a white social worker?" and "Would you rather go to an agency where the director is Negro or to one where the director is white?" About 78 percent of the respondents said they had no preference. Only 10–11 percent said they strongly preferred a black worker or agency director.

Backner encountered this problem over a three-year period as a counselor in the City College of New York's SEEK program, established to help high school graduates

---

[27] *See,* for example, Jerome A. Sattler, "Racial 'Experimenter Effects' in Experimentation, Testing, Interviewing and Psychotherapy," *Psychological Bulletin,* Vol. 73, No. 2 (February 1970), pp. 137–160.

[28] Robert R. Carkhuff and Richard Pierce, "Differential Effects of Therapist's Race and Social Class Upon Patient Depth of Self-Exploration in the Initial Clinical Interview," *Journal of Consulting Psychology,* Vol. 31, No. 6 (December 1967), pp. 632–634. *See also* Eugene C. Bryant, Isaac Gardner, and Morton Goldman, "References on Racial Attitudes as Affected by Interviewers of Different Ethnic Groups," *Journal of Social Psychology,* Vol. 70, No. 1 (October 1966), pp. 95–100.

[29] Sumati Dubey, "Blacks' Preference for Black Professionals, Businessmen and Religious Leaders," *Public Opinion Quarterly,* Vol. 34, No. 1 (Spring 1970), pp. 113–116.

from poverty areas with problems encountered in college.[30] Eighty percent of the students in the program were black and 15 percent were Puerto Rican. Backner was constantly admonished by students that "a white counselor can never really undertand the black experience" and that "no black brother or black sister is really going to talk to whitey." However, the results of a questionnaire completed by about half of the 325 students in the program tended to substantiate the staff's impression that although the students responded negatively to white counselors in general, they reacted differently to their own white counselors. One item asked, "What quality in your counselor would make you feel most comfortable?" Only 12.7 percent of the respondents said that a counselor of the same racial background was the most important consideration. In response to the question, "Which SEEK teachers, counselors, and tutors are most effective and helpful to you?" 4.9 percent of the students checked "teacher, counselor, or student with the same ethnic and racial background," whereas 42 percent checked "those whose ability as teachers, counselors, tutors seems good."

In a subsequent survey of all SEEK students, using a mail questionnaire that was completed anonymously and returned by 45 percent of the students, the relevant question was, "Your own counselor's ethnic background (a) should be the same as yours, (b) doesn't matter." Although 25.8 percent of the respondents answered that their counselors should have the same background, 68.4 percent said it did not matter. Subsequent studies indicated that when a student felt ethnicity was important, he was often expressing his feelings about the counselor as a person rather than a white person. However, in another study in which respondents had the opportunity to view racially different counselors via video tapes in a standard interview based on a script, blacks selected black counselors and whites selected whites.[31]

Brieland showed that client preference was dependent on certain conditions.[32] Black and white social work students asked black ghetto residents the following question: "If both were equally good, would you prefer that the (doctor, caseworker, teacher, lawyer, parents' group leader) be Negro (Black, Colored) or White?" One interesting result demonstrated the important effects of similarity or dissimilarity between interviewer–interviewee pairs. The white interviewers had a significantly larger percentage of respondents who said they had no preference as compared with black interviewers to whom respondents confessed they preferred a black doctor, caseworker, teacher, and so forth. However, only 55 percent of the respondents interviewed by black interviewers said they preferred a black caseworker, and 45 percent had no preference or preferred a white caseworker. The basis for respondents' preference for a black caseworker, other factors being equal, was that a black interviewer was more likely to be interested in his problems, less likely to talk down to him or make him feel worthless, more likely to give him a feeling of hope, and more likely to know the meaning of poverty.

A second question, which introduced the factor of competence, asked the respondent

[30] Burton L. Backner, "Counseling Black Students: Any Place for Whitey?" *Journal of Higher Education,* Vol. 41, No. 8 (November 1970), pp. 630–637.

[31] Richard J. Stranges and Anthony C. Riccio, "Counselee Preferences for Counselors: Some Implications for Counselor Education," *Counselor Education and Supervision,* Vol. 10, No. 3 (Fall 1970), pp. 39–45.

[32] Donald Brieland, "Black Identity and the Helping Person," *Children,* Vol. 16, No. 5 (September–October 1969), pp. 170–176.

to state his preference for a black or white worker if the white worker was better qualified. A large percentage of those who preferred "equally good" black caseworkers preferred a white caseworker if his qualifications were better. Competence, then, proved to be more important than race in determining black respondents' caseworker preferences.

Barrett's and Perlmutter's study of black clients' responses to black and white counselors at the Philadelphia Opportunities Industrialization Center—which offers training, placement, and vocational guidance services—supports Brieland's findings.[33] Although black clients preferred black counselors in the abstract (the interviewers in the study were black), actual ongoing client-counselor contact indicated that competence was a more crucial and significant variable than race. However, Barrett and Perlmutter suggest that the importance of matching may be greater when the problems discussed focus on personal concerns rather than on concrete services and when the client initially contacts the agency.

CONCLUSION

After making the usual cautious provisos about the contradictory nature of the findings, the tentativeness of conclusions, the deficiencies in methodology, the dangers of extrapolation, and so forth, what do all these findings seem to say? They seem to say that although nonwhite workers may be necessary for nonwhite clients in some instances and therapeutically desirable in others, white workers can work and have worked effectively with nonwhite clients. They seem to say that although race is important, the nature of the interpersonal relationship established between two people is more important than skin color and that although there are disadvantages to racially mixed worker-client contacts, there are special advantages. Conversely, there are special advantages to racial similarity and there are countervailing disadvantages. In other words, the problem is not as clear cut as might be supposed.

Not only is the situation equivocal, it is complex. To talk in terms of white and nonwhite is to simplify dichotomously a variegated situation that includes many kinds of whites and nonwhites. For example, interview interaction with a lower-class black male militant is quite different from interview interaction with a middle-class female black integrationist.

Findings like the ones reviewed here are understandably resisted, resented, and likely to be rejected because of the political implications that can be drawn from them. Nonwhite community leaders, in fighting for control of social service institutions in their communities, point to the special advantages to community residents of nonwhite staff and administration. Some studies tend to suggest that the need for nonwhite staff and administration is not that urgent. However, this ignores the current underrepresentation in social agencies of nonwhite workers and administrators, the clear preference of some nonwhite clients for a worker of similar racial background, the fact that many clients need workers of similar racial background as sources of identification for change, and the fact that although white workers may be able to understand and empathize with the nonwhite experience, nonwhite workers achieve this sooner, more thoroughly, and at less cost to the relationship.

---

[33] Franklin T. Barrett and Felice Perlmutter, "Black Clients and White Workers: A Report from the Field," *Child Welfare*, Vol. 50, No. 1 (January 1972), pp. 19–24.

Group Application Interviews in a Family Agency

ALBERTINA MABLEY

WHEN THE suggestion was made that our agency conduct group application interviews for people requesting family casework service, it seemed that this could not be done without violating some of the basic principles of casework practice. We were concerned about how we could safeguard individual privacy, whether a beginning relationship could be established with the applicants, and whether we could maintain an appropriately individualized focus. Two factors were influential in our decision to experiment with the suggestion: the pressure of an increasing waiting list and our participation for two years in meetings of the Family Agency Study Group, which had provided training in group treatment and stimulated our interest in group process.*

The application group was initiated in a district office where the waiting period was about two months. We began by arranging three application meetings at two-week intervals. We spaced the meetings in this way to allow time for any necessary individual interview before the worker met with a new group. We decided that no fees would be charged for these first meetings because we were uncertain about how much help could be given in an hour and a half with unselected applicants. When an applicant telephoned to request service, we followed our usual practice of having one of the caseworkers give him an appointment. He was given the time of one of the group application meetings and the worker's name; he was not, however, told that he would be attending a group meeting because we thought that the anticipation of the group meeting might create undue anxiety and lead to cancellations. Also, we did not want the usual absences falsely attributed to negative feelings about a group meeting.

At the time appointed for the meeting the worker introduced herself to each of the applicants in the reception room and invited them to come to the conference room together. Once they were assembled, she explained that we had no plan to continue this group but that we hoped to save time and repetition by seeing them together and knew that an added advantage of a group session was that their questions could stimulate and help each other to decide whether to proceed with their applications. The response of the group members was one of appreciation for our effort to be efficient and make the best use of time. They expressed this feeling again when we talked of the waiting list. The worker's statement that the various members' questions might be useful to others was given considerable verbal acknowledgment and encouraged freedom on the part of the applicants in making inquiries.

From such timid beginnings, we have progressed. We currently have two application group meetings each week. Every applicant is scheduled for one of them, except those applicants who have had considerable previous contact with the agency, those who are referred to us as the representative of Travelers Aid service in the community, and those who have been judged from the telephone contact to be acutely disturbed. After the first three meetings, we were satisfied that our applicants benefited from the group application, and so fees were established.

After the first six meetings we began informing the applicants that they would be

* This group was a committee of the United Community Services of Metropolitan Detroit, composed of staff representatives of the eight family agencies in the Detroit area. Emanuel Hallowitz, assistant professor of psychiatry at the Albert Einstein College of Medicine, served as group treatment consultant to the study group.

SOCIAL CASEWORK, March 1966, Vol. 47, No. 3, pp. 158-164.

seen first in a group meeting where service would be planned. The giving of this information has in no way affected the number of applicants who fail to keep appointments. The group meetings have varied in size from two to ten members, the average being five persons in a group.

We were concerned about the possibility of an applicant's encountering a personal acquaintance at a meeting but decided that most people would be able to handle such a predicament. We never discovered the reason for the agitation of one applicant who found herself part of one of our largest and first groups, and who insisted her appointment was with the worker with whom she had talked on the telephone about an appointment. It was apparent she would persist in avoiding the group or leave, and so another staff member saw her. On the other hand, we have found that some applicants try to discover associations with others and thus establish connections.

The Mechanics of Application

Face sheet information is secured by asking the applicants to fill in a simplified data sheet, and they seem to welcome this procedure as a way of settling into the group and binding their natural anxiety. We usually tell them this written information is confidential and that we wish to have it even if we decide together by the close of the meeting that some other plan would be more appropriate and desirable than continuing contacts with the agency. Frequently, the group members exchange remarks about the difficulty in recalling birth dates or some other information called for on the data sheet, and these comments also serve to reduce strain and tension.

There are always questions about gross income and fees, and we have observed surprising freedom in discussions of business ventures that cause fluctuations in income. In addition, applicants ask about joint incomes and voluntarily and frankly discuss why both husband and wife are working. This gives the worker an opportunity to discuss our reasons for charging fees, the agency's source of income, and our primary responsibility for helping families whether or not they can pay a fee. The applicants set their own fees, using our fee chart as a guide. Their questions bring answers from the caseworker that demonstrate the thoughtfulness and flexibility of the agency policies.

Mrs. A, twenty years of age, was applying for marital counseling. She told the group her husband was dictatorial, demanding, and irrational. He gave her no funds and even took from her the money she earned by baby sitting. She said she could pay only a one-dollar fee although she knew her husband's earnings warranted her paying more. The worker suggested the fee could be adjusted after contact had been established with Mr. A and asked whether Mrs. A could really manage to pay a dollar. Mrs. A explained that she had a dollar because she had planned to get her coat from the cleaners, but thought she could manage without it. The worker suggested that she get the coat and that the application fee be waived.

Mr. B, a factory worker, pointed out that his potential income from his job was greater than his current earnings or his actual earnings during the past year. The worker asked how long he had been receiving his current income and why his income fluctuated. She helped him arrive at a fair estimate and told him his income could be reviewed with the ongoing worker and his fee changed as his situation changed. By this discussion she showed the group members they could expect reasonable and individualized consideration.

The subject of the waiting list—usually introduced later in the meeting—always stimulates questions and comments. Applicants usually say that they have come to the agency because their problems are critical. Their feelings about having to wait are relieved, however, as they are discussed in the group. In one meeting, after a discussion of the necessity of giving priority to some situations, a very controlling applicant, who had previously spoken at length of her tenseness and distress and need for immediate individual help, pointed out that another applicant's situation was obviously an emergency that should get immediate attention. She added that she knew the worker could not do everything at once. In another meeting when several couples were present who had been discussing their marital problems, one woman, who had shown empathy in the discussion, patted another on the shoulder as they were leaving and said, "You are having such a terrible time. I hope you get appointments before I do." There is always sympathy for, and understanding of, the priority given to adolescents and their parents. Recently a young woman, who had heard another mother tell of her concerns about an adolescent daughter who had been expelled from school, remarked that her children were only four and six years old and could more readily wait for help than the troubled adolescent.

We feel the discussions in application meetings have provided real understanding of the waiting list and have presented it to the clients in a much more desirable light than does the usual explanation, which frequently carries some aspects of rejection.

Support

At the point of application it is usual practice in agencies to give applicants support in seeking help, to make an effort to alleviate their immediate distress. We have found that group application meetings are often more effective in accomplishing this objective than individual sessions. As soon as some members begin to reveal their problems, the others know that they are not alone with their difficulties. The feelings of concern that are expressed as the meeting proceeds and even the advice that is sometimes offered give the applicants additional support. One day, for example, an elderly "good Baptist" suggested to a young divorcee, then illegitimately pregnant, that she should learn more about the father of the expected baby before she married him. The note of concern as someone identified the group member's expressed feeling—in this case, ambivalence and confusion—made her feel accepted and understood. Meanwhile, others in the group who have the same general problem are stimulated to share the experiences that have given them understanding of their feelings.

In another group session, for example, two middle-class professional couples were comparing their marital problems when a third couple arrived late. The late-comers were of a lower socioeconomic class, the man being a factory worker. His wife had just been released from jail for fighting. She described a life of great deprivation and loneliness. When invited to join in the discussion, the newcomers poured out their distress and accounts of their friction, which had reached the point at which the wife had thrown breakable objects at her husband. In response, one of the other women commented on "how bad you feel afterward." With amazement, the third woman said, "Yes, I'm already missing some of my pretty things." The first two couples continued their discussion and, as the group broke up, the woman in the third couple said to the worker, "I didn't know other people had trouble like this." She surely had experienced understanding and acceptance greater than one worker could give.

Comments about feelings of despair or not knowing what to do always occur in a group and provide an easy opening for the worker to introduce a discussion of the difficulty most people have in making the decision to come to the agency for help. Some applicants say that it has been similar to admitting that there is another side to their problem and that perhaps they are partly wrong. Others talk of the guilt they feel at not being able to manage on their own. Many speak of having delayed application for as long as their situation could be tolerated. There have been applicants who have said little but have participated by nodding and weeping as others told of their troubled feelings.

Mrs. T, a most attractive and well-dressed young woman, was unable to talk in one of our first group meetings. She made several attempts to speak about her marital problems but each time choked up, shook her head, and remained silent. The worker said she must feel very hurt, alone, and frustrated, and Mrs. T nodded and smiled. Others were immediately stimulated to talk about situations in their lives that had caused similar feelings.

When Mrs. T came for her first individual appointment with a caseworker, she had even greater difficulty in talking at first, but she was determined to work on her problems. She said that prior to the application meeting she had been so hurt and upset by her husband's rejection that she had been unable to do anything. She said she thought the meeting had helped her to see her situation in perspective. Following the group session she had been able to function: she had enrolled for the second term of a nursing course she was taking, participated in planned activities with her children, and begun to think more clearly again. She had found the support she needed in the group meeting although very little attention had been directed specifically to her and her own verbal participation had been so limited.

Some of the support most applicants need is given by discussion of the strength that is required to ask for help and the reasons people are afraid to ask questions. Many times there has been a woman in the group who has said that her husband objects to seeking help and insists that they solve their own problem. She does not know what to do about this. Reactions of the other group members make it clear that they have all faced this problem in some way or another: they speak of their disagreements, agreements to use the agency as part of a compromise, negative feelings about being referred by an authoritative source, their expectations of the agency, and so forth. For the caseworker, such a discussion provides an opportunity to assure the group members they are self-determining individuals and the only ones who can change their situations. The worker can then discuss what they can realistically expect of agency service. Sometimes this introduces the choices the applicants will be making as clients about individual or joint interviews, family interviews, or group treatment. Incidentally, the worker is often able to identify applicants who seem ready to use group treatment.

Occasionally, we have discovered that an objection to being seen in a group at application is a reflection of resistance to seeking any agency help. We usually state the fact that no one will be asked to reveal anything he does not wish to disclose and that we believe a group discussion can be helpful. We have permitted, and often encouraged, an angry applicant to express his negative feelings at the group meeting. Some of the applicants have been critical of others in the group and have verbally separated themselves from the group. One man said, "How could any of these people possibly be interested in my very personal problem or help me?" We have experienced having resistance to the group expressed by one applicant and added to by the others present. Then the discussion can be guided to the topic of general resistance to asking for help with personal problems, a feeling common to all. Usually some group members then describe their own feelings of resistance, and as the exchange continues, even the most resistive members of the group are drawn in and accepted. In every meeting we have had, the resistive, angry person has taken part in the discussion eventually. When an applicant has found it necessary to speak to the worker alone after the group session, it has almost always been about a sexual problem or some other matter better suited for discussion in an individual interview. Many such problems have been spoken of in the groups, but usually because the applicant is feeling great pressures and lacks controls.

Clarification of the Problem

Another goal at application time is the clarification of the applicant's problem and the identification of those aspects of it on which he should work. A discussion of problems is frequently initiated by the clients themselves: it is quite common for a group member, on reaching the space on the data sheet headed "Problem," to cry out: "Problems, I have so many I wouldn't know what to put down." The worker suggests that the group talk about problems. The response varies, but it always comes—usually in the form of a hesitant, frank description of family friction by one person, which stimulates associations and comparisons by another applicant. The identification of one applicant with another on the basis of their problems happens readily with married couples who observe likenesses in their experiences and also with parents of adolescents who are experiencing similar concerns, frustrations, and hurts. Frequently applicants with very different problems find likenesses in their feelings about early life experiences or experiences with their extended families.

Sometimes this kind of discussion leads to an outpouring of problems, almost as if the speaker were unaware of how others might feel about what was being said. When this happens the worker may have to point out the general aspects of the problem several times before the troubled person can let others speak. His doing so enables group discussion to take place and is a first step in assisting the overwhelmed applicant to sort out what he is feeling and begin to think. Finally, as mentioned earlier, the worker's suggestions of talking of problems may lead the resistive applicant to denounce the worker and agency for expecting strangers to share personal matters, but often there is an ensuing discussion of resistance, acceptance of anger, and, finally, the applicant's problems.

In any application group the members observe the worker's acceptance of the various problems and hear the worker's questions, which are aimed at seeking more understanding of each problem. They are freer to observe the worker as he deals with others, and thus they gain a special understanding of agency service. Throughout, the client is given new glimpses of his own problem, and frequently he begins to focus his feelings.

Disposition of the Application

The worker must obtain enough information in the application meeting to know what the applicants' problems are and then be able to make appropriate disposition of each application. We have found that we are able to identify those situations in which referrals to other agencies are indicated. In addition, we have been able to identify the problems that need immediate exploration—those, for example, that involve mental disturbance, acute environmental situations, or time limits.

Additional Observations

We find the group meeting gives a realistic opportunity for observing the ego functioning of the applicants. It immediately becomes apparent whether an applicant has the ability to hear what another member of the group says and to respond with logical comments. Moreover, an individual's ability to participate and to empathize with another member and understand his feelings about his problems is evident. Much is revealed about the functioning of a group member as he draws upon his memory of past experiences and relates those experiences to the situations under discussion. Often a young married couple is in a group with parents seeking help with the behavior of their adolescent child. When a younger person identifies quickly with the concerns of the troubled parent and at the same time draws on his fairly recent experiences in growing up to try to help the parent understand what his child is feeling, he demonstrates his perception, judgment, and integration. If he does so at the expense of having to delay the consideration of his own problems until later in the meeting, we also learn about his tolerance of frustration, his controls, and his attitudes toward outside pressures.

Every aspect of an applicant's interaction with the group members denotes something about how he relates to others. For instance, one very self-centered, troubled young woman poured out her problems without regard to the propriety of what she said but was unable to sustain interest when the discussion moved to the problems of others. She became restless and played with her gloves. An applicant's lack of sensitivity about the probable effect on others of what he is saying stands out in the problem-oriented group discussion and serves as an indicator of the person's judgment and relatedness. There are others who find it difficult to talk but participate with their interest, tears, and smiles, showing awareness and responsiveness to the group situation.

It is more difficult to identify the functioning of the individual who almost completely withdraws. Though we can observe his passive reaction, we do not know what he is thinking. We usually see such an individual briefly after the session to clarify the meaning of his withdrawal.

The behavior of the applicant who bids for group attention stands out in a group setting. Similarly, the group meeting enables the worker to evaluate the reasonableness of the individuals as they exchange ideas, tolerate things said by others, and accept the rules the worker establishes. He can also observe the members' responsiveness to group pressures and expectations.

Descriptions of two applicants who would generally not be considered suitable for group application illustrate the value of a group meeting in supplying diagnostic information and a beneficial experience for the client.

Mrs. C came to a group meeting that was attended by four other women. She filled in her information sheet clearly and without difficulty. She spoke about her husband's income, mentioning what she thought the gross income was; she seemed anxious about her accuracy and asked if she could notify us later. Following this, she was silent but listened intently and smiled at appropriate times. Three of the women compared and shared their experiences with their husbands, who were alcoholic in different degrees. The worker asked Mrs. C if she understood what the other women were discussing. Mrs. C answered that Mr. C did not drink but that he, too, seemed "sick of his marriage." She then told of his secretive behavior. She felt he was plotting something against her, and she said in rather vague terms that she guessed he received his orders from the Communist party. Suddenly, she realized that other members of the group were looking at her, and she began to gather her belongings, saying that Mr. C came home early for dinner and she thought she should be going home to prepare it. The worker said that everyone would be leaving soon and invited her to remain. She smiled and stayed to the end.

To the other women, the worker remarked that Mrs. C had understood their feelings about their husbands' withdrawal, and they immediately resumed the discussion of this and other difficulties. At the close of the meeting Mrs. C said she had enjoyed it, gave the worker permission to telephone Mr. C and her attorney, and made an appointment with the worker for the following week. The worker was reassured sufficiently by Mrs. C's handling of the information sheet, her alertness to the meaning of the discussion, and her obvious pleasure at being accepted for the whole meeting hour, to be able to take the necessary time to plan how to proceed with the case. Mrs. C gained assurance from the group experience and continued her contact with the agency.

A professional woman who was a widow sought counseling because she was feeling discouraged and defeated. Only after she had been scheduled for a group application meeting did we learn of her marked depression. In the group meeting, she talked of her despair and insurmountable responsibilities, but she was very responsive to others in the group. She was alert, never unduly anxious, and seemed able to relate to others. Her behavior indicated she was cognizant of the impression she thought she was making on other people. The caseworker was impressed with the ego strengths she observed in this prospective client. After the session the applicant sought out the worker to protest the scheduled fee. As she talked to the worker alone for ten minutes, she spelled out her troubles and verbalized her dependency and depression. There was a hysterical quality to her speech. In view of her recent observation of this woman in the group situation, the worker was able to recognize the manipulative way in which the applicant was using her feelings. The worker was understanding but brief and unwavering in maintaining the plan for appointments and the fee.

This experience helped the worker a few days later when she received a call from a person in the community who was very distressed about the seriousness of the applicant's depression. The worker could appreciate the pressures the potential client put upon any person in an individual encounter, and she could assure the caller that she was certain her friend had resources within herself that she would use. The applicant did find specific things to do to help herself while waiting, and she later used casework help effectively.

Evaluation

The information gained in group application seems to more than balance the data not obtained. We do not learn as much of the history of the problems or of the applicants' early life experiences as we would learn in an individual interview; however, we frequently learn some of the early history as applicants refer back to the reasons for their feelings or behavior. The relationship to the application worker is, of course, diluted in a group situation. It may be true, however, that the group application meeting is beneficial in guarding against too much revelation in a first interview. Moreover, applicants do not have as much of a problem in separating from the group application worker as they do from a worker with whom they have had an individual session, and they are less likely to have an illusion that they have solved their problems in one interview. The presenting problems are less comprehensively reviewed in a group session than in an individual interview, but we find we can secure all the information we need at the time as well as receive signed permission to obtain additional pertinent information while the applicant awaits service.

The number of applicants who follow through with their request for agency service is impressive. Out of fifty-eight people representing forty-two families seen in thirteen group meetings during the first three months of our experiment, one family was referred to the court, several were given emergency service, and twenty-four families were offered ongoing casework service. When appointments were offered, twenty-three of the twenty-four accepted; the couple who did not wish further appointments had made application for help twice in past years and had never continued. In contrasting the responses of applicants held on a priority waiting list at the central office with the response of our district waiting list, we found that 72 per cent and 96 per cent, respectively, continued. The result of group application interviews as manifested in a desire for continued service is encouraging.

Our experiences lead us to conclude that in a group application meeting we can accomplish the aims of an individual application interview. We have learned that it was our apprehensiveness that made us doubt the advisability of having troubled applicants, from a variety of backgrounds, meet in a group. We were unduly concerned about the sensitivity of the applicants. We find that they know how to defend themselves in various ways if they feel uncomfortable or are threatened. The caseworker's acceptance of their behavior and the use of whatever information is given to demonstrate the understanding and flexibility of the agency is as easily, and frequently more effectively, demonstrated in a group meeting. Our experience in group application meetings has convinced us that this is another way of being helpful to clients and reducing job pressures.

Student Process Recording: A Plea for Structure

MARGARET DWYER and MARTHA URBANOWSKI

IN SPITE OF the substantial gains made in refining the methods of social work education, one of the most central elements in the students' field instruction remains virtually unchanged—process recording. We think that a more structured kind of recording should be taught by field instructors, both because it is less time-consuming and because it is educationally sounder. With that aim in view, this article is intended to outline an approach to student recording that has been used successfully in the Loyola University School of Social Work.

The thesis presented here is that intellectual clarity and logical structure, both of which are accounted essential in classroom teaching and learning, should be accorded the same importance in field work instruction, and that they are particularly appropriate in student process recording.

The Value of Process Recording

Is it possible for social work educators to agree on the meaning of the term *process recording* as used in field work instruction, or is the term vague, undefined, and subject to widely different interpretations? There may be at least general agreement that process recording is the written description of the dynamic interaction that has taken place in an interview. This description of the interaction is expected to contain factual information, student observations, and an account of both the client's and the student's responses and activity. The recording is expanded, however, to encompass a detailed analysis of the student's observations of, and reactions to, the interview—an analysis that includes his diagnostic thinking and planning. His earliest training in recording, therefore, gives special emphasis to reporting a wealth of detail and places relatively little stress on the structure of the written account.

It is difficult to devise a satisfactory substitute for process recording for the beginning student. Although it is time-consuming, frustrating, and difficult for the student, it does have certain values for his professional learning and growth. It forces him to rethink each of his interviews with the consciousness that his experiences and his interaction with his clients must come through clearly to the field instructor who reads his records. Therefore, it plays an important part in providing direction and a structural framework for the supervisory conference. It gives the field work instructor an opportunity to individualize both the student and the clients with whom he is working, and it is a basic tool for stimulating communication and self-awareness on the part of the student.

Process recording enables the field instructor to assess quickly the student's ability to respond to a client's feelings, and it permits the instructor and the student jointly to identify the student's weaknesses and strengths without the student's feeling threatened or exposed. His recording also reflects the extent to which he is able to integrate knowledge and theory gained from previous experience, classroom courses, and outside reading. It also gives him an opportunity to gain the ease and freedom in written expression that are important for his professional development. But the extent to which recording becomes a vehicle for the student's continued growth or a roadblock to his advancement depends upon how it is used as a teaching device.

Problems To Be Faced

The core of the difficulty is that discursive, extremely detailed recording does not equip

SOCIAL CASEWORK, May 1965, Vol. 46, No. 5, pp. 283-286.

the student to meet the professional demands that will be made of him later. Since he invests so much of his field work time in recording, one should be able to expect that, by the end of two years' training, he would be able to formulate his thoughts clearly in writing. Most agency administrators agree, however, that recent graduates, generally, are not able to do this. Moreover, most trained workers confess they are not adept in recording and feel considerable resistance to it. Many students complete their training unable to think without a pencil in their hand and are burdened with the compulsive need to be detailed. When they become agency staff members, recording continues to consume a disproportionate amount of their time, with the not infrequent result that they try to escape from this reality by postponing it until it has reached unmanageable proportions. The new graduate is often unable to make the transition from the recording required by the educational process and the recording he is expected to produce as a professional worker.

In an article on supervisory teaching, Fred Berl stated that "the learning process has five stages through which each learner goes, regardless of his individual characteristics or his level of skill: beginning or orientation; defining the learning problem; struggling with the learning problem in the supervisor-worker relationship; making a breakthrough to independent functioning; and evaluating the learning process itself." [1] It appears to us that unstructured process recording, as described earlier, is especially useful in the first stage of the learning process but that it gradually diminishes in value throughout the other four stages. Field instructors have not been able to use it as a means of identifying the student's learning patterns, or as an aid in the formulation of educational goals. Furthermore, it has not proved its worth in helping the student develop his ability to see cause-and-effect relationships, to identify pertinent information, or to conceptualize his thinking.

The manual of field instruction of the Loyola University School of Social Work states: "As in the classroom courses, the content of field instruction needs to be identified and planfully communicated to the students. . . . Coverage of content poses special problems to the field instructor. Unlike the classroom instructor who can plan the teaching of content in a chronological order and effectively control the logical and sequential order of class content, the field instructor very often must select teaching content according to the needs of the case." [2] Consequently, the field instructor is dependent, in large measure, on the content of the student's recording in teaching the elements of casework. Although teaching content may have to be limited by the cases assigned, the field instructor can move fairly easily from the specific to the general. Without some structure, the student may feel lost and cling desperately to detail.

Why Structure Is Necessary

The question to be answered is this: How can process recording be retained as a valuable tool for learning without becoming a handicap? We believe that the answer lies in introducing *structure* into student recording. Students often ask for structure, and they have both a need for it and a right to it. Unfortunately, however, a student's request for structure is too frequently depreciated as stemming from a preprofessional attitude acquired during his undergraduate training.

There was a time when the social work profession considered itself too "human" to want to be allied with a structural approach. Social work education has now advanced beyond this "anti-intellectual" phase insofar as curriculum and classroom instruction are concerned; but equal progress has not been made in field work. Consequently, the curriculum has moved rapidly ahead while field work has remained in a stagnant backwater outside the main stream of social work education. This was clearly demonstrated by the absence of any concentration on field work in the entire thirteen volumes of *The Social Work Curriculum Study*. And recently two educators made this observation: "While there is almost universal conviction that field experience does in fact *educate*, there is by no means general acceptance of the notion that it can and must carry a full *educational* commitment in order to discharge fully its educational responsibilities."[3]

Because field instructors have not been helped to make the transition from the problem-solving focus of casework to the educational focus of field work teaching, they have clung to detailed recording. Many of them fear that, if the student is expected to structure his recording, there will be an unfortunate carry-over to his interviews with clients, which will result in a rigid, stereotyped client-worker relationship and a loss of "the human touch." Actually, the opposite is true. Structured recording can help the student clarify his thinking about the purpose of an interview and his role in it. It can serve as a basic instrument in guiding his learning and in helping him to conceptualize his thinking and organize his ongoing casework activities. His investment in this phase of the learning process tends to cushion the pain that often accompanies self-evaluation and helps him to assume greater responsibility for his own learning. We do not believe that an emphasis on structure in recording hampers the student's development of the human touch in his field work. It is the obligation of the field instructor to create an educational climate in which the student can feel comfortable in recording and develop a positive attitude toward it as a learning device and a professional skill.

An Approach to Structured Recording

It is essential that the beginning student be provided with an operational framework that can be adapted to his own particular needs and his own rate of growth and development. The following outline of recording content has been offered as a guide by the Loyola School of Social Work to its field work instructors. It has been successfully tested over a considerable period of time, and we think that it provides sufficient structure to aid the student to think in a disciplined and organized manner, while at the same time allowing him to exercise freedom of choice and creativity.

Purpose of Interview. The student should be directed toward formulating a statement of purpose that is concise, clear, and specific in relation to the proposed interview. It should show the relatedness between this interview and the previous interview and should also reflect the student's awareness of the particular function of the agency and of the client's capacity and motivation.

Observations. This section of the record will vary in length and content in accordance with the stage of the student-client relationship. More detail is likely to be needed in relation to the initial contacts. The student should record his general impressions of the physical and emotional climate at the outset of the interview and, more specifically, its impact on the client. Significant changes in the client's appearance and surroundings are also important.

Content. This part of the record should be devoted to the actual description of the interaction during the interview. However, the traditional emphasis on detail and total recall should be discouraged, and the student should be helped to be selective. As the student develops the ability to conceptualize and to organize his writing, both his recording and his casework practice become more focused. The length of this section of his recording depends on his stage of development and his learning patterns. Some students need to be helped to expand the section while others have to learn to be more concise. Although each student develops his own style of writing, this section should include the following:

1. A description of how the interview began
2. Pertinent factual information and responses of both the client and the student in relation to it
3. A description of the feeling content of the interview, on the part of both the client and the student
4. Notes on the client's preparation for the next interview and a description of how the interview ended.

Impressions. As early as the student's written review of the first case record assigned, he should be asked to make a statement of his impressions based on the facts. This process gradually develops into diagnostic thinking as he begins to integrate course content and gains understanding of the interaction between himself and the client.

Worker's Role. This section should highlight the student's activity in the interview and reflect his use of the casework skills and techniques he has acquired. He should record his own evaluation of his effectiveness as a helping person in each interview or group of interviews.

Plan. The student should make a brief statement of his plans for the next interview and record some of his thoughts about the long-range goals for his client.

It is an accepted premise in social work that the one-to-one relationship is an enabling factor in learning and plays an important part in the student's development of attitudes, values, and philosophy. Therefore, it must be continually kept in mind that the student's ability to risk himself in recording, as in his total performance, will be largely dependent on his relationship with his field work instructor. Students differ in regard to the time at which they are ready to become more selective in their recording of the "content" of the interview. Since each student is unique in his life experiences, in his previous acquaintance with social work, in his personal talents, and in his cultural background, the way in which the field instructor uses recording in teaching him must be tailored to his individual needs. What his needs are can be assessed as part of the ongoing educational diagnosis, and the requirements for his recording can be adjusted accordingly. The average first-year student can be expected to become more selective during the second quarter of field work—to record in two or three pages what earlier required five or six. Greater selectivity in recording the content of the interview has a two-fold result: (1) It is less time-consuming, and (2) it is an aid to concise, disciplined thinking. The student should continue to record material on the purpose of the interview, his impressions, his role, and his plan, but he may have to record his observations and detailed content only for the first few interviews of a newly assigned case, or when there appear to be special problems or significant changes, either on his own part or on the part of the client. This approach to recording enhances his later adjustment to the professional demands of an agency and enables him to see recording in its true perspective, as an aid to his practice rather than as a burden.

Conclusion

If one accepts the premise that the primary role of the field work instructor is education, then it follows that a certain amount of structure is essential. Field work instruction can no longer afford to exist in a vacuum, divorced from the rest of the curriculum. The field work component of the curriculum is undergoing critical examination in all schools of social work, and we have taken a fresh look at only one of its tools—recording. The disproportionate amount of time spent on this facet of training has limited the number of the student's contacts with clients and the time available for additional experiences, such as group meetings and staff consultations, which might more adequately prepare him to meet the demands of professional practice.

The major responsibility for improving the over-all content of field instruction rests with the schools of social work; they should take more leadership in helping field instructors become identified with educational objectives. Since field work instructors carry such a heavy responsibility in the educational process, it behooves them to rethink, clarify, and revitalize the function of recording as a teaching tool. What is needed is a more structured approach, but one that will not stifle the student's quest for smoothness and for his own individual recording style.

REFERENCES

[1] Fred Berl, "The Content and Method of Supervisory Teaching," SOCIAL CASEWORK, Vol. XLIV, November 1963, p. 520.

[2] *Loyola University School of Social Work Manual of Field Instruction,* Loyola University, Chicago, Illinois, 1963, p. 25.

[3] Bess S. Dana and Mildred Sikkema, "Field Instruction—Fact and Fantasy," in *Education for Social Work,* proceedings, twelfth annual program meeting, Council on Social Work Education, January 29–February 1, 1964, Council on Social Work Education, New York, 1964, pp. 90–101.

GROUP ACTIVITIES AND ASSIGNMENTS

Rumor clinic: to illustrate the distortions in communicating information from the original source through several individuals to a final destination. (for a model rumor clinic cf. Pfeiffer, J. William and John E. Jones, A Handbook of Structured Experiences for Human Relations Training, Iowa City, University Associates Press, 1970, Vol. II, pp. 14-17.)

Discuss the impact of cultural differences between the communicator and individuals and groups.

Nonverbal Communication Exercise (cf. IBID., Pfeiffer and Jones, Vol. I, pp. 109-111)

Give a written report of your observations and the information you gathered on one of the following: A family--its profile information and interaction; a group of children in a playground, a school, a day care center, etc.; a person in a Welfare Department waiting room, hospital waiting room, or employment agency.

SELECTED BIBLIOGRAPHY

Briar, Scott, "The Casework Predicament," Social Work, 13 (1), 1968, pp. 5-11.

Burns, M.E. and P.H. Glasser, "Similarities and Differences In Casework and Group Work Practice," Social Service Review, 37 (4), 1963, pp. 416-428.

Frings, John, "Experimental Systems of Recording," Social Casework, 38 (2), 1957, pp. 55-63.

Galper, Jeffry, "Nonverbal Communication Exercise In Groups," Social Work, 15 (2), 1970, pp. 71-78.

Gyarfas, Mary, "Social Science, Technology, and Social Work: A Caseworker's View," Social Service Review, 43 (3), 1969, pp. 259-273.

Hartman, Ann, "But What Is Social Casework," Social Casework, 52 (7), 1971, pp. 411-419.

Krause, M., "Comparative Effects On Continuance of Four Experimental Intake Procedures," Social Casework, 47 (10), 1966, pp. 515-519.

Mabley, Albertina, "Group Application Interviews In a Family Agency," Social Casework, 47 (3), 1966, pp. 158-63.

Parnicky, J., D. Anderson, C. Nakao, W. Thomas, "A Study of the Effectiveness of Referrals," Social Casework, 42 (12), 1961, pp. 494-501.

Payne, James, "Ombudsman Roles for Social Work," Social Work, 17 (1), 1972, pp. 94-100.

Scherz, F. H., "Intake: Concept and Process," Social Casework, 43 (3), 1962, pp. 120-125.

Selma, Arnold, "Confidential Communication and the Social Worker," Social Work, 15 (1), 1970, pp. 61-67.

Shattuck, G.M., J.M. Martin, "New Professional Work Roles and Their Integration Into A Social Agency Structure," Social Work, 14 (3), 1969, pp. 13-20.

Shyne, Ann, "Evaluation of Results In Social Welfare," Social Work, 8 (4),1963, pp. 26-33.

Simmons, R.E., "The Brief Interview As A Means of Increasing Service," Social Casework, 47 (7), 1966, pp. 429-432.

"The Social Worker As Advocate: Champion of Social Victims" Social Work, (14) 2, 1969, pp. 16-22.

Zentner, Ervin, "The Use of Letters to Sustain the Casework Process," Social Casework, 48 (3), 1967, pp. 135-140.

DATA COLLECTION

Although interviewing as discussed in the last chapter is perhaps the most important data collection tool used by the change agent, it must be placed in perspective with other techniques which are contingent on the systems that are suggested by a particular problem. A problem-centered approach to social work practice allows the worker to determine on the basis of the given specific situation, the types of systems he may work with and through to effect the desired changes. The general practitioner should know what data will be relevant to the problem he is working with. He should have the skill to collect data about various systems by using the appropriate tools of interviewing, observation, surveys, written material, etc.

Too often the change agent system has determined the client system, the action system, and the target system. A worker functioning in a casework agency often is conditioned to view the problem presented by a client as an individual problem which may involve members of his family. Although he may collect data related to the social situation of the person, the data usually does not extend outside the individual or family system to other systems that are contributing to the problem. This will in turn limit the systems in which the worker might intervene to effect change. Social work literature in the '50's and early '60s was concerned with "putting the social back into social work." This thrust was more often than not a reaction to a too psychoanalytically oriented approach to study, diagnosis, and treatment of individual and group problems. However the information about the social situation of the client was usually confined to the data collection and analysis phase of the process. It was not until the late 1960's that the data collected were not focused on the pathology of the individual and group, but were used to intervene in other systems that were impinging on the client system.

For example, a mother heading a one parent family living in a public housing project might be showing signs of severe depression. She might be helped on an individual basis to cope with her feelings. However if the data is collected on the person in the problem situation, it might well indicate that intervention should take place not only on an individual level, but should be directed more at the housing system itself. The change agent might discover that there are a number of women in the project experiencing the same type of problems. His original client might be helped much more effectively by joining with other tenants (action system) to make the housing project (target system) a less depressing place to live. In each case, although the change agent system remains the same, the client system, the action system, and the target system change, and the data to be gathered are from a broader base.

Germain's article, "Social Study: Past and Future," examines the evolution of social study and reveals that the spirit of scientific inquiry on which the study rests is more than ever necessary in the face of constantly changing needs. It suggest that the worker with a scientific orientation will always think analytically.

The general practitioner is often going to be working with client systems in crisis situations. The Pasewark, Albers article, "Crisis Intervention: Theory in Search of a Program," draws on the contributions of Erikson, Lindemann, and Caplan to crisis intervention theory. It describes the three cornerstones of the theory: the concept of developmental crises, transient personality disorders precipitated by unusual environmental stress and the public mental health model of primary, secondary, and tertiary prevention and ways to apply the concepts to the helping services.

In Duckworth's article, "A Project in Crisis Intervention," a family agency demonstrates that more people, especially in the low income bracket, could be served in crisis intervention. The caseworker's time was limited to brief help with an identified problem in fifty-one cases. The interviews with the individuals centered on the reason for the person applying to the agency at that particular time. Heavy demands were placed on the worker adapting interviewing techniques to particular problems and making the maximum use of outside resources, a role which is particularly appropriate for the general practitioner.

The "Use and Misuse of Groups" by Helen Levinson, although primarily a research report of a number of articles that have appeared on groups in social work journals, offers a framework that should be useful for collecting data with a task oriented or developmental group.

Since the majority of the work with community groups done by BSW workers would be done at the neighborhood level, data collection demands a knowledge of the composition and problems of this particular system. The article by Fellin and Litwak defines the various components and actions that make up a neighborhood as well as suggesting strategies for effecting change.

Social Study: Past and Future

CAREL B. GERMAIN

NEW APPROACHES to the practice of social casework are now being considered, implemented, and evaluated in all sectors of the profession. The impetus for innovation derives from a number of sources, including the application of crisis concepts in various areas of practice, the growing use of family treatment, the efforts to develop more effective modes of intervention in work with the poor, the concern about treatment dropout and treatment failure, and the need to use the limited supply of trained personnel more productively. Innovation is an appropriate professional response to new knowledge, to the emergence of new problems and needs, and to the impact of social change on old problems and needs. Nevertheless, the implications of innovation must be recognized. And certain implications in current new approaches seem to cast doubt on long-accepted notions of the psychosocial study as a formalized process essential to the diagnostic understanding on which treatment intervention is based.

The crisis approach assumes a time-limited period of upset, when the usual coping capacity is weakened, anxiety is high, and the individual or family is most accessible to help. Immediacy of preventive or restorative intervention is seen as paramount; a period of study and exploration as a basis for action appears inconsistent with the concept of crisis.

Similarly, family treatment appears to emphasize the here-and-now interaction of family members as the arena for the caseworker's intervention, and longitudinal study-diagnosis of the individual family members is eliminated or at least subordinated to a horizontal focus on current transactions, communication patterns, and role relationships. The successes and economies of this approach give weight to prevalent doubts about the usefulness of social study as it has been conceptualized.

Experiences in the use of reaching-out techniques over the past decade and in contemporary efforts to understand and apply social and cultural differentials in casework practice have led to the realization that social study pursued in traditional terms is often experienced by the poor or lower-class client as a frustration and rejection.

Recent research findings have suggested that the dropout problem in the early phase of contact may be referred, in part, to difference in the objectives of caseworker and client, in that the caseworker's goals in the early interviews have been traditionally related to the gathering of information, albeit in a therapeutically oriented way, whereas the client's goal has been to secure immediate help with the presenting problem. Too often the caseworker is left with facts, we are told, but no client. Moreover, concerns about the manpower shortage carry the implication that the days of long-term treatment are over and with them the interview hours spent on study and exploration in order to uncover the "real" problem underlying the request for help.

Perhaps these emphases on speeding up the helping process mean that study, as it has been conceived and taught, is no longer appropriate or even possible. They may represent a growing polarity between theory and practice, and it seems urgent that social casework re-examine its tenets and assumptions concerning social study. Are we so in the grip of yesterday that we are clinging in

SOCIAL CASEWORK, July 1968, Vol. 49, No. 7, pp. 403-409.

theory to a time-honored principle no longer valid for the requirements of current and future practice? Or, at the other extreme, are we in danger of discarding, through expedience and disuse, what is actually a necessary component in all casework?

It is my conviction that study continues to be an essential element in a scientifically based practice. Indeed, the spirit of scientific inquiry on which study rests is more than ever necessary in the face of the constant change in social needs and conditions that now confronts the caseworker. Yet it must be study that serves today's demands, not yesterday's ideologies.

In order to reshape the study process, the first task is to identify the fundamental concepts in the traditional model of study. They will be identified in this article as relevance, salience, and individualization. It will be suggested that the resolution of practice dilemmas that emerge as these concepts are modified may depend on broadening conceptions of casework practice.[1] The study process will be recast within the framework of systems theory. Attention will be drawn to ways in which such a recast study process can match up with new treatment modalities to deliver services that make more productive use of time and resources for the client, the agency, and the worker.

Relevance, Salience, and Individualization

Mary Richmond set forth the principles of social investigation that gave to social study its initial shape and direction.[2] According to her model, the caseworker's first responsibility in planning treatment was to secure any and all facts that, taken together, would reveal the client's personality and his situation. Thus, the beginning thread of a scientific orientation appeared in the insistence on a factual base that, through logical and inferential reasoning, would lead to a plan of action. It was as if knowledge of all the evidence would reveal the cause of the problem and hence its remedy; consequently, every source of information was to be utilized.

In the light of increased experience and accretions of knowledge, particularly from psychoanalysis, the routine gathering of massive amounts of data gradually gave way to a more discriminating approach. Social history was obtained with more understanding of its relation to personality dynamics. Concepts clarifying the ego's functions in relation to social reality and to inner forces led away from the earlier preoccupation with repressed content to what is still the unit of attention, the person-in-situation. The impact of these developments on study culminated in Gordon Hamilton's conceptual model.[3]

Whereas Richmond had urged the exhaustive collection of facts followed by separation of the significant from the insignificant, Hamilton introduced the concept of relevance. Sources of data were respecified as the client's own account, the reports of collaterals, documentary evidence, findings of experts, and the worker's observations. Viewed in terms of newly defined psychological and environmental dimensions, they were to be tapped selectively according to the nature of the problem, the wish of the client, the purpose of the agency, and the availability and preventive value of the information itself. Study, guided by professional knowledge, was to be related quantitatively to the degree of intervention indicated and the difficulty of establishing the diagnosis. An important distinction was made between history-taking for diagnosis in the early contacts and the use of history for abreaction in the treatment phase.

Hamilton described two types of social study, the *patterned* type and the *clue* type. The most clearly conceptualized examples of the patterned type are the eligibility study made in public assistance work and the psychogenetic study made in cases focused on behavior disorders or emotional disturbances. In such studies priorities are assigned to certain areas considered relevant, and

[1] See Morris S. Schwartz and Charlotte G. Schwartz, *Social Approaches to Mental Patient Care*, Columbia University Press, New York, 1964.

[2] Mary E. Richmond, *Social Diagnosis*, Russell Sage Foundation, New York, 1917, and Mary E. Richmond, *What Is Social Case Work?*, Russell Sage Foundation, New York, 1922.

[3] Gordon Hamilton, *Theory and Practice of Social Case Work* (2nd ed., rev.), Columbia University Press, New York, 1951. See especially Chapter VII, pp. 181–212.

these areas are held in the foreground of attention. In making the clue type of social study, the worker feels his way on the basis of the request and clues, consciously and unconsciously furnished, in order to collect facts relevant to the problem. It has been recently pointed out, however, that, "as Miss Hamilton suggests, clue and pattern are really interrelated and are perhaps more indicative of ways of envisaging the process of securing data than they are clear-cut types of study. The patterned study may involve a matter of priorities, but it is best developed on a basis of explaining the relevance of the inquiry to the request, and with the client's participation, than on a questionnaire basis. Similarly, the clue approach involves a concept of pattern since criteria for relevance give significance to the clue. Further, the worker controls this approach by injecting attention to priority of subjects for exploration at appropriate points." [4]

The scientific orientation that began in Richmond's approach to social study is firm and clear in the Hamilton model. Since the model requires systematic inquiry into relevant facts, it is useful in considering the model to note *Webster's* definition of *relevant* as "bearing upon, or properly applying to, the case in hand; of a nature to afford evidence tending to prove or to disprove the matters in issue. . . ." [5] It follows that the way in which the problem is cast determines which data are relevant and where the emphasis and direction of inquiry will lie. How the problem is defined, and to some extent the mode of intervention available or selected, determines what data will be perceived as relevant and consequently observed, collected, and interpreted for professional judgment. An inquiry into a set of circumstances viewed as indicative of a personality disturbance, for example, will result in the collection and interpretation of certain data. These data will be quite different from those collected and interpreted when the same set of circumstances is viewed as indicative of a disjunction between the individual and his familial, organizational, or cultural system or between the individual and his physical environment.

An observation underscored in Hamilton's work but sometimes lost sight of in practice had been made as long ago as 1936 by Fern Lowry, namely, that "the decision what to treat frequently demands greater skill than the decision how to treat." [6] As Lowry suggests, early dropout and treatment failure is frequently attributed to the client or to external factors when it should be attributed, rather, to the caseworker's tendency to assume responsibility for every discoverable need. Such a tendency may even conflict with the client's wish for immediate help in a specific area. Accordingly, Lowry urges that the impulse to treat every need and the urge to cure be restrained.[7] From such a standpoint, study is not an inquiry into all areas and needs.

The work of Schwartz and Schwartz introduces the concept of salience [8]—and *Webster's* defines *salient* as "prominent; conspicuous; noticeable. . . ." [9] A salient feature, then, is one that has an emphatic quality that thrusts itself into attention.

According to the foregoing concepts of relevance and salience, treatment is not properly focused on the total person. It becomes, in fact, more individualized and differential when it is particularized for particular clients having particular needs or problems in particular situations.[10] Individualization is based on choice among needs, modes of treatment, and possible goals. From this perspective, social study must become more individualized in order to specify the salient need or needs for which social casework has professional accountability. Specifying the salient need, however, is not

[4] Lucille N. Austin, on "clue and pattern," as discussed in a doctoral seminar in social casework, Columbia University School of Social Work, New York, Spring 1966.

[5] *Webster's New International Dictionary of the English Language* (2nd ed.), G. & C. Merriam Co., Springfield, Massachusetts, 1950, p. 2104.

[6] Fern Lowry, "The Client's Needs As the Basis for Differential Approach in Treatment," in *Differential Approach in Case Work Treatment*, Family Welfare Association of America, New York, 1936, p. 8.

[7] *Ibid.*, p. 9.

[8] Schwartz and Schwartz, *op. cit.*, pp. 111–35.

[9] *Webster's New International Dictionary of the English Language* (2nd ed.), *op. cit.*, p. 2204.

[10] Schwartz and Schwartz, *op. cit.*, p. 124.

the same as partializing the problem. What is described here is still an organismic approach in which the caseworker remains constantly aware of the whole, and the changing relationships of the parts to the whole, while singling out salient need for individualized treatment.

Although caseworkers have long known of the importance of the role of norms in the assessment of functioning within specific social and cultural contexts, the concept of salience requires a shift in the concept of normalcy and a shift from setting treatment goals in terms of cure. Some shift has already occurred insofar as goals are conceptualized as restoration of a prior level of social functioning or return to a previous equilibrium. A further shift away from notions of cure is required so that some resolution of the presenting problem, easing of precipitating stress, and even remission of symptoms, for example, can be embraced as goals. These become appropriate additions to the array of possible goals as new models of casework intervention develop in response to new knowledge and new conditions. The individual and social value of such goals, in relation to conservation of the client's resources and to manpower issues, seems clear. Moreover, the resemblance of these goals to the processes of natural life situations is striking.

Broadening the Conceptions of Help

In social casework theory and education, if not always in practice, study-diagnosis-treatment has been conceptualized on a psychotherapeutic model in which the worker—and, it is hoped, the client—"will peer down the long avenue of the client's past life," as John Dollard puts it, "to see how the present event matured."[11] This conceptualization has often led to searching for, and giving primacy to, the problems underlying the presenting request, or even unrelated to it.

The dilemma that presents itself when such an approach is viewed in the light of the foregoing discussion may be resolved through broadening the conceptions of casework help within the framework proposed by Schwartz and Schwartz. They distinguish between *treatment* as conventionally accepted clinical procedures and *help* as a large variety of attempts to influence clients in a therapeutic direction. They suggest that the conceptions of help should—

> include considerations such as a wider arena within which help might proceed, a different conception of who and what is to be helped, and a different view of the conditions and processes that affect therapeutic progress. . . . Thus, broadening the conceptions of help involves some reorientation. From looking upon the process exclusively as a clinical activity, directed at a disease entity, and undertaken within the boundaries of the conventionally defined therapist-patient relationship, the change is to seeing it, in addition, as a socio-psychological process that attempts to deal with problems in living that are not necessarily serious or well-defined emotional disorders.[12]

The authors advance four objectives to be achieved in broadening the conceptions of help. They are interrelated, and although each may be discussed separately for heuristic purposes, each can only be understood in relation to the other three. These objectives are "reconceptualizing the unit of help, changing the . . . object of help, expanding the role of helper, and re-orienting . . . [the] approach to help processes."[13]

The Unit of Help

The unit of attention in social casework has been the person-situation, although history reveals a shifting in emphasis at times from one to the other side of the hyphen. The newer ego concepts have made possible the appropriate study of psychosocial factors in social functioning. Newly conceptualized elements of the dynamic environment—such as role, class, ethnic and other reference groups, value orientations, family structure, and the agency as a social system—have permitted more accurate definitions of the situation.[14] In spite of much effort, however,

[11] John Dollard, *Criteria for the Life History,* Yale University Press, New Haven, Connecticut, 1935, p. 27.

[12] Morris S. Schwartz and Charlotte G. Schwartz, *Social Approaches to Mental Patient Care,* Columbia University Press, New York, 1964, p. 85.

[13] *Ibid.*

[14] Herman Stein, "The Concept of the Social Environment in Social Work Practice," *Smith College Studies in Social Work,* Vol. XXX, June 1960, pp. 187–210.

there has until recently been no way to integrate psychological and social phenomena without invoking the fallacy of reductionism. In this regard, general systems theory offers a fruitful approach to reconceptualizing the unit of attention in a way that will permit a valid redefinition of social study.

The Object of Help

Caseworkers have tended to modify their traditional stance in relation to the client whenever the family, rather than the individual, has been viewed as client—and have frequently misconstrued family-focused treatment of individuals as family treatment. Much work lies ahead in developing, from the knowledge and experience of casework itself, useful study-diagnostic concepts and derivative treatment principles and techniques for the family as a social system.

Also required is an enlarged definition of the object of help to encompass not merely the personality, but the whole human being within a fluid, real-life situation, in order to utilize the therapeutic potential of life processes, adaptive and coping capacities, and social supports.

Still another possibility lies in viewing the agency itself as the object of change or as an instrument for change rather than as a given in the situation. Such a view has some similarity to conceptions of milieu therapy as applied in hospitals and other institutions; it implies the use of organizational structure and the organizational roles of clients and workers within the agency to effect organizational or individual change. Given such a view, social study would embrace a consideration of the impact on clients of organizational variables, of the potential of those variables for fostering or inhibiting growth, and of sources of organizational resistance to change.

The Helper

The discipline of social casework has moved in several ways toward redefining the role of the worker from that of clinician-therapist to that of helper. Whereas the formal, instrumental, functionally specific role was traditionally the only one available to the caseworker, a more informal, expressive, functionally diffuse role has been evolving. Its inception was in the development of reaching-out techniques in several fields of practice. And the dimensions of the role have become clearer in the course of current attempts to reduce social distance, which are based on increasingly sophisticated knowledge of socialization experiences and life styles in deprived groups.

In addition, there has been expansion in the leadership role of the caseworker on service teams, which may include homemakers, volunteers, case aides, and indigenous helpers. Such a team approach appears to offer varied experiences and interpersonal relationships for clients with salient needs in those areas. Continued experimentation and research in programs in which one practitioner makes combined use of casework, group work, and community organization methods are also expected to expand the caseworker's repertory of roles.

The Help Processes

Conventional treatment procedures require verbal skills, introspection, and motivation, which are not infrequently lacking among clients of casework services. Now, however, the idea of help is being broadened to include informal processes and activities. New uses of the home visit are being developed; searches are being made for ways to provide experiences in a social context that will promote growth and maturation in the client; and new techniques of concretization and demonstration are being utilized.[15] In such efforts the relationship offered the client is viewed as a training ground for living and for assuming social roles in more rewarding ways. The caseworker supports adaptive responses and progressive forces, rather than uncovering coping failures, since the latter tactic tends to foster transference and the attendant regressive needs.

The concept of casework help has been broadened to include the provision of consultation services, and, increasingly, caseworkers are being enlisted to provide con-

[15] See, for example, Louise S. Bandler, "Casework with Multiproblem Families," in *Social Work Practice, 1964*, Columbia University Press, New York, 1964, pp. 158–71.

sultation to community caretakers with respect to the needs and responses of their clientele, either as specific individuals or total groups. Those being helped are not cast in the role of client and are not subject to its prescriptions and proscriptions. They may be merely present, perhaps in a helping arena, such as a day care center, a school, or a sheltered workshop.

These broadened conceptions of help call for new models of intervention and new ways to provide help more appropriately and effectively to supplement the psychotherapeutic model and increase the caseworker's flexibility and adaptiveness. Some, such as the crisis model[16] and the life model,[17] are now being developed. They furnish new ways of conceptualizing needs and problems and new methods and techniques of intervention. The relevance and salience of data vary with a shift from one model to another. For example, it may be necessary to reconceptualize certain disturbances as life crises, maturational or situational, or as role transitions imposing new statuses and ego tasks or as psychosocial disabilities requiring help in developing social competence. Defining problems in these terms demands that study produce new kinds of environmental data for the understanding and utilization of life processes as treatment media. Implicit is an emphasis on rapidity in the collection of data so that decisions can be reached to take action that is timely in terms of the model.

A Systems Approach

Because systems theory, as a way of viewing biological, psychological, and social phenomena, cuts across disciplines and bodies of knowledge, its constructs may be useful for the identification of the relevant and salient data in individualized study. The unit of attention is reformulated as a field of action in which the client—his biological and personality subsystems—is in transaction with a variety of biological, psychological, cultural, and social systems within a specific physical, cultural, and historical environment. Though there are important differences among these types of systems, all, as open systems, have important properties in common.[18] Some of these characteristics have to do with the input, transformation, and output of energy from and to the environment, which highlight the interdependence of systems, exchanges across boundaries, and degrees of openness to the environment. Other features pertain to the maintenance of a steady state or dynamic homeostasis—that is, the preservation of the general character of the system—and these highlight feedback processes, subsystem dynamics, and the relation between growth and survival. These and other characteristics draw attention to the functional and dysfunctional consequences, the reciprocal effects and reverberations that occur in the field of systems as the result of the operations of each. Similar observations can be made concerning the relation of its parts to any single system.

In contrast to the two-dimensional person-situation approach, this conception offers a wide range of system variables and encourages a holistic view. It leads to a focus on the disruptive factors in the usual steady state and on the mechanisms for restitution, coping, adaptation, and innovation in all systems. The systems perspective also places the agency as a social system and the worker and the client in the same transactional field. The helping relationship has a larger purview, which adds the reciprocal influences of the roles, norms, and values of several transacting social systems to the clinical aspects of the relationship. The worker's entrance into the client's field

16 Developments in the crisis model are found in Howard J. Parad (ed.), *Crisis Intervention: Selected Readings,* Family Service Association of America, New York, 1965.

17 Bernard Bandler, "The Concept of Ego-Supportive Psychotherapy," in *Ego-Oriented Casework: Problems and Perspectives,* Howard J. Parad and Roger R. Miller (eds.), Family Service Association of America, New York, 1963, pp. 27–44.

18 For further discussion of the characteristics and operations of open systems, see, for example, Daniel Katz and Robert L. Kahn, *The Social Psychology of Organizations,* John Wiley & Sons, New York, 1966, pp. 14–70, and Roy R. Grinker (ed.), *Toward a Unified Theory of Human Behavior,* Basic Books, New York, 1967. All the material in this work is valuable. See also Gordon Hearn, *Theory Building in Social Work,* University of Toronto Press, Toronto, 1958, pp. 38–51.

changes it *de facto,* not only through his effect as an observer on the observed but also through the reverberations of his entrance through the various other systems in the client's field, particularly secondary role networks. Similarly, the client's organizational roles have an impact on agency role-sets, whether they are designed by client groups as in some current public welfare agencies or by other agencies that have provided for planned participation for citizen-clients. In either instance, Heinz Hartmann's view of adaptation, which takes into account the individual's potential for contributing to the modification of existing environments and the creation of new ones, is more likely to be implemented through the systems approach.

Conclusions

We tend to observe and recognize as relevant what is closest to our conceptual model, and the systems perspective allows more indicators of salient and relevant variables to filter through the worker's perceptual screen. This does not mean that in any one case the entire field is covered.[19] On the contrary, the systems perspective enables the worker to comprehend the salient features of the problem as it is systemically conceived, to recognize relevant data within the relevant system or systems, and to reach professional judgments more rapidly. Paradoxically, it enlarges the unit of attention while it sharpens the focus by suggesting additional possible points of entry to effect change, as well as by illuminating the feasibility of change in specific systems. In a systems approach, a rapid gathering of relevant facts related to the salient features of the presenting need requires, however, greater breadth of knowledge, more skill in diagnosis, and greater capacity for communication, relationship, and self-awareness than are required in a traditional person-situation approach. Rapidity requires confidence in a knowledge base amplified to include all systems, their characteristics and linkages. Even in the first interview, the caseworker's broad knowledge is available to lead him to an understanding of the psychological and social commonalities revealed empirically through verbal and nonverbal clues. Increased knowledge and skill permit him to rely on these clues and signs as indicators that it is not then necessary to explore many phenomena and large areas of the client's experience. As Joseph Eaton has pointed out, this kind of professional confidence and security calls for tolerance of some degree of uncertainty and error.[20]

No matter what types of casework intervention may arise from broadened conceptions of help, the worker with a scientific orientation will always think diagnostically, using logical procedures with respect to evidence, inferential reasoning, and the relating of empirical data to theory and knowledge. He will make disciplined use of prognosis and evaluation, as formulated by Hamilton, against which predicted probable outcomes are measured. Careful analysis will be made of cases that do not have the expected outcome in order to uncover previously unknown variables, which may themselves add to the refinement of study. The worker will be guided in study, as in the total helping process, by social work values. His effectiveness will be enhanced by diversified patterns of communication, differential roles, and helping relationships that give attention to the emotional, cultural, and cognitive forces in growth and change.

For the new demands of practice, social study remains the scientific inquiry Hamilton conceptualized, but it is becoming accelerated and more sharply relevant in its focus on salient system variables. Its newer form and content must go hand in hand with newer treatment modes, newer levels of intervention, and broader conceptions of the flexible helping process that is social casework.

[19] This view departs from that suggested in a pioneer paper, Werner A. Lutz, *Concepts and Principles Underlying Social Casework Practice,* "Social Work Practice in Medical Care and Rehabilitation Settings, Monograph III," Medical Social Work Section, National Association of Social Workers, Washington, D.C., 1956, pp. 72–75. In contrast, the present article is an attempt to apply systems theory to more models than the clinical.

[20] Joseph W. Eaton, "Science, 'Art,' and Uncertainty in Social Work," *Social Work,* Vol. III, July 1958, p. 10.

Crisis intervention: theory in search of a program

by Richard A. Pasewark
and Dale A. Albers

Tremendous strides have been made in the field of public health in recent decades. Many former scourges, threatening young or old or both, have been drastically cut down or even practically eliminated—such as tuberculosis, polio, malaria, and typhoid fever. The mental health field cannot point proudly to similar dramatic advances.

Can some of the same concepts and basic techniques that have proved successful in public health be applied effectively on a wide scale to the field of mental health? The authors believe that this can be done through crisis intervention.

Crisis intervention has been developing over a number of years. Workers using the crisis approach have reported many instances of success in dealing with problems arising from specific situations and events such as illegitimacy, pregnancy and birth, suicide and other deaths, and poverty.[1] However, there is a notable absence of programs either totally or primarily oriented to this approach.

To substantiate the viewpoint that general application of crisis intervention can revitalize the mental health field and offer hope for successful primary prevention of mental disorders, an explanation is presented of what crisis theory is, how it developed, and how it might be applied broadly to mental health and the helping services.

The development of crisis intervention theory owes much to Erikson, Lindemann, and Caplan—all associated with Harvard University or the Harvard Medical School. They evolved three cornerstones of the theory: the concept of developmental crises, redefinition of transient personality disorders as life crises having a predictable pattern, and application of the public health model to mental health.

Erikson contributed the idea that in nor-

[1] *See* Karen A. Signell, "The Crisis of Unwed Motherhood: A Consultation Approach," *Community Mental Health Journal,* Vol. 5, No. 4 (August 1969), pp. 304–313; Gerald Caplan, "Mental Hygiene Work with Expectant Mothers," *Mental Hygiene,* Vol. 35, No. 1 (January 1951), pp. 41–50; Gerald Caplan, Edward A. Mason, and David M. Kaplan, "Four Studies of Crisis in Parents of Prematures," *Community Mental Health Journal,* Vol.

Reprinted with permission of the National Association of Social Workers, from SOCIAL WORK, Vol. 17, No. 2 (March 1972), pp. 70-77.

mal growth the individual experiences several specific developmental crises that he must surmount if he is to become a mature, integrated adult. He defined crisis as "a necessary turning point, a crucial moment, when development must move one way or another, marshaling resources of growth, recovery, and further differentiation."[2] He identified eight such types of developmental crises occurring during the normal span of life from infancy through childhood, adolescence, and maturity, to old age and senescence.

Lindemann's interest focused on transient personality disorders—precipitated by unusual environmental stress. The assumption is that removing stress will ameliorate or eliminate the observed behavioral symptoms. Lindemann was especially concerned with grief reactions following a loved one's death and concluded that an individual had to make an adjustment to the crisis such a death precipitated. His investigations contributed to crisis theory the idea that reactions to crisis follow a predictable pattern and have specific, identifiable stages.[3]

Caplan was a forceful advocate of crisis intervention theory. A major thrust of his work was toward applying public health principles to community mental health problems. Specifically, Caplan was concerned with primary, secondary, and tertiary prevention and ways to apply these public health concepts to mental health activities.[4]

Primary prevention aims to reduce the incidence of a disorder by altering the environment so that it restrains the disease process or by making the individual less susceptible. Secondary prevention tries to keep a mild disorder from becoming a severe one. Early case-finding and treatment are stressed. Tertiary prevention aims to keep a serious disorder from producing permanent disability. All three endeavor to prevent any individual from being a source of contagion.

In essence, a crisis might be considered analogous to a learning dilemma. In both the person experiences a new situation or event for which he has no adequate coping behaviors. The strategy in crisis intervention is to provide the individual with appropriate behavioral patterns that will enable him to deal effectively with the specific crisis. Crisis theorists have not delineated the mode of intervention; one assumes that the techniques to be used remain the prerogative of the intervenor.

A number of overt or tacit assumptions are made in crisis theory, such as:

Crisis is not a pathological experience. Acute symptoms manifested in crisis do not necessarily indicate previous personality disturbance or reflect current pathology. Instead they mirror first a dearth of available mechanisms for dealing with the situation, then groping behavior that seeks to resolve it effectively, and eventually the behavior adopted for coping with the crisis. The basic optimism of the theory is seen in the point of view that a person's troubled behavior in a crisis may reflect struggle with a current problem rather than past or present deviation from the normal. In some ways, this assumption is reminiscent of Jung's view of psychiatric disturbance as symptomatic of the organism's dissatisfaction with a current developmental state and of the flux in personality as it attempts to deal with the situation.[5]

1, No. 2 (Summer 1965), pp. 149–161; Edwin S. Shneidman and Norman L. Farberow, "The Los Angeles Suicide Prevention Center: A Demonstration of Public Health Feasibilities," *American Journal of Public Health*, Vol. 55, No. 1 (January 1965), pp. 21–26; Erich Lindemann, "Symptomatology and Management of Acute Grief," *American Journal of Psychiatry*, Vol. 101, No. 2 (September 1944), pp. 141–148; Erich Lindemann, Warren Vaughn, and Manon McGinnis, "Preventive Intervention in a Four Year Old Child Whose Father Committed Suicide," in Caplan, ed., *Emotional Problems of Early Childhood* (New York: Basic Books, 1955), pp. 5–30; and Harris B. Peck, Seymour R. Kaplan, and Melvin Roman, "Prevention, Treatment, and Social Action: A Strategy of Intervention in a Disadvantaged Urban Area," *American Journal of Orthopsychiatry*, Vol. 36, No. 1 (January 1966), pp. 57–69.

[2] Erik H. Erikson, *Identity: Youth and Crisis* (New York: W. W. Norton & Co., 1968), p. 16.

[3] Op. cit.

[4] Gerald Caplan, *Principles of Preventive Psychiatry* (New York: Basic Books, 1964), pp. 35–127.

Crises are temporary and therefore self-limiting. All crises must come to an end; none continues indefinitely. Some adjustment is made to the event be it adequate or inadequate. It is assumed that different categories of crises have different temporal histories. For example, the crisis precipitated by the death of a loved one differs in length from that caused by the incarceration of a spouse or son.

Each type of crisis pursues a course made up of typical, identifiable stages. Crisis behaviors and reaction patterns can be anticipated. Further, each crisis category has an individualized progression that is theoretically discrete from that of all others. For example, Lindemann distinguished the following successive stages in grief and bereavement: (1) disbelief, (2) denial, (3) symptoms of grief or bereavement that include (a) somatic distress, (b) preoccupation with images of the deceased, (c) guilt, (d) hostility toward the deceased and others such as physicians, nurses, and friends, and (e) loss of typical patterns of conduct and emergence of such behaviors as withdrawal, lack of initiative, and dependence, (4) emancipation from bondage to the deceased, (5) readjustment to an environment in which the deceased is missing, and (6) formation of new interpersonal relationships and behavior patterns.[6] It is normal for a person to experience each stage of crisis. In fact, omission of any stage in the progression suggests that he may not be coping adequately with the crisis.

The individual in crisis is especially amenable to help. Crisis is a critical period during which the individual actively seeks new resources and activities. He is therefore prone to accept help and to learn and incorporate new behaviors.

A small amount of assistance makes it possible for a person to surmount a crisis. This assumption holds that only limited resources and assistance must be expended in the intervention process. Old defenses are weakened and resistance to the development of new behaviors is diminished.

Weathering a current crisis permits the individual to cope more effectively with future crises. This is probably the most important assumption made in crisis theory. Problem-solving behaviors learned in the immediate situation can be applied effectively to subsequently encountered crises. It may be presumed that inadequate reactions can make future adjustments to new crises less effective.

Various workers in crisis theory have categorized the different types of crises that can be experienced. Caplan, Hill, and Eliot have probably evolved the most meaningful classification systems.

Caplan identifies two categories.[7] The first group includes crises precipitated by changes in the everyday course of living—such as entry into school, birth of a sibling, emergence of heterosexual interests, marriage, birth of a child, retirement, and death. The second category includes crises occasioned by unusually hazardous events—such as acute or chronic illness, accidents, or family dislocations—which might occur to an individual, a member of his immediate or extended family, or a close associate.

Hill also names two categories, but places greater stress on the family as the focus of crisis.[8] His first group includes crises precipitated by extrafamilial events, such as war, flood, economic depression, or religious persecution. Crises in his second

[5] Carl G. Jung, "Two Essays on Analytical Psychology," in Herbert Read, Michael Fordham, and Gerhard Adler, eds., *The Collected Works of C. G. Jung*, Vol. 7 (New York: Pantheon Books, 1966), p. 10.

[6] Lindemann, op. cit.

[7] *Principles of Preventive Psychiatry*, pp. 34–55.

[8] Reuben Hill, "Generic Features of Families Under Stress," *Social Casework*, Vol. 39, Nos. 2–3 (February–March 1958), pp. 139–150.

category are precipitated by intrafamilial events or situations, such as desertion, alcoholism, or infidelity. Hill believes that extrafamilial crises tend to solidify the family and enhance its crisis-meeting resources but that intrafamilial crises typically lead to its demoralization.

Eliot lists four categories also built around the family unit.[9] In the first, crises of "dismemberment," loss of a family member is experienced either through death or from extended separation because of war, imprisonment, employment dislocation, or hospitalization for physical or mental disorders.

His second category, crises of "ascension," involves an unplanned addition to the family unit. Examples are an unwanted pregnancy, an illegitimate birth, the return of a deserting father, or the unwanted addition of a stepsibling, a stepparent, or an aged parent.

In Eliot's third category, crises of demoralization, the family unit remains the same size, but one of its members experiences an undesirable event or condition. These crises include a husband's or father's nonsupport, infidelity, alcoholism, drug addiction, delinquency, unemployment, vocational demotion, or mental disorder. Eliot's fourth class embraces crises of demoralization accompanied by either dismemberment or ascension (loss or addition of a family member). Examples are a runaway adolescent, a father's desertion, divorce, imprisonment, suicide, homicide, or institutionalization for a mental disorder.

STAGES OF CRISIS

In the sequence of interactions leading up to the state of perceived crisis, an objective event first takes place, such as the death of a loved one, unemployment of the breadwinner, or birth of a child.[10] The event then interacts with the individual's or group's crisis-meeting resources, which may be excellent, adequate, poor, or nonexistent. From this interaction, a definition of the event is made. The same event might be defined similarly or quite differently by different individuals or families. For instance, because of varying crisis-meeting resources and extenuating circumstances, a breadwinner's sudden unemployment might be defined as a severe, moderate, or mild crisis or even as no crisis at all.

If defining the event leads to a perception of crisis, then a period of disorganization inevitably follows. This is characterized by various maladaptive behaviors or psychiatric syndromes such as grief, withdrawal, inactivity, or heightened anxiety. There is exaggerated use of currently available defense systems and behaviors that are not suited to the crisis situation. Because the individual is experiencing difficulty in his groping and problem-solving behavior, he tends to be more receptive to outside assistance and resources during this period.

The period of disorganization is followed by a period of reorganization, which has clearly identifiable phases. In the initial phase of correct cognitive perception, the problem is maintained at a conscious level. For example, in the case of death the individual recognizes that feelings of dependency and support can no longer be anchored to the deceased. During the next phase, management of affect through awareness of feelings, there is an appropriate acceptance and release of feelings associated with the crisis. After the death of a loved one, emotions such as remorse, guilt, and hostility are accepted and find suitable expression.

The last phase is the development of patterns for seeking and using help. The individual begins to adopt constructive means for dealing with the problem and uses other persons and organizations to help him in this task. For example, the widow may use the state employment agency to find a job or, encouraged by a friend, she may

[9] T. D. Eliot, "Handling Family Strains and Shocks," in Howard Becker and Reuben Hill, eds., *Family, Marriage, and Parenthood* (Boston: D. C. Heath & Co., 1955), pp. 616–641.

[10] The following description of the stages of crisis is derived from the work of Hill, op. cit.; and Lydia Rapoport, "The State of Crisis: Some Theoretical Considerations," *Social Service Review*, Vol. 36, No. 2 (June 1962), pp. 212–213.

become active in volunteer associations to fill the void created by her husband's death. At the end of this phase, habitual behavioral patterns have developed that allow flexible use of persons and external resources not only in crisis but in ordinary situations. Essentially, the individual's horizons and resources have expanded. In other words, the level of reorganization achieved after crisis is higher than the precrisis behavior level. However, this does not always occur. The reorganization level can be the same as, lower, or higher than the precrisis level.

Various writers have cataloged the following characteristics that seem to be associated with an individual's or a family's ability to cope successfully with crisis-producing events: [11] (1) behavioral adaptability and flexibility within the family, (2) affection among family members, (3) good marital adjustment between husband and wife, (4) companionable parent-child relations, (5) family members' participation in decision-making, (6) wife's participation in husband's social activities, (7) nonmarginal economic status, (8) individual's or family's direct or vicarious experience with the type of crisis encountered, (9) objective knowledge of facets of a specific crisis before it occurs—which presupposes the individual's or group's capacity to discuss openly feelings about events that might precipitate crisis, such as drug abuse or impending birth, marriage, or death—(10) established patterns of interaction with the extended family, neighbors, and friends.[12]

Two conclusions emerge from a study of this list. First, an individual needs and may even require other persons to surmount a crisis. These persons may be members of the immediate or extended family, friends, or social workers. Second, facilitating communication between the individual and these persons mitigates the severity of the crisis.

PRIMARY PREVENTION

The principles of crisis intervention, practically applied, have profound implications for mental health and the helping services. Crisis concepts seem particularly applicable to primary and secondary prevention efforts.

In primary prevention, the intervenor may direct his efforts chiefly toward eliminating or minimizing events capable of inducing crisis. Distinction should be made between different classes of events. There are some events that, with present knowledge, can be eliminated or minimized by appropriate social action. Unemployment and marginal economic circumstances might be practically abolished by vast social and economic reforms. The possibility of war might be greatly reduced by forming an international government invested with viable responsibility. Birth injuries, some forms of mental retardation, and certain types of illness leading to death might be prevented through expanded medical services. Birth of children can be prevented through contraception or abortion. Accident control might reduce accidental deaths. Premarital counseling might prevent certain divorces. Increased use of community facilities and homebound programs for the mentally ill could minimize family separations occurring from hospitalization.

Knowledge is currently lacking about ways to prevent or minimize certain events. Among these would be death resulting from

[11] *See* Caplan, *Principles of Preventive Psychiatry*, pp. 44–48; Hill, op. cit., p. 148; Rapoport, op. cit., p. 216; Jay L. Rooney, "Special Stress on Low-Income Families," *Social Casework*, Vol. 39, Nos. 2–3 (February–March, 1958), pp. 150–158.

[12] Individuals and families best able to surmount the crisis of separation in Great Britain during World War II frequently mentioned friends, neighbors, and relatives who provided assistance. Much to the chagrin of the helping professions, these families rarely mentioned that the church, physicians, or social agencies played a significant role in their adjustment. *See* Hill, op. cit., p. 148.

certain disease processes and aging, hospitalization for various forms of physical and mental illness, and many divorces. Optimistically, increased knowledge should extend life and promote health and marital well-being so that most of these events should eventually be classified in the first category.

There are also events that cannot be prevented, including those that people would not wish to prevent even if they could. Among these are the broad developmental crises experienced in life, such as birth, adolescence, marriage, and retirement.

Effective primary prevention measures, besides influencing events, may strengthen the individual's or group's crisis-meeting resources. The intervenor's efforts would be directed toward developing patterns of interpersonal relations that aim to increase family members' communcation, individual and group experience with crises, and accessibility to social resources at appropriate crisis points.

Increasing communication within family units might prove to be essentially educational. Procedures used could include premarital, marital, and ongoing educative group counseling and discussions emphasizing the necessity of familial communication, ways to maintain it, and ways to avoid communication breakdown.

Increasing the experience with crises might also be an educative task. Efforts would be directed toward permitting individuals to experience "sham" crises. To a greater degree than at present, the helping professions would be concerned with preparing premarital groups, groups of expectant parents, and drug groups to handle experiences likely to be encountered. These programs would focus not only on presenting factual information about the event but also on dealing with the resultant crisis. Thus the focus of a drug group would not be limited to incidence rates, laws, and physiological effects related to drugs. The group would also discuss anticipated personal and familial crises, such as that which might occur when a mother discovers a "joint" in her son's jacket pocket. They would "experience" these crises also through such techniques as role-playing, psychodrama, and sensitivity sessions. Similar programs might be developed on mental disorders, retirement, death, and many other topics. These mock experiences would be somewhat comparable to the childhood fantasies that Erikson regards as valuable preparation for future roles.[13]

To make social resources more readily accessible to individuals in crisis, two approaches seem feasible. First, currently available personnel and services might be brought closer. To accomplish this, the helping professions would have to assume a more active stance than at present. Rather than passively waiting for the client experiencing crisis to be referred or voluntarily come to the social work agency, manpower resources would be deployed to locales in which crises were most likely to occur. For example, rather than establishing a network of mental health centers, mental health personnel would be located in potential crisis sites, such as day care centers, schools, obstetrical wards, and community centers in slum areas. A second complementary approach would be to identify crisis-prone individuals and then mobilize resources to provide them with readily accessible services. In this area, development of "risk registers" might be fruitful. Thus a crisis-prone pregnant woman would, on reporting to her physician, find a group of persons ready to assist her in pregnancy—the alerted physician himself, the pediatrician who would eventually care for her newborn child, the public health nurse who could provide pre- and postnatal care, perhaps even a mental health worker to involve her in group discussions, and a housekeeper aide to assist her during the difficult early postnatal months. If the intervenor can affect either the event or the individual's crisis resources, the event's defini-

[13] Erik H. Erikson, *Insight and Responsibility* (New York: W. W. Norton & Co., 1964), pp. 120–121.

tion and the nature of the perceived crisis will be altered considerably.

SECONDARY PREVENTION

Applying crisis theory to secondary prevention is basically dealing with the intervenor's role when an event is already experienced as a crisis. The efforts that might be taken roughly parallel the phases in the period of reorganization.

Establishing or facilitating communication. In crisis situations communication between family members is often lacking or blocked. For example, a family's discovery that a son or daughter is to be the parent of an illegitimate child or is a drug-user frequently causes abrupt cessation of communication between family members and the offender. In such cases, professional skills and resources might well be most efficaciously used to try to restore disrupted family communication and initiate contacts with community agencies potentially able to assist in the crisis.

Individuals experiencing crisis often have no previous knowledge of, let alone contacts with, agencies providing assistance. A case in point is that of parents who give birth to a retarded child. They may be unaware of the immediate help available through the National Association for Retarded Children and the crippled children's division of the local health department. Nor are such parents necessarily aware of help obtainable later from state vocational rehabilitation agencies for training activities. Similarly, a woman of 40, suddenly widowed, may not know about such community resources as state unemployment or child welfare services. A paramount role of helping persons in time of crisis, and probably one of the more meaningful ones, would be to help the individual identify and get in touch with community social agencies most able to provide assistance.

Assisting the individual or family to perceive the event correctly and to understand it. Cases in point would be the parents of a youth apprehended for possession of marijuana and the parents whose unmarried daughter tells them she is pregnant. In the former instance, the intervenor might help the parents recognize the conflict between law and reality in drug use and understand other "reality-myth" distinctions concerning drug use and abuse. In the latter instance, the intervenor could explain the effects of the birth on the daughter and the family and present various alternatives for dealing with the situation.

Assisting the individual or family to manage emotions and feelings, keep affects conscious, and deal with them openly. In the cases of the drug offender and the unmarried mother, the intervenor might best serve by helping those involved to recognize and express feelings of shame and to realize how this emotion is related to their hostile reactions. The intervenor might also provide appropriate means for releasing these sentiments in discussion.

CONCLUSIONS

At the time when mental health workers are critically reexamining modes of service delivery, the application of crisis theory principles to mental health seems especially worthy of attention. More than most approaches and models, it offers a consistent view of mental health problems and suggests guidelines for the direction and thrust of mental health efforts. Essentially, it advocates an active and preventive stance—eliminating specific events associated with crisis, enhancing crisis-meeting resources before crisis is experienced, and intervening actively in crisis before maladaptive problem-solving patterns develop.

There are a number of reasons, however, why the crisis approach has not been widely adopted in the mental health field. First, it seems reasonable to suppose that a much greater commitment in finances and personnel would be required to implement crisis theory principles than is now made in mental health efforts. Current efforts, lip service to the contrary, focus primarily on tertiary prevention endeavors.

Second, widespread adoption of the crisis

approach is risky. Despite reported successes in various limited endeavors, there is no conclusive evidence that such promising results will in fact be realized if the crisis model is generally adopted and resources are directed to the primary prevention efforts it involves.

Third, implementing crisis principles would demand a rather abrupt adjustment by mental health workers. They would have to become much more aggressive. They would have to make active efforts to eliminate or minimize crisis-producing events by altering social situations. They would have to intervene in the social scene to increase the crisis-resistance resources of normal individuals before society or these individuals themselves realized the need of such assistance. They would have to seek out actively individuals at an early stage of personal disorganization. In many ways the mental health worker's role would become that of social architect. Considerable question exists within the field itself about whether such intervention is an appropriate function of the mental health technician and professional.[14] The lay public is as yet unaware of this potential role.

Fourth, adoption of crisis principles would also raise considerable question concerning the wisdom of the field's present investment in the community mental health center model. Crisis theory principles at least create doubt concerning the efficacy of the community mental health center model for deploying services, in fact create doubt about whether these centers offer the most appropriate and effective means of dealing with mental health problems. Thus crisis intervention, although it has much to offer, is still a theory in search of a program.

---

[14] *See* Dale Albers and Richard A. Pasewark, "How New are the New Comprehensive Mental Health Centers," in Willard F. Richan, ed., *Human Services and Social Work Responsibility* (New York: National Association of Social Workers, 1969), pp. 148–155; H. Warren Dunham, "Community Psychiatry: The Newest Therapeutic Bandwagon," *Archives of General Psychiatry*, Vol. 12, No. 3 (March 1965), pp. 303–313; David M. Mechanic, "Community Psychiatry: Some Sociological Perspectives and Implications," in Leigh M. Roberts, Seymour L. Halleck, and Martin B. Loeb, eds., *Community Psychiatry* (Madison: University of Wisconsin Press, 1966), pp. 201–222; Richard A. Pasewark and Max W. Rardin, "Theoretical Models in Community Mental Health," *Mental Hygiene*, Vol. 55, No. 3 (July 1971), pp. 358–364.

A Project in Crisis Intervention

GRACE L. DUCKWORTH

CRISIS INTERVENTION theory is of particular interest to family service agencies, in which the focus has always been on solving problems rather than on reconstructing the client's personality. In fact, family agency caseworkers think of themselves as being already engaged in the practice of crisis intervention, in the sense that they are primarily concerned with working out situational stresses that occur in the lives of their clients. Crisis intervention theory, however, adds a new dimension to their thinking about the helping process.

Literature in the field of crisis intervention suggests that if applicants are seen immediately, on the day they first apply, or within a few days afterward, the casework process can be greatly intensified and speeded up. A few interviews given at the onset of a crisis when the client is in a heightened state of anxiety and receptivity to help may be more beneficial to him than long-term treatment given at a later time. Brief service, sharply tailored to the client's particular needs and limited to discussion of the immediate problem to be solved, may be all that is necessary if properly timed. Such an approach, if it can be built into the family agency's program, may well provide a new avenue to serving more people and serving them better.

The staff at the West End Family Counseling Service, for which the ratio of caseworkers to population served is approximately one and a half to every 100,000, became interested in crisis intervention as a way of making the best possible use of the limited staff time available. A number of questions were raised. Can the crisis intervention approach be used with all agency applicants? Can a few interviews really restore equilibrium? Can a standard length of service be established for the resolution of crises, even though they are of different kinds? In order to find some answers to these questions, the agency decided to undertake a small pilot project in crisis intervention.*

Outline of the Project

A caseworker with several years' experience in family casework was hired part time specifically to conduct the project. She came to the office on Mondays and Thursdays each week, working a total of twelve hours a week. Monday hours were from 1 P.M. to 8:30 P.M. and Thursday hours were from 9 A.M. to 2:30 P.M., so that a full range of appointment times was made available to clients.

The time span of the project covered two phases. Phase I ran from July 14, 1965, to September 13, 1965, a total of eight weeks. Phase II ran from September 13, 1965, to January 3, 1966, covering sixteen weeks.

Selection of clients to be included in the study was made as follows: At the start of the study each applicant who telephoned or came to the office asking for an appointment was given an appointment with the project caseworker at the earliest possible time. When possible, the appointment was made for the same day or within forty-eight hours. All appointments were scheduled within four days of the first contact by the client. It was assumed that *all* applicants who contacted the agency did so because they were faced with a crisis of some kind. To test this assumption, applicants were screened only to the extent of determining that they lived in the area.

Applicants were given appointments in turn until the project schedule was filled. After that, whenever there was an open

* The project was financed by two grants from The Price Foundation, Inc.

SOCIAL CASEWORK, April 1967, Vol. 48, No. 4, pp. 227-231.

hour, the next applicant was assigned to the project. All appointments were made by the supervising caseworker, usually by telephone.

All clients included in the project were new to the agency or had not been seen in the agency for more than a year. Two applicants who were reapplying for more help after having terminated less than a year before were eliminated from the project and were instead given appointments with the caseworker who had seen them previously. Except for these two, all applicants who happened to apply when the project started, or when there was an opening in the project worker's schedule, were assigned to the project caseload.

Various interviewing methods were used. Marriage partners were seen individually or jointly; various combinations of parents and children were interviewed together; and some interviews with whole families were held. The interviews were spaced at various intervals—once or twice a week, once every two weeks, and so forth. During Phase I, the first eight weeks of the project, the service was limited to a maximum of six interviews for each case. During Phase II, the next sixteen weeks of the project, service was limited by offering clients "brief help with this particular problem" rather than by setting an arbitrary limit on the number of interviews. This was done to test and compare the two different ways of structuring the brief service to be made available to the client.

Fees were charged according to the agency's regular sliding scale: 11 families paid no fee; 3 paid the maximum of $15.00; and the remaining families were about evenly distributed at all levels in between. The average fee paid was $4.25 an interview.

Twelve weeks after completion of the project, follow-up questionnaires were mailed to all the families included in the project. These questionnaires asked for the clients' evaluation of the help received.

Findings

Within the course of the project, the project caseworker carried 51 cases—individual persons, separated couples, couples living together, and family groups; 15 cases fell within Phase I and 36 within Phase II. In all, 176 interviews were held, an average of about 3.5 per case.

Of the problems presented in the project caseload, marital problems constituted 35 per cent; individual personality disturbance, 26 per cent; and parent-child problems, 39 per cent. It should be noted that, as compared with other family service caseloads, there was a somewhat high percentage of cases involving individual personality problems, because there is no tax-supported psychiatric clinic in the area. It should also be noted that in Phase II of the project there was an inordinately high proportion of parent-child problems, 50 per cent, because of the typically sharp increase in school referrals during the fall and winter months.

The different structuring of Phases I and II did not have an appreciable effect on the progress of the cases, except that the slightly more open-ended approach in Phase II did result in a slightly higher proportion of cases in which between three and six interviews were held. Over-all, for the entire project, slightly more than 50 per cent of the cases were terminated after one or two interviews. Moreover, in Phases I and II, respectively, 87 per cent and 91 per cent of the cases were terminated after six interviews.

In Phase I two cases involving clients with acute anxiety reactions went beyond the six-interview maximum. In both cases the client had been seen twice a week for three weeks. In each case it was necessary to add two more interviews, spaced a week apart, to reach a comfortable point of termination. In Phase II three cases involving extended crises could not be satisfactorily brought to the point of transfer or termination within the span of the project. These three families had had between nine and thirteen interviews by the close of the project but were continued by the project caseworker beyond that point.

The outcome or disposition of the cases served in the project was as follows: service consisting of clarification only, 14; resolution of crisis, no further service needed, 19; diagnosis of crisis, referral to other source of help, 6; resolution of crisis, transfer to regular caseload for further treatment, 2;

resolution of crisis, placement on waiting list for further treatment, 3; withdrawal after little or no improvement, 4; extension of crisis beyond project, continuation of treatment by project caseworker, 3.

In the 14 cases, 27 per cent, in which the client was helped only to clarify his problem and the agency's role in the treatment of such problems was spelled out, the client either declined further appointments or canceled them if scheduled. In several of these cases the wife withdrew on the ground that she did not want to come alone and knew that her husband would not. It is assumed that the brief service was helpful to these clients, who had had only sketchy information about the agency in advance and little or no previous counseling. It is impossible to say how they viewed the help. Only one responded to the questionnaire. She said that the one interview she had had was not helpful, because she knew she had a severe psychiatric problem but only brief help and a possible referral had been offered by the agency.

In 19 cases, or 37 per cent, the crisis was successfully resolved and further treatment was not needed. An additional 5 families achieved sufficient restoration of equilibrium to sustain transfer to a regular worker in the agency or placement on the agency's waiting list for the further service that was needed. If 6 referrals to outside sources of help are included as satisfactory resolutions of the immediate crisis, 30 of the clients, nearly 60 per cent, experienced successful resolution of their crises within the span of the project.

In 48 out of the 51 cases, or 94 per cent, the brief service approach seemed applicable. Of the 3 cases that could not be dealt with in the short time span of the project, 2 involved psychiatric problems that would have been referred to a psychiatric clinic if one had been available. In the third case the marital crisis was extended by the mother's flight from the home for several weeks. In each of these cases, the elongated nature of the crisis was recognized within the first few interviews. At that time the cases could have been transferred to a regular caseworker in the agency, thus holding to the design of the project, but it was decided that the clients should be carried through the crisis by the project worker.

In the follow-up questionnaires that were sent, the following questions were asked: (1) Did you like the way the counselor interviewed you? (2) Did the counseling you received help you with the problem you came in about? (3) Did you receive as many interviews as you wanted? (4) If you felt the need to talk with someone again about a problem, would you come back to West End Family Counseling Service? Unfortunately, only 15, or about 30 per cent, of the questionnaires were completed and returned—but the responses were conspicuously consistent. Of the 15 respondents, between 12 and 14 chose the most positive response offered for each question.

Implications

This project was undertaken as a trial run, on a small scale, of the crisis intervention approach, to see how it would work in the agency, from the standpoint of the agency, the caseworker, and the client. The information obtained does not lend itself to quantitative statistical analysis. Nevertheless, some subjective comparisons can be made with previous experience in which the intake method involved a weeding-out process through the use of a written application form and a waiting period of from two to six weeks before the first interview.

The theory that more people can be served through the crisis intervention method is borne out by the study. The project caseworker, working less than half time, served 51 families during the five-and-a-half month period; this is about the same number she formerly served working full time with the same kind of caseload in a similar agency. Moreover, the crisis intervention method enables the agency to serve more peple in low-income brackets. The fact that about 22 per cent of the families in the project paid no fee, which means that they were either receiving public assistance or had a subsistence-level income, indicates that fewer of these low-income families are lost to the agency when they are offered immediate appointments without any red tape.

Because the agency receives four new applications a day, on the average, the twelve hours a week devoted to the crisis intervention project was far from enough to keep up with the current applications. The fact that the cases did turn out to be very brief, for the most part, and still produced a very satisfactory number of successes indicates that agency service could be broadened considerably by devoting a substantial proportion of staff time to this kind of service.

Presenting problems covered a wide range of family difficulties and types of crises. Among them were anxiety reactions, school phobia, mental breakdown, alcoholism, delinquency, and situational stresses of various kinds. With few exceptions, the crises tended to be resolved within six to eight weeks, if resolution of the crisis is taken to mean that the clients felt a sense of equilibrium and could terminate comfortably. In some cases nothing new or significant had occurred and the reality stresses had not been removed; yet the clients felt better. For example, a young couple with three children and a long history of poverty, unemployment, and mental breakdown had come for marital counseling because the husband was out of work and was becoming discouraged and demoralized and because they were at the point of separation. By the end of six interviews he was still out of work and on relief and debts were still piling up, but the couple felt better. They said, "We don't fight so much," meaning "We can bear it now." Other types of resolutions were more clear-cut: anxiety symptoms subsided; a boy stopped stealing; a mentally ill client voluntarily entered a hospital; a phobic child went back to school; and a wife accepted her husband's drinking and he became less violent.

A crisis intervention approach makes heavy demands on the caseworker, who must diagnose quickly, adapt interviewing techniques to the client's particular problem, and make maximum use of outside resources. On the other hand, it is also very exhilarating. There is no question about the greater accessibility of people in crisis. Moreover, resistance can be cut through much more quickly if the worker uses the crisis approach; client and caseworker become mobilized, saying, in effect, "Let's roll up our sleeves and see what can be done in the short time we have." In addition, setting limited, short-term goals creates a feeling of optimism, and in many instances there is a sense of progress from week to week.

Crises differ in intensity and duration. At one end of the scale in the project there was an applicant who had been referred by the local rehabilitation office because he was dissatisfied with the training he was receiving. Upon exploration it appeared he had real reason to be dissatisfied. He was not aware of any emotional problems; he just came to the agency because he was told to. His "crisis" was resolved in one interview. At the other end of the scale was a single man forty-five years of age who had quit his job and was unable to find another, although he had a college degree and was in good physical health. This man was so anxious and depressed that he was almost immobilized; if he had not had help when he did, he would have had to go into a mental hospital. His crisis could not be resolved until he found employment. In this case, it took seven weeks.

Conclusion

During interviews in which the crisis approach is used, the caseworker must focus on the reason for the client's applying to the agency *at that particular time*. In some cases in the project it was difficult to pinpoint one factor in the situation that turned a chronic stress into a crisis. Often the clients would say, "It just kept getting worse until it got this bad," and no amount of exploration would turn up a new, or triggering, force that had propelled them in at that time. Whenever the precipitating factor could be identified, the treatment took on a more clear-cut, manageable character and was therefore more likely to be successful.

The project caseworker found it more comfortable to structure the working plan with the client by estimating the number of times they would need to meet and explaining it could not be more than six. This method seemed to convey a clear and well-defined blueprint. The alternative, used in Phase II, of defining the task and explaining that there could be only "a few interviews" over "a brief period of time" to get the client over the immediate hump produced the same results. The preference for setting a certain number of interviews, with an arbitrary maximum, may have been a personal one of the caseworker. Whichever way the contract is stated, the crisis intervention stance prevents long-term involvement, holds the client's dependency to a minimum, and keeps the interviews oriented to a particular goal.

It would be desirable for family agencies to refine their knowledge about crisis intervention techniques and learn more about the implications of the method for policy and practice. For example, if it is not possible to apply crisis intervention methods of intake to all clients, what are the criteria for determining which ones will be seen immediately and which ones will be asked to wait? Can the crisis intervention approach be used in short-term group treatment? What are the long-range benefits to the client of brief emergency treatment compared with the benefits of longer-term treatment? These are some of the questions we hope to study in the future.

When sixty-one articles on social work with client groups were analyzed, a number of shortcomings in the way workers used groups appeared consistently. The most significant finding was that although collective effort for changing the clients' environment was clearly needed in many instances, the predominant focus was on changing individual behavior.

Use and misuse of groups

by Helen M. Levinson

Helen M. Levinson, MSS, is a social worker at the Charles Peberdy, Jr., Child Psychiatry Clinic, Hahnemann Hospital and Medical College, Philadelphia, Pennsylvania. *The author thanks Jeffrey Galper for his suggestions on and encouragement with this article.*

The use of groups by social workers is on the upswing, and practitioners increasingly report their experiences in the social work journals. However, when the articles on client groups are examined closely, some important shortcomings emerge. These weaknesses are generally of two types. First, the potential of groups is underutilized. Most groups led by social workers are oriented toward treatment of individuals, rather than achieving common goals, and, concomitantly, much of the potential of "group process" is neglected. Second, workers tend to impose their agenda (treatment of individuals) on groups of clients even when some other need is clearly evident. When used, task-oriented activity is regarded as a technique for promoting personal growth, and actual task achievement (in which the group is putatively engaged) is secondary to therapeutic goals.

This article summarizes the author's analysis of sixty-one articles on groups that appeared in *Social Casework* and *Social Work* between 1955 and 1970.[1] In approaching her survey, she raised the following questions in relation to each article: (1) What was the worker's stated purpose for the group, and how was the group organized to carry out its purpose? (2) Did the worker's purpose and that of the group coincide or differ and what was the nature of this similarity or divergence?

The first question was posed to uncover the essential nature of the groups in terms of purpose, function, and structure.[2] The second was asked because of concern about the effectiveness of groups run by social workers, which is reflected to some extent by the convergence or divergence of purpose between worker and group members and the nature of this similarity or difference.

The author discusses these questions in detail and then summarizes the information gathered from the sixty-one articles. Specific articles are also reviewed to bring the social workers' approach to groups more sharply into focus. Finally, she draws conclusions and proposes a more useful method for working with client groups.

Reprinted with permission of the National Association of Social Workers, from SOCIAL WORK, Vol. 18, No. 1, (January 1973), pp. 66-73.

GROUP PURPOSE

Social workers who report on their work with groups frequently state their purposes in the following ways: to "improve functioning" of group members, strengthen "personality," and develop "the client's capacity to function more adequately." [3] A more useful scheme to characterize group purpose is based on the following dimensions: "task-growth" and "common goal–individual goal."

Falck characterizes groups as task oriented or growth oriented.[4] A task orientation indicates that the group's purpose is to accomplish a job, be it an action, a policy, or an objective. A growth orientation refers to a group's concern with the participants' personal development.

Tropp prefers to distinguish groups on the basis of common goals and individual goals: ". . . a common goal would have to be defined as a goal which the members share for the group as a whole. . . ." [5] The goal is "corporate" or "collective" and is arrived at through group decision-making or the leader's prescription. In contrast, in an individual-goal group, each member prescribes for himself, or has prescribed for him, what he will seek to achieve in the group.

The task-growth distinction alone is inadequate to describe a group's purpose. It fails to differentiate between a group of students who are working on individual projects and happen to be in the same room and a group of students who are planning a group action. Furthermore, growth-oriented groups may engage in task activity, and task-oriented groups must meet members' personal needs to some extent to survive. Although growth and task elements are present in all groups, one element is likely to dominate in a particular group. Likewise, the distinction between Tropp's common goal and individual goal is, by itself, insufficient to characterize group purpose. It fails to take into account the predominance of a "task" or "growth" interest in a group at a particular time. It is evident that the immediate concern of some individual-goal groups is with task achievement, e.g., in a class, while others are concerned with self-development, e.g., in a traditional therapy group. Therefore, to discern group purpose in the articles discussed here, both task-growth and common goal–individual goal distinctions will be used. (See Table 1.)

Individual-goal group with a task focus. Members of a class or a play group are intent on accomplishing a job. As Tropp points out, in a class the goals of participants may be similar, but they are not common for the group as a whole: i.e., decisions are ". . . essentially made by the instructor." [6] A play group is a "combination of individuals seeking personal pleasure through recreation." [7]

Common-goal group with a task focus. The work crew or team is also intent on job accomplishment. But goals are shared by all members, although assigned by a foreman or captain. The mutual interest group also seeks to accomplish a job, although, unlike the work crew or team, common goals are not prescribed; they are arrived at through agreement of members.

Individual-goal group with a growth focus. Treatment groups seek to improve the psychological and social functioning of members, which is referred to here as "growth." As Tropp indicates, members'

TABLE 1. CLASSIFICATION OF GROUPS BY PURPOSE [a]

Types of Goals	Task Focus	Growth Focus
Individual goals	Class Play group	Treatment group, e.g., psychotherapy, counseling, recreation, and education groups
Common goals	Work crew Team Mutual interest group	Training group

[a] With the exception of "training group," the nomenclature and definitions are taken from Emanuel Tropp, "The Group Intent and Group Structure: Essential Criteria for Group Work Practice," *Journal of Jewish Community Service*, 4 (March 1965), pp. 235–236.

goals are similar but not common. This is illustrated by the fact that each member's needs are evaluated and individual goals are established prior to the group's first meeting.[8]

Common-goal group with a growth focus. A training group of "family" members is composed of people who interrelate in some way in everyday life: for instance, people who work together. The group seeks to improve the interactions among its members and ultimately its capacity to achieve goals as a unit. Therefore, the focus is on growth, and goals may be said to be common because they are shared (ideally) by all members.

Group purpose, in the articles discussed here, will be defined by investigating the descriptions and applications of this two-way classification. In addition, the groups will be evaluated in terms of the way they were organized to carry out their purposes. In other words, their function and structure will be analyzed. Tropp defines a group's function as ". . . what the group members are supposed to do to carry out [their] purpose." [9] If the group's purpose is individual growth, it may be achieved through discussion, films, games, political activity, and so on.

The group's structure concerns organization—or, as Tropp puts it, *how* the group will carry out its purposes.[10] An attempt will be made to distinguish between groups that were organized on the basis of group process and those that were not.

"Group process" refers to characteristics or properties of the group as a whole. When people come together for a vaguely defined purpose, the authority for developing the group is in the hands of its members, and little or no structure is assigned, certain fairly predictable events follow. There is a struggle to develop leadership, evolve goals. agree on operational procedures, acquire unity, deal with conflict, engage heteronomous influences, and meet members' personal needs. These events, which involve the group as a whole, are known as group process.

In contrast, in groups in which structure, procedure, leadership, and so forth are assigned, members do not engage in the imperatives of group process. Characteristically, interaction occurs mostly between the worker and individual group members, and interaction among members is ". . . not compelling but optional, non-committal and transitory." [11]

When group process is not utilized, much of a group's potential is wasted. Thus the sixty-one articles were reviewed to discern the extent to which social workers utilized group processes.

AGREEMENT OF PURPOSE

Both in individual social work practice and social work with groups, the clients' and workers' purposes are not necessarily the same. In some settings, group purpose is defined by the situation and is more likely to be obvious to all concerned—for instance, the therapeutic purpose of a group of patients who meet with a psychiatric social worker in a mental hospital. One would expect divergence of purpose to be more evident among groups in settings such as housing projects and public assistance agencies, where groups are not ostensibly developed for the purpose of treatment. In these cases, the nature of the divergence of purpose can be ascertained by looking for stress between task or growth achievement and between common goals and individual goals.

Several patterns concerning the consequences of agreement or disagreement of purpose between worker and group members were evident in the articles reviewed. The following were most common: (1) The purposes of the workers and members were in accord.[12] These groups tended to operate optimally to achieve their purpose. (2) The purposes of the worker and members diverged and the worker went along with the group's purpose.[13] These groups also tended to operate optimally to achieve their purposes. (3) The worker ascribed group purpose and the members concurred.[14] Usually this took place in an authoritarian setting. It is questionable whether a group can operate optimally in this pattern.[15] (4) The worker ascribed purposes that were rejected by the members, and the group eventually dissolved.[16]

Having delineated the questions on group purpose and agreement of purposes between worker and group members, it is now possible to apply them to the sixty-one articles reviewed. To do this, an overall summary of the articles is given, followed by a more detailed review of selected articles.

Group purpose, function, and structure. The groups described in fifty-five articles manifested an individual goal–growth orientation. Twelve of these groups were not ostensibly developed as therapy groups; but, on closer examination, they were found to involve some kind of treatment.[17] Four articles described groups with a common goal–task orientation. One described groups with a common goal–growth orientation, and one described groups with an individual goal–task focus.

Forty-five groups functioned entirely through discussion; ten combined discussion with recreational activities. Two functioned only through recreation, and four utilized discussion and the pursuit of joint actions.

Twenty-seven articles did not address group structure. Twenty-six groups were worker centered: i.e., primary interaction took place between the worker and individual members; the worker was directive, took a leadership role, and so on. In only seven articles was group process fully utilized, i.e., the groups were truly group centered.

Divergence or correspondence of purpose between members and workers. Discussion of workers' and members' perceptions of group purpose was absent in most of the articles. This question was not addressed at all in thirty-three, or, if it was raised, divergence or correspondence could not be clearly discerned. In thirteen cases, workers' and members' goals were clearly in accord. In two, serious discrepancies were found between workers' and members' perceptions of group purposes, and the worker acquiesced to the group. In eleven cases, the worker ascribed group purpose and the group acquiesced. (This usually occurred in authoritarian settings.) In two, the worker ascribed group purpose and the group dissolved or membership dropped considerably (presumably because members' purposes did not coincide with the worker's.

In five cases in which divergence was clearly evident, the worker tended to stress therapeutic goals for individuals while the members sought to change their external environmental conditions. In two instances in which divergence was evident, group members expected more structure in terms of receiving practical information from the workers, while the workers perceived the groups in terms of treatment goals.

REPRESENTATIVE GROUPS

The following representative groups deal with four types of clients: welfare recipients, unmarried mothers, the aged, and tenants. To demonstrate more clearly the nature of groups led by social workers, those that were *not* ostensibly developed as treatment groups (i.e., they were not located in psychiatric settings) are highlighted. This focus illustrates that common goal–task oriented activity is not generally used, although it might be most viable, and that when it is used, the worker often views it as a means to therapeutic ends. These two evaluative criteria are applied, to the extent possible, to each article in the following discussion.

Welfare recipients. Five articles discussed groups composed of welfare recipients.[18] All of them involved individual treatment and stressed the goal of satisfactory client adjustment to the welfare system.

For example, Green's purpose in working with a group of unemployed fathers was to promote ". . . increased self-esteem, motivation to seek employment, and insight into behavior and attitudes that inhibit effective functioning." [19] In the present author's scheme, group purpose would therefore be characterized as the accomplishment of individual goals, with a growth focus. In the four other articles that dealt with welfare clients, common goal–task oriented activity, which might have opposed agency purpose, was absent. Green's group functioned through discussion: "Ventilating feelings, trying new roles, and time-limited problem solving were emphasized." [20] Although Green did not address group structure directly, one can cull from his description that sessions fluctuated between being group centered and worker centered, with the leaders acting sometimes as facilitators and limit-setters and at other times in a more directive capacity.

Green stated that after several meetings, the group was able to establish its purpose —which seemed to be along the lines of the one he established. Whether there was any difference between the members' perception of group purpose and Green's is not clear, although in this and other authoritarian settings, what the leader had in mind presumably had a strong influence on what the group did.

Unmarried mothers. Barclay's purpose in working with a group of unmarried welfare mothers was to reach out to these women who were ". . . without family ties . . . [were] unfamiliar with the community and almost completely socially isolated." [21] Although not explicitly stated, her purpose could be classified as the attainment of individual goals, with an emphasis on personal growth. The group functioned exclusively through discussion, although its structure is unclear to the reader. Barclay did refer to group process, but only in terms of the support that members received from each other and the group solidarity that developed. Although Barclay stated that she hoped to discover where ". . . these women were in relation to their life situation and to focus on concerns common to all," she did not explain the group's expectations or whether they were similar to her own. However, she did say that ". . . there was great emphasis during the early meetings on environmental concerns . . ." and that "for a long time . . . [they] did not talk about the worries and concerns unique to their situation. . . ." [22] Here again, the worker's orientation strongly influenced the group's direction.

The aged. Three articles described work with the aged. In two, there was evidence of common-goal activity with a task focus. In one case, however, this was seen primarily as a means to therapeutic ends.

In Silverstein's discussion about a group of elderly "floor captains" in a city housing project for the aged, there was a definite change in purpose from an individual goal-growth orientation to common goals and task achievement.[23] In other words, there was a shift from discussion of personal attitudes, reactions, and so forth to development of trust and camaraderie, which enabled joint action to meet common needs.

Activity within the group consisted of discussion. However, the group's focus was expanded to include dealing with housing officials and then larger community and bureaucratic structures. The group was structured so that the worker acted as leader. Silverstein does not deal directly with what she and the members considered to be the group's purposes at the outset or whether their purposes eventually converged or differed. But it can be assumed that her orientation toward common-goal activity strongly influenced the group's movement toward common actions. As she states: ". . . the group becomes a channel through which members share and explore their concerns and experiences. This may lead not only to peer group analysis and support but also to joint action. . . ." [24]

Forman stated that his purpose in intervening in a Golden Age Club was to have all members participate in decision-making and to move them away from their recreational activities toward task achievement. In other words, he viewed his intervention in terms of promoting

> conflict, controversy, and confrontation [because] productive conflict has an invigorating and stimulating effect on older people and can stimulate group movement.[25]

According to the present author's scheme, Forman sought to move the group toward common-goal–task-oriented activity. Yet he was less interested in task accomplishment per se than in using common-goal activity as a technique to promote personal growth:

> The goal of this effort—reduced transportation rates—has not as yet been attained. However, many tangible results have been achieved. . . . relationships between [senior citizens] groups have begun to develop. . . . Much gratification and ego strength have come from meeting with state and national leaders. . . . The older adults have learned that their opinions count, that others respect their thinking, and that they have a continuing contribution to make.[26]

Thus although his task was not accomplished, Forman believed that an important amount of personal growth was achieved. But because he did not discuss the differences or similarities between his and the members' perceptions for the group, it is impossible to tell whether the group shared his perspective. Given the material in the description, no conclusions can be drawn as to how the group was structured, although Forman says that he acted as a catalyst in moving the group away from its former mode of functioning.

Tenants. Shapiro described her attempt to organize a group of single, unattached, low-income tenants for the purpose of helping them to achieve ". . . a positive self-image and mutually protective relationships," "extend individual capacities to want help," and "withstand the frustration of seeking it." At their first meeting

> the tenants gradually began to come forward with suggestions for a recreation program, a separate reading service and knitting room for women, television, [and] church services. . . . There was no response to the worker's query about group therapy. . . .[27]

Although Shapiro's perception of group purpose consisted of a treatment or individual goal–growth orientation, the members' purpose centered on common goal–task achievement. Thus the divergence of group purpose (which is not dealt with in many of the articles) was made explicit. After the group rejected treatment, it engaged in activity leading to task achievement. The author did not address other questions.

Bateman and Stern described a housing court clinic that corresponds most closely to group treatment. The group was composed of tenants who had repeatedly violated housing codes and had been given the choice of paying a heavy fine or attending the clinic. It is noteworthy that landlords who repeatedly violated the same codes were excluded from the group because they had the "education and sophistication to behave in a responsible manner if they chose to do so." [28]

The clinic's express purpose was educational, e.g., to give the tenants information about safety, tenants' rights, care of their homes, and so on. However, the class progressed beyond the educational function to discussions about members' general lifestyles, presumably to bring about reflection and change in this area. As Bateman and Stern pointed out:

> Class members were encouraged and helped to express the kinds of feelings they had experienced during the court hearing, the reasons for such feelings, and the methods used to control or resolve them.[29]

COMMENTARY

The characteristics of the groups described in the sixty-one articles can be summarized as follows:

1. The majority of the groups were oriented toward treatment of individuals. Their purposes were described in terms of attaining personal growth by assigning individual goals to group members. Few groups were engaged in common-goal activity with a task focus. Most groups functioned through discussion only. The majority of articles did not address themselves to group structure at all; many groups were found to be worker centered. The recognition and utilization of group process took place only in a small number of groups.
2. In more than half the articles, the authors did not address the question of members' perceptions of group purpose and how these perceptions did or did not correspond to their own. When the existence of divergence was clearly stated, the divergence tended to occur because the worker stressed therapeutic goals and the members stressed environmental change.

These findings suggest that social workers grossly underutilize the potential of groups. It is curious that the groups described in the articles were oriented so heavily toward treatment, even though some other need was clearly present. The author does not mean to imply that all groups should be common goal–task oriented. However, this approach would be more viable in many group settings in which, at present, only the therapeutic approach is used.

The author also suggests that common goal–task oriented activity should not be viewed as a technique for promoting personal growth—or, as Empey says, "as an incidental means to the realization of more abstract therapeutic objectives." [30] Rather, task achievement should be valued for its effects beyond personal development.

Finally, social workers neglect much of the potential of group process. This was evident both in the number of articles that described worker-centered groups and the number in which group process was not mentioned at all.

The tremendous waste of the potential of the group situation—as well as the need to turn away from focusing solely on treatment when working with groups—has also been discussed by other authors.[31] This article, however, attempts to underline these shortcomings with concrete data supplied by social workers themselves.

NOTES AND REFERENCES

1. The authors listed their professional specialties as follows: casework, 15; group work, 9; community organization, 1; general, 9; youth work, 1; interdisciplinary, 1; and unspecified, 25.
2. Emanuel Tropp, "The Group: In Life and in Social Work," *Social Casework,* 49 (May 1968), pp. 267–274.
3. Emanuel Hallowitz and Bernice Stephens, "Group Therapy with Fathers," *Social Casework,* 40 (April 1959), p. 184; and Gertrude J. Conrad and Harry K. Elkins, "The First Eighteen Months of Group Counselling in a Family Service Agency," *Social Casework,* 40 (March 1959), p. 124.
4. *See,* for example, Hans Falck, "The Use of Groups in the Practice of Social Work," *Social Casework,* 44 (February 1963), p. 64.
5. Emanuel Tropp, "Group Intent and Group Structure: Essential Criteria for Group Work Practice," *Journal of Jewish Communal Service,* 41 (March 1965), p. 234.
6. Ibid., p. 235.
7. Ibid., p. 235.
8. *See,* for example, Ada S. Cyrus, "Group Treatment of Ten Disadvantaged Mothers," *Social Casework,* 48 (February 1967), p. 81.
9. "The Group: In Life and in Social Work," p. 271.

10. Ibid.

11. Tropp, "Group Intent and Group Structure," p. 239.

12. *See,* for example, Catherine R. Collier and Anne Campbell, "A Post-Adoption Discussion Series," *Social Casework,* 41 (April 1960), p. 192.

13. *See,* for example, Joan Shapiro, "Single Room Occupancy: Community of the Alone," *Social Work,* 11 (October 1966), pp. 24–33.

14. *See,* for example, Muriel N. Rogers, "A Group Educational Program for Marginally Adjusted Families," *Social Casework,* 43 (March 1962), pp. 178–184.

15. For a discussion of this issue, *see* Ralph White and Ronald Lippitt, "Leader Behavior and Member Reaction in Three 'Social Climates,'" in Dorwin Cartwright and Alvin Zander, eds., *Group Dynamics* (New York: Harper & Row, 1960), pp. 527–553.

16. *See* Gertrude Conrad, "Development of a Group Counseling Program in a Family Service Agency," *Social Casework,* 39 (December 1958), pp. 560–564.

17. *See,* for example, Lillian E. Barclay, "A Group Approach to Young Unwed Mothers," *Social Casework,* 50 (July 1969), pp. 379–384; and Philip Green, "Group Work with Welfare Recipients," *Social Work,* 15 (October 1970), pp. 3–4.

18. Barclay, op. cit.; Cyrus, op. cit.; Green, op. cit.; C. W. Bell and H. L Kaplan, "Public-Voluntary Sponsorship of a Mothers' Group," *Social Casework,* 45 (January 1964), pp. 21–25; and Louise P. Shoemaker, "Social Group Work in the ADC Program," *Social Work,* 8 (January 1963), pp. 30–36.

19. Op. cit., p. 3.

20. Ibid.

21. Barclay, op. cit., p. 379.

22. Ibid., pp. 380 and 382.

23. Sandra Silverstein, "A New Venture in Group Work with the Aged," *Social Casework,* 50 (December 1969), pp. 553–580.

24. Ibid., p. 576.

25. Mark Forman, "Conflict, Controversy, and Confrontation in Group Work with Older Adults," *Social Work,* 12 (January 1967), p. 84.

26. Ibid.

27. Op. cit., pp. 24–25.

28. Richard W. Bateman and Herbert J. Stern, "Baltimore's Housing Court Clinic," *Social Work,* 6 (October 1961), p. 44.

29. Ibid., p. 46.

30. Lamar Empey, "Sociological Perspectives and Small Group Work," *Social Service Review,* 42 (December 1968), p. 461.

31. *See,* for example, ibid.; Tropp, "The Group: In Life and in Social Work"; Falck, op. cit.; Robert Glass, "The Current Dilemma in Social Group Work Methodology, *Journal of Jewish Communal Service,*" 44 (June 1968), pp. 310–315; and Hyman Weiner, "Social Change and Social Group Work Practice," *Social Work,* 9 (July 1964), pp. 106–112.

BY PHILLIP FELLIN AND EUGENE LITWAK

The Neighborhood in Urban American Society

■ ***The influence of the neighborhood primary group in urban society is explored through the identification of mechanisms that serve to overcome problems in social relations resulting from mobility, heterogeneity, and impersonality. This discussion provides a basis for the development of selected diagnostic approaches and intervention strategies for social work practice.*** ■

While the social work profession traditionally has been concerned with understanding man's social environment, an emphasis on effecting change in this environment has most recently emerged through involvement in programs for delinquency control, educational improvement, community action, and urban renewal. Specific attention in these programs has been directed toward the neighborhood primary group and its role in urban American society. This concern about and interest in the neighborhood serve as an impetus for the examination of theoretical formulations and empirical findings of the social sciences that deal with this social unit. This knowledge serves to identify major problems confronting the neighborhood primary group in contemporary society and provides a basis for initial neighborhood assessment to guide social work intervention.

VIABILITY OF THE NEIGHBORHOOD

The sociological literature reveals two contrasting views of the role of the neighborhood in urban society. One approach, represented in the writings of Wirth, Simmel, Park, and Theodorson, stresses the decline in importance of neighborhood primary group relations as society becomes industrialized and urbanized.[1] This position is most clearly expressed by Wirth's classic consideration of "Urbanism as a Way of Life," in which it is argued that all primary groups as bases for social solidarity become weak or disappear owing to the size, density, and heterogeneity of population in the urban environment. Parsons is in only partial agreement with this position when he maintains that only the nuclear family retains selected functions that require primary relations, i.e., provision of primary socialization of children and stabilization of adult personalities.[2] All these theorists, either explicitly or implicitly, suggest that increased urbanization and bureaucratization of society are accompanied by second-

PHILLIP FELLIN, Ph.D., *is Associate Professor, and* **EUGENE LITWAK, Ph.D.,** *is Professor of Social Welfare Research, University of Michigan School of Social Work, Ann Arbor, Michigan.*

[1] Louis Wirth, "Urbanism as a Way of Life," and George Simmel, "The Metropolis and Mental Life," in Paul K. Hatt and Albert J. Reiss, Jr., eds., *Cities and Society: The Revised Reader in Urban Sociology* (New York: Free Press of Glencoe, 1957), pp. 46–63 and 635–646 respectively; Robert E. Park, *Human Communities* (Glencoe, Ill.: Free Press, 1952); and G. A. Theodorson, "Acceptance of Industrialization and Its Attendant Consequences," *American Sociological Review*, Vol. 18, No. 5 (October 1953), pp. 477–484.

[2] Talcott Parsons, "The Social Structure of the Family," in Ruth N. Anshen, ed., *The Family: Its Function and Destiny* (New York: Harper & Row, 1949), pp. 190 *ff.*; Parsons and Robert F. Bales, *Family, Socialization and Interaction Process* (New York: Free Press of Glencoe, 1955), pp. 3–19.

Reprinted with permission of the National Association of Social Workers, from SOCIAL WORK, Vol. 13, No. 3 (July 1968), pp. 72-80.

ary contacts and secondary types of social control, with the neighborhood losing its traditional functions in community life.

In contrast to this position, there is considerable evidence that neighborhood primary groups play a significant role in the attainment of individual and social goals in American society. For example, Greer and Kube found in Los Angeles that rather than a decrease in primary relations, "as the neighborhood grows more characteristically urban, friendship and kinship become a larger proportion of all social interactions." [3] Bonjean's recent study of the neighborhood integration of managers, businessmen, and workers in an industrial community indicates the existence of much less "isolation" than is generally ascribed to the urban neighborhood, with the average respondent knowing five or more neighbors well enough to call on.[4] In the area of urban renewal, Davies notes that "in New York City the role of neighborhood groups in urban renewal decision-making has increased steadily." [5] Additional studies reported in the sociological literature that focus on social contacts of neighbors, exchange of services and resources, and neighborhood identification also substantiate the viability of the urban neighborhood.[6]

Another area in which the significance of neighborhood and local community is demonstrated concerns the behavior and social control of youths. Thus, Reiss and Rhodes report a relationship between the status structure of the residential community and the delinquency life changes of boys at each ascribed social class level.[7] These authors show that the risk of a boy who resides in a high-status residential community becoming delinquent is minimal, regardless of his family's economic status. Children from both wealthy and poor families are more likely to become delinquent if they live in low-status areas. In another delinquency study, Maccoby investigated the degree to which two low-income neighborhoods were integrated in terms of common values, contacts, and neighborhood identification.[8] She found support for the proposition that delinquency rates were lower in the more integrated areas. Kobrin also deals with the extent to which delinquency is a product of the cultural processes of the local community, i.e., high-delinquency areas.[9] He characterizes the neighborhood in terms of the relationship of conventional and criminal value systems to

[3] Scott Greer and Ella Kube, "Urbanism and Social Structure: A Los Angeles Study," in Marvin Sussman, ed., *Community Structure and Analysis* (New York: Thomas Y. Crowell Co., 1959), pp. 93–112.

[4] Charles M. Bonjean, "Mass, Class, and the Industrial Community: A Comparative Analysis of Managers, Businessmen, and Workers," *American Journal of Sociology*, Vol. 72, No. 5 (September 1966), pp. 149–162.

[5] J. Clarence Davies III, *Neighborhood Groups and Urban Renewal* (New York: Columbia University Press, 1966), p. 205.

[6] Morris Axelrod, "Urban Structure and Social Participation," *American Sociological Review*, Vol. 21, No. 1 (February 1956), pp. 13–18; Theodore Caplow and R. Forman, "Neighborhood Interaction in a Homogeneous Community," *American Sociological Review*, Vol. 15, No. 3 (June 1950), pp. 357–366; Leon Festinger, Stanley Schachter, and Kurt Back, *Social Pressures in Informal Groups: A Study of Human Factors in Housing* (New York: Harper & Bros., 1950); Phillip Fellin and Eugene Litwak, "Neighborhood Cohesion Under Conditions of Mobility," *American Sociological Review*, Vol. 28, No. 3 (June 1963), pp. 364–376; Wendell Bell and Marion D. Boat, "Urban Neighborhoods and Informal Social Relations," *American Journal of Sociology*, Vol. 63, No. 1 (January 1957), pp. 391–398; Eugene Litwak, "Voluntary Association and Neighborhood Primary Groups," *American Sociological Review*, Vol. 25, No. 2 (April 1960), pp. 258–266.

[7] Albert J. Reiss, Jr., and Albert L. Rhodes, "The Distribution of Juvenile Delinquency in the Social Class Structure," *American Sociological Review*, Vol. 26, No. 5 (October 1961), pp. 720–732.

[8] Eleanor E. Maccoby *et al.*, "Community Integration and the Social Control of Delinquency," *Journal of Social Issues*, Vol. 14, No. 3 (July 1958), pp. 38–51.

[9] Solomon Kobrin, "The Conflict of Values in Delinquency Areas," in Herman D. Stein and Richard A. Cloward, eds., *Social Perspectives on Behavior* (New York: Free Press of Glencoe, 1958), pp. 498–505.

each other, i.e., the degree to which they are integrated and the consequences for boys in these areas who move between delinquent and nondelinquent roles. In each of these studies the neighborhood is viewed as a major controlling variable in regard to the occurrence of deviant behavior.

A third area in which the influence of neighborhood as a social context has been demonstrated concerns the educational aspirations of youths. Studies by Wilson, Turner, and Michael clearly identify neighborhood environments as having considerable influence on the ambitions and college plans of youths.[10] A recent study by Sewell and Armer further investigates the hypothesis that neighborhood socioeconomic status has a significant impact on the individual's educational plans. Their evidence suggests that while the effects of neighborhood have sometimes been overstated in past formulations, the neighborhood contributes significantly to the explanation of differential educational aspirations of high school youths.[11]

These studies relating neighborhood to social contacts, delinquency, and educational aspirations are cited to illustrate areas in which the neighborhood primary group constitutes a significant force in the social environment. Some of the major underlying reasons that have been advanced to suggest that the neighborhood is likely to play a minimal role in urban industrialized society will now be explored.

PROBLEMS OF NEIGHBORHOOD COHESION

Mobility. Technological innovation accompanied by occupational and geographic mobility has been considered a major factor in reducing neighborhood cohesion. In addition, urban society fosters social mobility, with education, occupational roles, and personal talents providing routes for movement. With social mobility, individuals must learn new patterns of behavior as they leave old groups, create new interaction patterns, and meet the demands of new social systems, e.g., occupational, neighborhood, and community. Since it generally has been assumed that relatively permanent membership is a condition of group cohesion, the question becomes one of how well the neighborhood primary group can function when members move in and out of the group. In prior studies the authors have proposed that negative effects of mobility are minimized when selected attributes of individuals and groups obtain.[12] These conditions, which allow quick integration into the neighborhood group and promote neighborhood cohesion, include the following:

1. The amount of training individuals have for integrating under conditions of change.
2. The extent to which reference group orientations permit mobility and integration.
3. The attitudes individuals have toward discussing problems relating to personality, i.e., communication norms.
4. The attitudes individuals have toward themselves as strangers in a neighborhood.
5. The presence of positive group norms toward integrating the stranger.
6. The avoidance of competition between significant primary groups.
7. The use of localized voluntary associations.

Empirical investigations of the ways in which these mechanisms operate in neighborhood primary groups provide evidence

---

[10] Alan B. Wilson, "Residential Segregation of Social Classes and Aspirations of High School Boys," *American Sociological Review*, Vol. 24, No. 6 (December 1959), pp. 843–844; Ralph H. Turner, *The Social Context of Ambition* (San Francisco: Chandler Publishing Co., 1964); John A. Michael, "High School Climates and Plans for Entering College," *Public Opinion Quarterly*, Vol. 24, No. 4 (Winter 1961), pp. 585–595.

[11] William H. Sewell and J. Michael Armer, "Neighborhood Context and College Plans," *American Sociological Review*, Vol. 31, No. 2 (April 1966), pp. 159–168. *See also* George Brager, "Organizing the Unaffiliated in a Low-Income Area," *Social Work*, Vol. 8, No. 2 (April 1963), pp. 34–40.

[12] Fellin and Litwak, *op. cit.*, p. 365.

that neighborhood cohesion is maintained and the negative effects of mobility are lessened by speeding up the process by which newcomers are socialized into the group.[13] Even though a person has a shorter time span in the group, because of rapid integration he may have the same social span as individuals in groups with a more stable population. Thus, there is some evidence to challenge the assumption that permanence is necessary for neighborhood integration.

Heterogeneity. Heterogeneity of population constitutes a second underlying problem thought to impede the development and maintenance of community cohesion.[14] Since the urban community consists of diverse kinds of people—with rural and urban backgrounds; ethnic, racial, and regional differences—the heterogeneous character of the community has been said to make cohesion difficult. However, this factor may be less valid today owing to the development of mass communication and the enlargement of the middle-class stratum in current society. The relevant question in regard to heterogeneity involves the extent to which values of people are different or contradictory. While value differences sometimes make communication between people difficult, differences may also serve complementary needs and lead to cohesion, e.g., husband-wife relationships. When values are contradictory and people are polarized along value positions, group cohesion is unlikely. However, extreme polarization of values is not common in our society, and when there are contradictions there are usually also areas of agreement. Contradictions are less likely to occur when there are common socialization devices such as relatively uniform educational and occupational experiences. Whyte notes that although people moving into Park Forest have minor differences, their basic values are likely to be the same.[15] While the extreme homogeneity proposed by the "mass society" theorists may not obtain, Bonjean's empirical work detects a leveling effect of bureaucratized urban society and enlargement of the middle stratum of the community, while at the same time a new upper stratum is created.[16]

When inconsistencies in values are present, they may lead to disruption in social relations unless mechanisms exist to make the differences tolerable. Thus, procedures for quick role socialization are necessary, such as provision of sufficient information regarding differences and procedures whereby role inconsistencies can be tolerated and conflict minimized. For example, role performance in neighborhood interactions may need to be clearly defined and separated out from other conflicting roles. This demands that newcomers to a neighborhood be quickly socialized to overcome conflict resulting from role discontinuities. In short, the traditional indicators of heterogeneity in urban neighborhoods—e.g., race, ethnic, and rural-urban background—are not necessarily disruptive in current society. Value differences are not likely to cover all areas of life, and contradictions in values may be balanced by agreements that may be emphasized to create cohesion.

Impersonality. A third major problem in regard to the maintenance of the local neighborhood group concerns the extent to which impersonality is imposed by the urban environment. From a theoretical perspective, Tonnies' writings indicate that as movement occurs from community (*Gemeinschaft*) to societal (*Gesellschaft*) relations, the personal relationship (i.e., "intimate, private, exclusive living together") of community gives way to the mechanical structure of society.[17] Wirth follows this approach in his writings on social relations

13 *Ibid.;* Litwak, *op. cit.*

14 *See* Robert C. Angell, "The Moral Integration of American Cities," *American Journal of Sociology*, Vol. 57, No. 4 (July 1951), pp. 1–140. *See also* Bonjean, *op. cit.*, pp. 149–162.

15 W. H. Whyte, Jr., *The Organization Man* (New York: Simon & Schuster, 1956).

16 *Op. cit.*, p. 157.

17 Frederick Tonnies, *Fundamental Concepts of Sociology*, C. P. Loomis, trans. (New York: American Book Co., 1940), pp. 18–28.

of the city, and concurs with Weber's contention that size and density of settlement bring about a lack of personal relationships in the neighborhood.[18] This situation is said to occur because of the nature of the contacts and the use of formal rather than personal controls. Thus, Simmel maintains that the metropolis promotes a structure of great impersonality, expressed in part through a blasé attitude in its inhabitants.[19] In contrast to this approach, other theorists point out that uniform problems are most efficiently handled in society through formal organizations that are characterized by impersonal relations.[20] However, there remain nonuniform tasks, both within and outside the formal organization, that can best be accomplished through personal relations. Parsons and Bales, for example, emphasize the need for personal relations in regard to tension management.[21] While this task is customarily carried out within the family, the involvement of neighbors on a personal basis provides another resource for individuals, with the social interaction serving to bring about cohesion in the group as well. The neighborhood provides individuals with opportunities for personal advice, extra resources, and aid on a short-term basis. Thus, even in a highly bureaucratized society, tasks of nonrepetitive, idiosyncratic nature remain that can best be handled through the personal relations of primary groups such as the family and the neighborhood. The neighborhood group not only serves an informal service function but provides for appropriate referrals for professional service. As Soyer has noted, the practice of casework in settlements is indicated for reaching problem families because of the local, informal, and personal nature of the setting.[22] The neighborhood group, then, may be cultivated by the social work practitioner as part of the "lay referral system" identified by Landy, as well as a structure that shares functions with formal organizations.[23]

NEIGHBORHOOD VERSUS FORMAL ORGANIZATIONS

Examination of underlying problems of maintaining a viable neighborhood group in urban society suggests further exploration of the general role of primary groups as contrasted with formal organizations in reaching societal goals. Primary groups such as the family and neighborhood were characterized by Cooley as having the dimensions of face-to-face, permanent, diffused, affective, and noninstrumental relations.[24] In contrast, formal organizations stress rules, specialized relations, mobility, and impersonal and instrumental relations.[25] In the light of these differences, it is useful to consider these organizational types in relation to the bases of social influence proposed by French and Raven.[26] In the use of expertise, formal organizations provide for problem-solving most efficiently in dealing with uniform tasks, while the neighborhood group is likely to be equal to or better than the formal organization when there is no real knowledge available, when problems are simple, and when they are idiosyncratic in nature. The neighborhood can handle problems of a diffuse nature

18 *Op. cit.*

19 *Op. cit.*, p. 638.

20 *See*, for example, Eugene Litwak, "Extended Kin Relations in an Industrial Society," in Ethel Shanas and Gordon F. Streib, eds., *Social Structure and the Family: Generational Relations* (Englewood Cliffs, N. J.: Prentice-Hall, 1965).

21 Parsons and Bales, *op. cit.*, pp. 3–19.

22 David Soyer, "Reaching Problem Families Through Settlement-Based Casework," *Social Work*, Vol. 6, No. 3 (July 1961), pp. 36–42.

23 D. Landy, "Problems of the Person Seeking Help in Our Culture," *Social Welfare Forum 1960* (New York: Columbia University Press, 1960).

24 Charles H. Cooley, "Primary Groups," in Paul Hare, Edgar F. Borgatta, and Robert F. Bales, eds., *Small Groups* (New York: Alfred A. Knopf, 1955), pp. 15–17.

25 Max Weber, "The Essentials of Bureaucratic Organization: An Ideal Type Construction," in Stein and Cloward, eds., *op. cit.*, pp. 564–571.

26 John R. P. French and Bertram Raven, "The Bases of Social Power," in Dorwin Cartwright, ed., *Studies in Social Power* (Ann Arbor: University of Michigan Press, 1959), pp. 155–165. This type of analysis is used in regard to the family in Litwak, "Extended Kin Relations in an Industrial Society."

and, owing to small size and common values, can gain quick consensus for action. Thus, a variety of crisis situations can be handled by the neighborhood group, such as emergency first aid, baby-sitting, and immediate advice.

Other forms of social influence, such as reward and punishment, referent power, and legitimation, have significance in primary groups owing to the immediate observability of behavior by members of these groups. For example, the neighbors observe behavior and respond to it according to neighborhood norms. Adherence to group expectations is likely to result in approval, social acceptance, and positive reinforcement of acceptable behavior. Thus, the neighborhood frequently defines normal and deviant behavior for the group and serves as a mechanism for social control. Social distance, isolation, and exclusion from formal and informal neighborhood associations may be introduced by group members as punishment for disapproved behavior.

Since the family also is in a position of social influence over its members and provides resources for them, it is necessary to consider the neighborhood in relation to the family as a primary group. The neighborhood's major function is likely to be the provision of resources additional to those supplied within the family. Since neighbors are physically close, they are in a position to provide immediate services and psychological support when these are not available from family and kinship groups. Also, as Mogulof has pointed out, the organized neighborhood group is in a position to influence the distribution of resources by formal organizations to meet neighborhood needs.[27]

NEIGHBORHOOD DIAGNOSIS

Examination of the role of the neighborhood in terms of mobility, heterogeneity, and impersonality in urban society has considerable implication for social work practice. We are alerted to organizational, value, and change dimensions of neighborhood primary groups that can be utilized in the construction of diagnostic categories. These in turn imply strategies for social work intervention.

The organizational base of neighborhoods may be identified in terms of the associational structure of informal contacts and of local formal organizations, e.g., voluntary groups. "Ideal types" of neighborhoods include those organized and unorganized in terms of their capacity to implement their values. Values, then, comprise a second major dimension for classifying neighborhoods. Neighborhood values such as orientation toward education and good citizenship may be viewed on a positive-negative continuum, based on the extent to which the values of a neighborhood group are or are not consistent with those of the general society. Combining these dimensions of organization and values leads to four types of neighborhoods, those with (1) positive values, organized to implement them, (2) positive values, unorganized, (3) negative values, organized to implement them, and (4) negative values, unorganized.

Whyte's Park Forest neighborhoods illustrate the first type, as do most middle-class suburbs.[28] Park Forest is described as having a highly organized complex of formal and informal relations, with families characterized as having positive values toward education, participation in community life, community improvement, and maintenance of law and order. This neighborhood type is also found in the stable working-class neighborhoods described by Miller and Riessman.[29] The neighborhood described by the "mass society" theorists illustrates the second type of neighborhood,

[27] Melvin B. Mogulof, "Involving Low-Income Neighborhoods in Antidelinquency Programs," *Social Work*, Vol. 10, No. 4 (October 1965), pp. 51–57.

[28] *Op. cit.*

[29] S. M. Miller and Frank Riessman, "The Working Class Sub-Culture: A New View," *Social Problems*, Vol. 9, No. 2 (Summer 1961).

in which the group is unorganized but maintains a positive orientation toward conventional societal values, e.g., the inner-city elite apartment-dwellers. The third type is represented in slum neighborhoods with high mobility and negative values and the criminal world neighborhoods and delinquency areas depicted by Kobrin.[30] The fourth type is illustrated by inner-city skid row and rooming-house areas, as well as by many high-rise low-income housing project areas.

In addition to neighborhood organization and values, a third diagnostic category concerns the capacity and orientation of the neighborhood group to handle social change. Thus, a neighborhood may be organized toward stability or change, or may be unorganized. The neighborhood organized for stability is illustrated by the "urban villagers" of Boston's West End, who attempted to maintain the traditional neighborhood, resisting differential mobility of members out of the group and seeking long-term identification and commitment to the neighborhood.[31] Alissi labels this type of group the "farm" system, with the exchange of mutual obligations bringing about organization and control. Alissi also notes that within such neighborhoods there exist other subsystems, such as those with predominantly mobile or deviant members.[32] The neighborhood organized for change is exemplified by the urban middle-class, bureaucratic occupational type of neighborhood, with members engaged in ordered change and oriented toward use of mechanisms for quick socialization of newcomers. For the family involved in occupational and geographic mobility, movement into the unorganized neighborhood or one organized for stability is likely to be dysfunctional in current society.

STRATEGIES OF SOCIAL WORK INTERVENTION

The scheme for neighborhood diagnosis presented is useful in determining strategies of social work intervention. For example, one major task of the social worker is to create and/or maintain linkage between formal organizations and the primary groups of family and neighborhood. Litwak and Meyer have identified a series of linking mechanisms that serve to bridge the gap between these two organizational types and balance their relationships at a middle position of social distance.[33] The professional social worker may take the role of a detached expert by direct participation in community primary groups. A second mechanism involves the social worker's use of the opinion leader in the community to influence members of the neighborhood group. Other approaches include the use of settlement house, voluntary association, messenger, mass media, and formal authority. These means of co-ordination are used by social workers to narrow or increase the social distance between the neighborhood primary group and formal organizations. The selection of linking mechanisms and the sequence in which they are used may be guided by the type of neighborhood to which intervention is directed. When the neighborhood group has deviant values, mechanisms of co-ordination that have initiative, intensity, and focused expertise are necessary. In contrast, with neighborhoods displaying positive values, use of mechanisms such as mass media and voluntary associations is likely to be most efficient.

For disorganized neighborhoods, Piven notes that efforts toward organization are necessary to provide a basis for converting

---

30 *Op. cit.*, pp. 498–505.

31 Herbert K. Gans, *The Urban Villagers: Group and Class in the Life of Italian-Americans* (New York: Free Press of Glencoe, 1962).

32 Albert S. Alissi, "Social Influences on Group Values," *Social Work*, Vol. 10, No. 1 (January 1965), pp. 14–22.

33 Eugene Litwak and Henry J. Meyer, "A Balance Theory of Coordination Between Bureaucratic Organizations and External Primary Groups," *Administrative Science Quarterly*, Vol. 11, No. 3 (June 1966), pp. 31–58.

individual needs and interests into a collective source of influence.[34] In a disorganized neighborhood with negative values, the social worker would seek to identify individuals with positive norms and organize them, provide expertise in developing leadership within the neighborhood, and promote participation by the residents. In organized neighborhoods with negative norms, it might be necessary to use a strategy of disorganization, followed by organization toward positive values. In the case of disorganized neighborhoods with positive values, major efforts would be directed toward identifying opinion leaders and creating organization. For organized neighborhoods with positive values, the major task would be to keep channels of communication between group members open, allowing members to support each other with positive norms.

Social work intervention in neighborhoods may also focus on helping members develop a facility for handling change. From an ecological point of view, several kinds of population change—i.e., racial or class change—occur in urban neighborhoods. Ravitz considers the nature of these changes and the roles for the social worker in relation to preparing these types of neighborhoods for change, such as use of voluntary associations.[35] Voluntary associations composed of neighbors may be organized to deal with local neighborhood issues. Greer and Orleans call organizations of this type "parapolitical," since they may become overtly political and serve as bases for opinion and action.[36] Such associations permit initiative in forming friendships, i.e., getting to know people. They also publicize local norms and sanctions and build neighborhood identity by permitting participation with neighbors around local issues.

Group activities within the neighborhood can also be structured to avoid competition with other primary groups and therefore aid in speeding up integration of newcomers into the neighborhood. If participation in the neighborhood takes place at the expense of family activities, one procedure for avoiding this competition is to incorporate the nuclear family as a unit into the neighborhood group. This means husband and wife share common friends among the neighbors and do things together. In low-income, highly mobile areas the social work task would be to assist newcomers in integrating and adjusting to the challenge of a changed environment, as well as to help individuals who aspire to move to middle-class areas.

NEIGHBORHOOD DEFINITION

The problems and potentials of maintaining the neighborhood group as a significant force in contemporary society have been discussed and some initial diagnostic approaches and intervention strategies for social work practice have been indicated. While the neighborhood has been defined in terms of primary group membership, this discussion points to additional aspects of neighborhood definition that need attention. For example, considerable descriptive data regarding neighborhoods are available through analysis of census tract characteristics. Thus, the social area analysis approach of Shevkey and Bell focuses on identification of economic, family, and ethnic characteristics as the basis for neighborhood typologies.[37] In this type of analysis, geographic boundaries are often used to define the limits of the neighborhood group.

However, as Greer has pointed out, neighborhoods take on additional meaning when they define fields of social interaction.[38]

[34] Frances Fox Piven, "Participation of Residents in Neighborhood Community Action Programs," *Social Work,* Vol. 11, No. 1 (January 1966), pp. 73–80.

[35] Mel J. Ravitz, "Preparing Neighborhoods for Change," in Sussman, ed., *op. cit.,* pp. 173–187.

[36] Scott Greer and Peter Orleans, "The Mass Society and the Parapolitical Structure," *American Sociological Review,* Vol. 27, No. 5 (October 1962), pp. 634–646.

[37] Eshref Shevkey and Wendell Bell, *Social Area Analysis* (Stanford: Stanford University Press, 1955).

[38] Scott Greer, "Socio-Political Structure of Suburbia," *American Sociological Review,* Vol. 25, No. 4 (August 1960), pp. 514–526.

Greer has proposed the use of units of household, neighborhood, local residential area, and municipality, with size increasing and primary relations decreasing from household to municipality. A variation of this approach is suggested by Spiro, who labels the household and immediate surrounding households the "nuclear" neighborhood, followed in size by the street or "block" neighborhood.[39] Next in size is the "service" neighborhood, including a combination of block units, with common areas of social interaction as well as services ranging from elementary school to shopping area. These definitions serve to differentiate neighborhood in terms of size (number of people and territory) and the nature of interactions likely within the areas.

[39] Shimon Spiro, "Definitions of Neighborhood." Paper prepared for Seminar on Community Cohesion, University of Michigan School of Social Work, 1966. (Mimeographed.) *See also* Richard Dewey, "The Neighborhood, Urban Ecology, and City Planning," in Hatt and Reiss, eds., *op. cit.*, pp. 783–790.

These dimensions of the neighborhood need to be taken into account in strategies for social work intervention. In the case of the block neighborhood, the task may center around the problems of communication, friendship development, maintenance of the site, mutual aid, and social order. However, the block unit may be too small and informal as an organizational base for other problems, and a combination of blocks may become the focus of intervention. Thus, creation of voluntary associations with a broad neighborhood base may be called for in order to supply adequate resources and organizational influence to reach neighborhood goals. In noting these variations in definition of the neighborhood unit, we are alerted to the importance of identifying the boundaries of the neighborhood as a target of change.

SUMMARY

Recognizing the need for neighborhood assessment as a guide for social work intervention, the authors have suggested ways in which the neighborhood can be defined and analyzed, i.e., in terms of associational structure, organization, values, and capacity for change. The potential influence of the neighborhood group is highlighted through identification of mechanisms that serve to overcome problems in social relations resulting from mobility, heterogeneity, and impersonality in urban society. It has been noted that the neighborhood group may complement formal organizations in reaching individual and societal goals, and that linkage problems between these organizational types constitute significant areas of social work intervention. It has not been suggested that the traditional rural neighborhood with all of Cooley's dimensions of primary groups can or should be re-established in the urban environment, but that the neighborhood primary group plays a significant role in contemporary society and constitutes an important focus for social work intervention.

GROUP ACTIVITIES AND ASSIGNMENTS

Break into triads and role play a one-to-one situation, just for the purpose of data collection about a person in a problem situation (eg. "Someone stole my welfare check..."; "I just can't take it any longer, my husband is driving me crazy..."; "Everybody hates me..."). Experiment with techniques of restatement, reflection, mirroring,etc. The third party should observe and give feedback to the helping agent.

Role play a first group session with: a group of teenagers who are having school problems; a group of welfare recipients living in public housing; a group of parents who are heads of one-parent-families who are having difficulties with their pre-teen children; etc. Let one member of the group act as a facilitator, two as observers and the rest as participants.

Role play: a group of inner-city people who are planning to confront the Welfare Department for changes in the Food Stamp program; a group of tenants in low-income housing who are being harassed by the management; a group of agency representatives who are exploring the need for homemaker services.

Write a process recording of your one-to-one data collection interview.

SELECTED BIBLIOGRAPHY

Alissi, A.S., "Social Influences on Group Values," Social Work, 10 (1), 1965, pp. 14-22.

Bernard, S.E., Durtagh, E., and Johnson, H.R., "The Neighborhood Service Organization: Specialist Social Welfare Innovation," Social Work, 13 (1), 1968, pp. 76-84.

Billingsley, Andrew and Billingsley, Amy, "Negro Family Life In America," Social Service Review, 39 (3), 1965, pp. 310-319.

Boehm, B., "Protective Services for Neglected Children," Social Work Practice, 1967, pp. 109-125.

Cohen, W.J., "What Every Social Worker Should Know About Political Action," Social Work, 11 (3), 1966, pp. 3-11.

French, John, "A Formal Theory of Social Power," Psychological Review, 63 (3), 1956, pp. 181-194.

Frey, L.A. and Kolodny, R., "Illusions and Realities In Current Social Work With Groups," Social Work, 9 (2), 1964, pp. 80-89.

Glasser, P.H., Navarre, E.L., "The Problems of Families In the AFDC Program," Children, 12 (4), 1965, pp. 151-6.

Goroff, N., "Social Group Work; An Intersystematic Frame of Reference," Journal of Jewish Communal Service, 47 (3), 1971, pp. 229-237.

Grosser, C.F., "Community Development Programs Serving the Urban Poor," Social Work, 10 (3), 1965, pp. 15-21.

Herre, E.A., "A Community Mobilizes to Protect Its Children," Public Welfare, 23 (2), 1965, pp. 93-97.

Lindsey, Inabel, "Race As A Factor In The Caseworker's Role," Social Casework, 27 (3), 1947, pp. 101-107.

Locklear, H., "American Indian Myths," Social Work, 18(3), pp. 72-81

Manning, S., "Cultural and Value Factors Affecting The Negroes Use of Agency Services," Social Work, 5 (4), 1960, pp. 3-13.

March, M.S., "The Neighborhood Center Concept," Public Welfare, 26 (2), 1968, pp. 97-111.

Marsh, C.P., "The Structure of Community Power and Community Decision Making," Adult Leadership, 13 (3), 1964, pp. 71-72.

Mayer, J.E., Rosenblatt, A., "The Client's Social Context: Its Effect On Continuance In Treatment," Social Casework, 45 (9), 1964, pp. 511-518.

Mizio, E., "White Worker Minority Client," Social Work, 18 (3), pp. 82- 86.

Purcell, F.P., Specht, H., "The House On Sixth Street," Social Work, 10 (4), pp. 69-75.

Rose, S.D., "A Behavioral Approach To The Group Treatment of Parents," Social Work, 14 (3), 1969, pp. 21-29.

Wachtel, D.D., "Structures of Community and Strategies for Organization," Social Work, 13 (1), 1968, pp. 85-91.

DATA ANALYSIS

Even as the change agent is collecting data he is beginning, at least tentatively, to analyze it. In other words, data collection and analysis are not necessarily discrete steps, but in many instances are overlapping. Data analysis is essentially "making sense" out of the data which has been collected. Depending on the system with which the change agent is working, data analysis requires a substantial knowledge of the appropriate theories. For example, in working with individuals, my own preference is a framework of a combination of ego psychology, role theory, and crisis intervention as articulated by Erikson and Lindemann in the previous chapter. Someone else who is more behaviorally oriented might well prefer to analyze the data from his particular perspective. Or again, someone else might be more eclectic in his approach. On dealing with groups the change agent must be well grounded in small group theory. Larger systems require a knowledge of concepts of power, power structures, conflict, etc. as well as the knowledge required to work with smaller systems. Hopefully these concepts will have been presented in other courses in the curriculum. The task of the methods course is to assist the student in operationalizing these concepts and in acquiring skill in practice.

As suggested in the previous chapter, crisis intervention theory can be a useful concept for the general practitioner. To use crisis intervention effectively in social work settings, objective criteria to determine whether the client is in a state of crisis and could benefit from this approach must be utilized in the initial encounter. Golan's article, "When Is a Client In Crisis?," reviews and defines four basic operational elements of a crisis situation. Various approaches from crisis theory and research in this area are examined in regard to when and how to use these elements. A crisis intervention model for initial interviews that can be applied selectively and flexibly in a large number of settings is outlined.

The Fausel article "The General Practitioner in the Undergraduate Social Welfare Program," adapts the Pincus and Minahan framework referred to in the previous chapter and describes the process involved in the analysis of data. It spells out in more detail the different systems the worker needs to be aware of as well as the phases of planned change.

Critical mistakes in the data analysis phase of the helping process can occur if the change agent does not take into account the cultural background of the client system. Ignacio Aguilar points out cultural values and patterns of behavior among Mexican-Americans, and barriers to assimilation in an alien society that demand adaptation on the part of the change agent if he is going to make any meaning of the data he is collecting. A case example of a Mexican-American family illustrates this.

A similar approach is taken by D. Corydon Hammond in his article "Cross-Cultural Rehabilitation." After pointing out a number of value differences between the Anglo culture and the native American culture, he describes seven areas in which a non-Indian might have difficulty in both relating to an Indian client system and in interpreting data. He then spells out eleven recommendations that should be helpful in analyzing information received from a client system of another ethnic background.

Emanuel Tropp's article, "The Group: In Life and In Social Work," gives a good, but brief review of group dynamics. He presents both Vinter's and Schwartz's approach to groups, and he delineates the essential features of social work with groups.

The article by Robert Pruger and Harry Specht presents one method of analyzing theories of community organization in a systematic way. They address themselves to the essential question: What methods produce what changes in what situations? Although primarily concerned with the Alinsky approach to effecting change in systems, the article offers a framework for analyzing specific ways in which systems are changed.

Naomi Golan

When is a client in crisis?

A model for an intake interview is proposed that can be applied flexibly and selectively by different workers in different settings

Crisis intervention has become a major treatment modality in a variety of social work settings. But it is often not easy to identify a crisis at the time of intake, when the crucial decision must be made whether or not to use this modality.

It is true that a worker sometimes meets with a clear-cut presenting problem that has been identified in the literature as a crisis.[1] And sometimes the setting itself not only defines the crisis but also contributes to its development and resolution.[2]

Most often, however, a social worker is presented with an undifferentiated, multifaceted problem situation, especially if he functions in an agency that provides a variety of services. Moreover, the intake worker's perception may be affected by the highly charged, anxiety laden atmosphere during the first interview. He may respond to bizarre, poignant, or emergent elements in the client's situation. He may be influenced by pressure from the referral source. Or he may react precipitously to the chronically crisis producing person who, feeling little anxiety himself, generates a sense of it in others.

A quietly desperate applicant, on the other hand, clinging to shreds of denial and determined not to give way to panic, may successfully mask a true crisis. Or a usually adequate person, confronted with the unexpected inadequacy of his customary problem solving methods in a crisis, may withdraw in the face of the probing information gathering process of the intake interview. Moreover, a nonverbal client may be unable to describe his predicament adequately and be turned away before it is even investigated as a possible crisis.

Given the premise that "a little help, rationally directed and purposefully focused at a strategic time, is more effective than more extensive help given at a period of less emotional accessibility,"[3] practitioners must be able to recognize a crisis in time to work with it, before maladaptive adjustments have set in and change producing anxiety has receded. In such situations two questions are paramount: How can a crisis situation be identified? How can the elements of the crisis situation be utilized? These questions were the basis of a research project conducted by

[1]See Howard J. Parad, ed., *Crisis Intervention: Selected Readings* (Family Service Association of America, New York, 1965).

[2]Jeannette R. Oppenheimer, Use of Crisis Intervention in Casework with the Cancer Patient and His Family, *Social Work*, 12:44–52 (April 1967).

[3]Lydia Rapoport, Crisis-Oriented Short-Term Casework, *Social Service Review*, 41:38 (March 1967).

SOCIAL CASEWORK, July 1969, Vol. 50, No. 7, pp. 389-394.

the author, upon which much of this article is based.[4]

Identifying a crisis

The first step in working with crises is to know what to look for. Four operational terms have been worked out, based on Donald Klein and Erich Lindemann's breakdown of the total emotional predicament;[5] Gerald Caplan's plotting of the phases in the development of a crisis;[6] and, particularly, Peter Sifneos' identification of the components of an emotional crisis.[7] The four elements are (1) the hazardous event, (2) the vulnerable state, (3) the precipitating factor, and (4) the state of active crisis (disequilibrium).

It should be made clear at the outset that these terms are diagnostic abstractions, that few clients seen in intake interviews actually present such an orderly, clear picture. As a matter of fact a psychosocial appraisal at any one time may show different members of the same family in different stages of individual crisis springing from and contributing to the total crisis situation: the application of an unmarried pregnant girl for help in planning for her baby may constitute for her a constructive resolution of a crisis that started with her adolescent struggle about her feminine role and reached the active state when she discovered she was pregnant and her boyfriend would not marry her. At the same time the mother may be in a vulnerable state, which could be precipitated into a state of active crisis by an attempt to involve her in the planning. The father may have been carefully shielded from the situation, which could cause him to perceive a request for participation as a hazardous event.

The duration of the process can be either telescoped or elongated. One event, such as the death of a mother, may be catastrophic enough to send the whole family into a state of disequilibrium. Or a series of hazardous events may occur over a period of months, each taking its toll, until the breaking point is reached: for example, the bankruptcy of a father's business, a son's withdrawal from college and his induction into military service, the breakup of a daughter's marriage, and the beginning of a mother's menopause.

Careful questioning focused on the client's current life situation—which is too often neglected—usually enables the intake worker to determine whether or not the client is in an incipient or active state of crisis. In such questioning, attention should be given to all four components of the crisis situation.

Hazardous event

The possible existence of a hazardous event should be explored at the outset, the term being defined as the initial external blow or internal change that triggers a chain of reactions leading to a crisis. If the original hazardous event cannot be identified through direct questioning, it can often be identified through an inferential reconstruction of events leading to the current situation. When such an event is discovered, it is useful in understanding its impact to identify it as either unanticipated or anticipated. Unanticipated hazardous events fall into three major categories: (1) a loss or impending loss to the applicant or a significant other, through death or desertion, illness or disability, for example; (2) the introduction of a new person into the social orbit, through the premature birth of a child or the return of a significant other after a prolonged absence, for example; and (3) involvement in community disasters or disruptions, such as fire or blizzard, urban renewal or depression. Anticipated hazardous events fall into two major categories: (1) developmental critical stages and (2) transition points, such as starting school, getting married, and retiring.

Thomas McGee suggests that such events

[4]Naomi Golan, Casework in Crisis: A Study of the Association of Selected Applicant Factors with Workers' Decisions on Cases Seen in Intake in Psychiatric Admission Services, doctoral dissertation (University of Chicago, Chicago, 1968).

[5]Donald C. Klein and Erich Lindemann, Preventive Intervention in Individual and Family Crisis Situations, in Gerald Caplan, ed., *Prevention of Mental Disorders in Children* (Basic Books, New York, 1961), 284.

[6]Gerald Caplan, *Principles of Preventive Psychiatry* (Basic Books, New York, 1964), 40–41.

[7]Peter E. Sifneos, A Concept of "Emotional Crisis," *Mental Hygiene*, 44:177 (April 1960).

can be assigned different priorities along a continuum. Normal developmental crises, which seldom require direct and immediate intervention, might be placed at the lower end of such a continuum; more immediately severe crises, such as the loss of a job combined with the death of a family member, might be placed at the upper end.[8]

Vulnerable state

The term *vulnerable state* refers to the individual's subjective reactions to the hazardous event either at the time of its occurrence or subsequently. In discussing vulnerable states Lydia Rapoport notes that the initial blow may be perceived in various ways: as a *threat,* either to instinctual needs or to the sense of physical or emotional integrity; as a *loss,* either of a person or of an ability or capacity; or as a *challenge.* Each of these states has its typical accompanying affect: threat calls forth a high level of anxiety; loss or deprivation is accompanied by depression or mourning; and challenge stimulates moderate anxiety and some hope and a release of energy for problem solving.[9]

Some corroboration of these alignments was obtained in the author's research project mentioned earlier: perception of the hazardous event as a loss was highly associated with feelings of depression, and perception of the hazardous event as a threat to integrity was significantly related to anxiety. Perception of the hazardous event as a threat to instinctual needs, however, called forth feelings of depression and anxiety almost equally, which seems to imply that a more complex assault is implicit in such an event. Though a crisis presents a problem in the current life situation of the client, it is indeed often linked with unresolved conflicts. The nature of the original conflict may well determine the individual's emotional reaction to the current situation.

Whereas any diagnostic formulation about underlying personality structure based on data gathered during a first interview would probably be highly inferential, it is certainly both relevant and appropriate to find out how the client has attempted to deal with the problems posed by the hazardous event before coming to the agency: it is probable that he has first resorted to habitual problem solving methods that are part of his customary life style and then, to meet rising tension, tried new emergency measures.[10]

Following is a classification of the ways in which applicants in the author's research project said or implied they had attempted to deal with the effects of the crisis situation within the recent past:

1. Carried on as usual; made no new effort.
2. Expressed grief in words or action or both (adopted depressive behavior).
3. Expressed anger by words or action or both (adopted aggressive behavior).
4. Escaped reality by words or action or both (slept excessively; fantasized; became psychotic; used alcohol or drugs).
5. Developed neurotic symptoms (adopted phobic behavior, compulsive rituals, hysteric manifestations).
6. Developed somatic symptoms (suffered from migraine, ulcers, dermatitis).
7. Engaged in reality oriented efforts to deal with the situation (cut down expenses; looked for a job; returned to the parental home).
8. Mobilized energies for new, growth producing activities (started training for a new career, innovated basic changes in the home).

Caplan has pointed out that when the usual homeostatic, direct problem solving mechanisms do not work and the problem is such that other methods that might be used to sidestep it cannot be used, the individual's tension rises and the process leading toward disequilibrium becomes accelerated.[11] Some individuals, however, although indicating

---

[8]Thomas F. McGee, Some Basic Considerations in Crisis Intervention, *Community Mental Health Journal,* 4:319 (August 1968).

[9]Rapoport, Crisis-Oriented . . . , 37.

[10]The ways by which individuals "go forth to do battle" have been variously described as coping devices, problem solving methods, grappling efforts, and so forth. It should be stressed that what is being examined is the effort made to deal with the situation, on a conscious or unconscious level, whether or not it actually solved the problem in the eyes of the caseworker, the family, or the community.

[11]Caplan, *Principles* . . . , 39.

Crisis intervention: model for an intake interview

I. Immediate focus on crisis situation

A. Nature of precipitating factor ascertained: kind, severity, scope, persons involved.

"What brought you in here?"
"What's happened to make you so upset?"

B. Applicant's current condition discussed and observed: dysfunction in feelings, thoughts, behavior; bodily performance and symptoms; disturbance in role networks.

"Can you tell me what's going on?"
"How are you getting along now?"

C. Original hazardous event identified, and subsequent events disclosed.

"Can you recall what started all this?"
"Did anything happen to you that made you feel different?"
"Did anything else happen after that to make you feel the same way?"

D. Nature and duration of vulnerable state ascertained: subjective reactions to hazardous event, earlier attempts to deal with problem.

"How did this affect you in the beginning?"
"When did you begin to feel so bad about it?"
"Did you do anything about it before you came here?"
"Did things get better after that?"

E. State of applicant evaluated, and treatment of choice determined.

II. Stimulation of cognitive awareness of crisis

A. Current situation discussed; feelings of loss, guilt, fear, and anxiety ventilated; and grief work encouraged as indicated.

"You must have felt very bad about this."

B. Subjective significance of situation explored; specific problem with which applicant is struggling clarified; link (actual or symbolic) to previous unresolved conflicts brought out.

"Why did this upset you so?"
"Why should it bother you when none of the rest felt so bad?"
"Was this the first time this happened to you?"

III. Attempt to partialize and focus situation

A. Problem formulated by applicant, and need defined by him.

B. Appraisal of current situation verbalized by worker, in workable terms.

C. Tentative problem to be worked on agreed upon; immediate goals defined; area for interventive action staked out; decision for action taken.

IV. Start of therapeutic intervention

A. Acceptable and available alternatives reviewed; specific, time limited treatment plan set up.

B. Involvement of significant others in role networks considered and agreed upon.

C. Other community resources to support treatment plan reviewed; referrals discussed.

that crisis situations have occurred in the past, show few signs of disequilibrium and display instead the aftereffects of maladaptive efforts to deal with the problems posed. Therefore, it is important at intake to secure some knowledge not only of the nature and extent of problem solving methods used previously but also of the degree to which such efforts have been adaptive or maladaptive.

Precipitating factor

The precipitating factor in a crisis situation is the final link in the chain of stress provoking events that converts a vulnerable state into a state of disequilibrium.[12] It is "the straw that breaks the camel's back." Accordingly, it is useful in any intake interview to find out what actually prompted the request for help at the particular time at which it was made, even though the true precipitating event is sometimes not directly linked to referral to the agency and therefore not immediately identifiable.

Theoretically, the precipitant can be internal pressure building up within the individual to a point of unbearable tension. Frequently, however, it is a relatively minor incident. Information about such an incident may be vital both for determining whether the applicant is actually experiencing a crisis and for evaluating his motivation. The precipitating factor is frequently the appropriate "handle" by which to pick up the case. It can also become the focus for immediate intervention.

State of active crisis

The term *state of active crisis* applies to the stage of disequilibrium, when tension and anxiety have risen to a peak and the individual's built-in homeostatic devices no longer operate. It is the key element in crisis theory and the criterion for determining whether crisis intervention is the appropriate approach.

Determining whether or not an individual is in a state of active crisis calls for an appraisal of his current state of dysfunctioning, both as subjectively reported by him and as objectively determined by the worker on the basis of personal observation and collateral information. Such an appraisal should take into account the four primary areas of reaction: affective, perceptive-cognitive, behavioral, and biophysiological. It should include an examination of the individual's dysfunctioning in terms of his vital social roles in his family, in his job, and in social and institutional networks and the reciprocal reactions of others. It should also include a judgment about the intensity and extent of the individual's discomfort and anxiety. And closely tied to such an assessment is an estimate of the seriousness of the person's condition in terms of possible danger to himself or others. A suicidal-homicidal potential is often held to be the prime determinant in deciding what action should be taken immediately—although it does not necessarily imply that a crisis situation exists.[13]

Another key factor in such an evaluation is information about how long the applicant has been in a state of active crisis. Since, according to Caplan, this stage is predictable and time limited, usually lasting up to six weeks,[14] such data could disclose whether the individual is still in a fluid state, during which limited intervention can produce dramatic and significant results, or has already settled into a new state of equilibrium, pathological or antisocial or limiting though it may be.

When to use crisis intervention

It is a far cry from identifying the elements of a crisis situation to utilizing such elements appropriately in the casework process. Howard Parad suggests that crisis intervention may be most validly applicable for the very strong or the very weak, for those requiring

---

[12]See M. Robert Harris, Betty L. Kalis, and Edith H. Freeman, Precipitating Stress: An Approach to Brief Therapy, *American Journal of Psychotherapy,* 17:465–71 (July 1963).

[13]See Naomi Golan, Helen Carey, and Erland Hyttinen, The Emerging Role of the Social Worker in a Psychiatric Emergency Service, *Community Mental Health Journal,* 5:55–61 (February 1969).

[14]Gerald Caplan, Concluding Discussion, in Gerald Caplan, ed., *Prevention of Mental . . . ,* 409.

only short periods of help and for those not motivated for continuing service.[15]

Robert Porter points out that the clients most responsive to crisis intervention are usually those for whom the onset of the psychosocial problem is clear-cut; whose prior level of adjustment was stable; for whom the crisis was generated out of a reciprocal role relationship; and who have some knowledge both of the social or behavioral difficulty for which they seek help and of the precipitating stress, even though they may not connect the two. He suggests that investigation of the crisis situation need not exceed the bounds of the client's current life situation, since examination of current social role relationships and environmental influences usually yields sufficient data.[16]

Often the focus of the applicant's request for service reveals the specific area of his discomfort. Requests generally fall into the following categories: (1) exploring the nature of the problem; (2) clarifying or changing the behavior, thoughts, or feelings of himself or a significant other; (3) clarifying or changing the interaction between himself and a significant other; (4) handling the consequences and aftereffects of earlier actions and interactions; (5) minimizing current discomfort; and (6) reducing environmental pressures. Findings in the author's research study showed that four out of five applicants were primarily interested either in minimizing discomfort or handling aftereffects of actions and interactions. At the point of intake, regardless of the nature of the problem, they were asking either for symptom relief or for reduction of external pressures. This finding substantiates Rapoport's contention that while not many people may be motivated to change their ways of behaving and feeling, all people in distress are motivated to obtain relief from suffering. This fact, she believes, is the proper starting point with people in crisis.[17]

Leaving aside the issue of defining "cure," it is certainly clear that a utilization of the dynamic force seeking the reestablishment of psychic equilibrium points to crisis intervention as the treatment of choice in a large number of cases, if the potential can be recognized in time.

Using the crisis model

Once the elements of a crisis have been identified and the appropriateness of crisis intervention has been determined, more is still required of the intake worker. The first phase—the diagnostic phase—has been discussed. To avoid presenting only a partial picture, a model for a full intake interview is presented also. It is by no means intended as a formula. It is hoped that it will provide useful guidelines that can be applied flexibly and selectively by different workers in different settings—and that it will in some measure answer the question, "It's a good idea, but what can you do with it?"

[15] Howard J. Parad, The Use of Time-Limited Crisis Intervention in Community Mental Health Programing, *Social Service Review*, 40:279 (September 1966).

[16] Robert A. Porter, Crisis Intervention and Social Work Models, *Community Mental Health Journal*, 2:17 (Spring 1966).

[17] Rapoport, Crisis-Oriented . . . , 43.

THE GENERAL PRACTITIONER IN THE UNDERGRADUATE SOCIAL WELFARE PROGRAM*

Donald F. Fausel

In recent years, the traditional boundaries between casework, group work and community organization, to say the least, have been strained. Controversy among practitioners, educators, and students of the social work education over the issue of methods—which methods should be taught and used in the field, has filled pages of journals and books, and occupied the time and thought of panelists and workshops during the last decade. The questions raised by the Milford Conference in the 1920's related to the generic vs. the specific approaches for fields of practice, are now being argued in terms of social work methods. Besides the individual methods orientations referred to above, one area of concern focuses on an expanded problem-solving orientation to social work practice. A practitioner using this more expanded problem-solving orientation has been said to be analogous to the general practitioner in medicine, while the practitioner using an individual methods orientation would have the medical specialist as a counterpart.[1] I believe with Gordon Hearn that social work, like medicine needs both general practitioners and specialists.

The Undergraduate Social Welfare Program at Arizona State University has adopted as its practice model, the social work generalist or general practitioner, i.e., an entry level worker who has begun to incorporate the values of the profession and has generic knowledge and skills to work across different size systems at appropriate interventive levels. Although not a clinician, his contacts with consumers in a multi-purpose service center or as a service worker in a welfare department are in a broad sense 'therapeutic.' Although not a group therapist, he might be called upon to work with a group of tenants in a housing project to facilitate their grievances against the management. Although not a policy-planner, he should be able to work with welfare mothers as they organize to effect some change in the welfare system. Part of his skill should be an awareness of his own limitations; that is the skill to identify those aspects of problems which are beyond his level of competency and to select the appropriate specialist for referral.[2]

To operationalize this orientation of the general practitioner, I

*Paper presented colloquium, Graduate School of Social Service Administration, Arizona State University, April 1973. Mimeographed.

ORIGINAL MANUSCRIPT, 1973.

have adapted the model presented by Pincus and Minaham.[3] Basic to this model is an understanding of the four systems in which the change agent carries out his role:

1. The change agent system—i.e., the organization that hires the worker—its structure, function, roles, hierarchy, policy, procedures, etc.
2. Client system—person, family, group, organization that engages his services as the change agent—the expected 'beneficiary' of his services.
3. Target system—person, family, group, organization or community at which the worker directs his change efforts. (It is an important task in determining those conditions, persons, systems, etc., that must be changed in order to benefit the client system.)
4. Action system—all of those persons and processes engaged in influencing the target system. In individual therapy we have the smallest possible action system—the client and the change agent. When the target system is larger, we might have a coalition of a number of people or groups which the change agent works with and through to effect change.

In situations where effecting change in the target system is beyond his competence, the general practitioner can become an important part of the action system as he acts as a catalyst to bring together appropriate specialists.

To relate this to a concrete situation: several welfare mothers living in an FHA 236 apartment complex individually complain to you as their service worker (change-agent system-DPW) about mistreatment by the management of the apartments. This mistreatment is causing them to be extremely anxious. A worker whose orientation is casework might give the individuals supportive treatment, hoping to relieve their anxieties. In which case, each individual is the target system, the worker and each individual is a separate action and the client system is the same as the action system and target system. A worker whose orientation is group work might get the mothers together to relieve their anxieties in a group. In which casę the target system, the action system and the client system are all the same. Or in either of the above orientations the change agent might advocate with the apartemnt management (target system) on an individual or a group basis.

The main difference in the approach of the general practitioner is in the choice of action and target system. Although he might see the mothers individually or as a group, he might also facilitate the formation of a resident action committee made up of a number of individuals living in the complex (action system) to put pressure on the administration (target system) to cease and desist their harassment of residents. In this move, expanded problem-solving orientation the client system has had the opportunity to become part of an action system (Resident Action Group) which hopefully has effected a change in their circumstances and provided a gratifying experience for them.

Obviously before the types of choices I am suggesting above could be made, the change agent along with the client system and the action system must follow a certain process. Again, Pincus and Minahan suggest five phases of planned change.

1. Recognition of the problem and initiating engagement of change-agent and client system.
2. Identification of client system, target system, change-agent system and action system related to the problem—and establish a contract with the client system.
3. Formulation of the action system.
4. Operation of the action system.
5. Evaluation.

The skills necessary to follow this process and which are generic to any size system with which you are working are communication skills, data collection, data analysis and intervention. All of these skills must be based on a knowledge foundation appropriate for the particular system being addressed. If the system is a micro-system, individual or small group, an eclectic framework of ego psychology, role theory and crisis intervention might form his theoretical framework. Larger systems, mezzo-systems or macro-systems, require a knowledge of concepts of power, conflict, power structures, etc.

I believe that this generic approach to methods could be incorporated in the curriculum of a quality undergraduate program or the first year graduate program with options to specialize in work with different size systems in the second year. At a point where graduate schools were more convinced of the quality of undergraduate accredited programs they might facilitate an undergraduate going directly into a specialty, as is being done at a number of graduate schools at the present time.

With a foundation in gneeric methods at an undergraduate or graduate level, the change agent would be less likely to perceive problems in the perspective of his own specialty. The worker whose expertise is in working with indifiduals should feel comfortable in working to effect change in those systems that are inpinging on his client system. As far back as the 1950's we talked a lot about putting the 'social' back in social work. In many instances, the 'social' that we put back did not go beyond the sytdy or diagnosis phase and rarely into the treatment phase.

If the profession is to be effective, there must be a more sophisticated assignment of takss for different levels of expertise and practice and a broader approach to problems presented by various size systems.

FOOTNOTES

1 Gordon Hearn, 'Towards a Unitary Conception of Social Work Practice,' (paper read at the Fourth Annual Student Social Work Conference, University of Washington, School of Social Work, May 10, 1963) pp. 3-4. (Mimeographed)

2 *Ibid.*

3 Allen Pincus and Anne Minahan, 'Toward a Model for Teaching a Basic First-Year Course in Methods of Social Work Practice,' *Innovations in Teaching Social Work Practice*; ed. Lilian Ripple (New York: CSWE, 1970), pp. 34-37.

Initial contacts with Mexican-American families

by Ignacio Aguilar

Schools of social work have, for the most part, been oblivious to the need for adapting methods of practice to minority groups. Rather they teach practice derived from a generic method that is dictated primarily by the majority. Yet much social work practice is carried out in the United States with minority groups and, too often, social workers apply it by a blanket method supposedly effective with all people.

Each minority group has its own problems and personality—derived from long-existing cultural and moral values, language, patterns of behavior, socioeconomic conditions, ethnic background, and many other factors. Social work practice in a minority community shows that besides the variations that must be made in the generic method to suit individuals, certain adaptations should be made in applying social work methods to the specific minority group.

During ten years' experience in a California community made up mainly of Mexican-Americans, the author learned from the people in the community how to adapt some of the key concepts and techniques of social work to the needs and the life-style of Mexican-Americans and how to avoid some common obstacles to the development of goodwill.

This article briefly outlines different cultural values and patterns of behavior—and barriers to assimilation in an alien society—which the social worker should consider in making initial contacts with Mexican-American families. How social work method was adapted in this initial contact phase in order to provide effective counseling is illustrated by a case example of work with a family in the author's community.

INITIAL CONTACT

There is no doubt that one of the most important and difficult processes in social work is the beginning phase, that is, starting to work with a client. Green and Maloney describe this phase as one in which

> . . . emotional interaction takes place. The worker focuses on an emotional en-

Reprinted with permission of the National Association of Social Workers, from SOCIAL WORK, Vol. 17, No. 3 (May 1972), pp. 66-70.

> gagement with a purpose, explores the possibilities of person(s), agency and worker finding a realistic *common purpose.* On the other hand, the client(s) naturally and rightly questions moving into a relationship with the worker.[1]

Since the first encounter determines the dynamics of the relationship and the kind and quality of the interaction between worker and client, a correct start is vital.

Awareness of differences, an understanding of why the differences exist, and experience in dealing with people of the specific minority group—all these are important to the social worker in establishing feelings of friendliness and confidence from the outset. Without them, a worker can unknowingly arouse antagonism or cause the client to withdraw in fear or confusion.

PATTERNS OF LIVING

The social worker in a Mexican-American community finds that his ways of work are strongly influenced by the people's patterns of living, which differ in many respects from those of people having a Protestant Anglo-Saxon background. Consideration of concepts, attitudes, and patterns of behavior that are likely to have a marked effect on the beginning stages of social work method can help to assure that vital correct start.

The leisurely opening. When Mexican-Americans meet to negotiate or arrange affairs, the first step is to set the climate or *ambiente.* A preliminary period of warm, informal, personal conversation precedes the discussion of the concerns that brought them together. Jumping into the middle of serious and controversial affairs—as many persons in the United States are inclined to do—seems confusing and even discourteous to most Mexican-Americans.

Language. Language is of course one of the main problems in working with non-English-speaking people. How can a social worker help people if he cannot communicate with them? How can a common purpose be established if that purpose cannot be discussed? How can a worker start where his clients are and proceed at a pace comfortable to them when he cannot even start at all? Obviously, for any social worker in a Spanish-speaking community, fluency in the language is a tremendous asset and for those dealing directly with clients it is a necessity—both for communicating and establishing rapport.

Attitude toward the law. Having to deal with the law is considered shameful by the average Mexican-American family, and the family members are disinclined to accept it as a common practice. The social worker needs to reassure his clients that dealing with the law offers them an honorable way of protecting their interests and legal rights. He will also have to explain their relation to such persons as probation officers and the police and tell them about legal services available to them. Knowledge of the basic elements of the Mexican system of law, as well as the system in the United States, will enable him to interpret these subjects more intelligibly to his clients.

Influence of religion. Religion plays an important role in the Mexican-American home and shapes the lives of the entire family. As Heller notes:

> Some observers have reported that the church continues to exercise a strong influence in the Mexican-American community. For example, Broom and Shevky contend that "the church is the principal agency of cultural conservatism for Mexicans in the United States and reinforces the separateness of the group." They specify that they have in mind not only the parish organization of the Catholic Church but also the Protestant Missions "with their functional sectarian attributes." There seems to be little doubt that the "religious factor" (to use Professor Lenski's phrase) plays an important role in the rate of acculturation of Mexican Americans.[2]

---

[1] Rose Green and Sara Maloney, "Characteristics of Movement in Phases of the Social Work Relationship." Unpublished paper, University of Southern California, Los Angeles, 1963. (Mimeographed.)

Role of the male. The concept of the male in society and in the family is important to the understanding of the person of Mexican ancestry. It is not only a concept of philosophy, it is a way of life, quite different from the "American way of life." Paz describes the *macho* concept as follows:

> The ideal manliness is never to "crack," never to back down. . . . Our masculine integrity is as much endangered by kindness as it is by hostility. Any opening in our defenses is a lessening of our manliness. . . . The Mexican macho—the male—is a hermetic being, closed up in himself, capable of guarding both himself and whatever has been confided to him.[3]

The traditional role of the husband and father in the Mexican-American family is explained by Heller, as follows:

> According to the traditional norms the husband is regarded as the authoritarian and patriarchal figure who is both the head and the master of the family, and the mother as the affectional figure in the family.[4]

The extended family. To Mexican-Americans the extended family is of great significance in their pattern of living; they take it for granted that in time of trouble they can always count on the family to help out. Again quoting Heller:

> Not only in size, but also in organization the Mexican American family displays an unusual persistence of traditional forms. It continues to be an extended type of family with strong ties spread through a number of generations in a large web of kinships. These ties impose obligations of mutual aid, respect and affection.[5]

BARRIERS TO COOPERATION

The social worker dealing with Mexican-Americans may well find that there are certain obstacles to be overcome before he can gain his clients' confidence and they can work together smoothly and effectively in endeavoring to solve problems. These obstacles may involve attitudes of other people with whom the Mexican-Americans associate or they may be related primarily to the clients' own attitudes.

Prejudice. Unfortunately, in many sections of the United States Mexican-Americans—especially the families of poor and unskilled workers—are likely to encounter prejudice. This can occur within the community at large, can reach out to the children in school, and can even be found among persons in the helping professions.

Unfriendly or antagonistic feelings conveyed by insensitive people in positions of authority hinder the progress of such families in becoming assimilated and assuming responsibility. These families with limited financial resources and limited knowledge of English are likely to become the target of prejudiced individuals reluctant to help those who do not fit readily into the mold of middle-class American society. Too often, help is not offered at all. Or it may be offered in such a way that acceptance requires departure from familiar behavioral patterns. Indeed, prejudice in its purest and ugliest manifestations becomes one of the most common problems the minorities face in their encounters with helping professionals. It can also be one of the social worker's greatest obstacles to building confidence.

The strange system. It is hard for the parents in a Mexican-American family to understand the "system" with which they have to deal as they endeavor to cope with their problems. It becomes in their minds a kind of hydra-headed creature, with authorities cropping up from all sides to make demands upon them and press in on their privacy. Yet these families have to learn how to deal with the system if they are to become active partners in the process of being helped. They have to learn how to ex-

---

[2] Celia S. Heller, *Mexican American Youth: Forgotten Youth at the Crossroads* (New York: Random House, 1966), p. 19.

[3] Octavio Paz, *The Labyrinth of Solitude*, Lysander Kamp, trans. (New York: Grove Press, 1962), pp. 29–31.

[4] Heller, op. cit., p. 34.

[5] Ibid., p. 34.

"Indeed, prejudice in its purest and ugliest manifestations becomes one of the most common problems the minorities face in their encounters with helping professionals."

ercise their rights and to assert their self-worth and esteem as human beings in a society they do not understand. As Hollis notes:

> This emphasis upon the innate worth of the individual is an extremely important, fundamental characteristic of casework. It is the ingredient that makes it possible to establish the relationship of trust that is so essential to effective treatment. From it grow the two essential characteristics of the caseworker's attitude toward his client: acceptance and belief in self-determination.[6]

For truly effective social work practice with minority groups, the social worker must learn as well as the client. Much more needs to be done in the way of teaching the uniqueness of the cultures of these groups to social workers and others in the helping professions if they are to provide worthwhile assistance to those who need the most help.

The following case illustration presents only the beginning stages in working with a typical family in a Mexican-American community in California. With further involvement, all other orthodox social work methods had to be modified somewhat in order to help the family fully.

CASE ILLUSTRATION

Family X is made up of the parents and three children: a girl 6 years old and two boys, aged 7 and 16. Mr. and Mrs. X were legally married at one time, but because of serious marital problems and pressures from Mrs. X's family were divorced three years ago. However, they managed to resolve their problems and came together again; the church never considered them divorced. The family lives in a small house in the back of a large empty lot that has not been taken care of properly. Weeds have taken over the majority of the land, so that they conceal the house.

The probation department referred Family X to the community center because neither the father nor the mother were able to communicate in English. The probation officer explained that this family needed counseling and also "someone who could speak their language." The parents were unable to control their 16-year-old son, Freddy, who had been placed on probation for running away from home regularly.

Mrs. X had been told to call the center for an appointment. This might have been sufficient to start the helping process for an Anglo-Saxon Protestant family; for a Mexican-American family it was not. Not only was it difficult for the family to overcome the shame of having to deal with the law, but Mr. X—who made all the decisions—had been disregarded by the probation officer. It was decided that establishing contact was up to the center, on the assumption that this would be difficult or impossible for Mrs. X.

ESTABLISHING CONTACT

The director of the community center called Mrs. X, identifying himself in Spanish as a social worker who knew that her son had been in some trouble, and explained that the center was a voluntary not a governmental agency. It was suggested that Mrs. X ask her husband if he could come with her to the center. She agreed to do so and to call back later in the evening when her husband came home from work, adding,

[6] Florence Hollis, *Casework: Psychosocial Therapy* (New York: Random House, 1964), p. 12.

"It is good to talk to someone who can speak Spanish." The fact that Mrs. X had been asked to consult her husband about a conference for the two of them put her in a situation in which she did not have to decide on her own. Her husband was now involved in the decision-making.

A few days later Mr. and Mrs. X came to the center for the interview. True to Latin custom, the first hour was leisurely, the talk mainly about familiar things that they could comfortably share with the worker. Conversation centered about Mexico, where they had lived until about two years before. They shared information about their respective families and mentioned how difficult it was for them to get used to the American way of life. Here they had no close relatives nearby to whom they could turn when problems arose. It was disconcerting for them to have to bother people outside the family.

ALIEN SURROUNDINGS

It was no wonder that Mr. and Mrs. X were having a hard time, not only with their son, but with the society surrounding them, which was completely alien to them and highly threatening to their way of life. In their own little house at the end of the big lot, hidden by the growing weeds, they had found an island isolated from the outside world—up to the time that their son had gotten into trouble. But then they had to face the world, and it was difficult to understand and more difficult to be understood.

They were not pressed to talk about their son's situation in detail. They decided to come back the following day to talk about this problem after the probation officer had come to see them.

The purposes in mind for this first interview were accomplished: to meet Mr. and Mrs. X personally and to establish a comfortable relationship that would lead to a partnership once they were able to share their problems with the social worker. The next step would be to share a common purpose, in this case, helping Freddy.

Mr. X was included in the helping process from the beginning. Had he been left out, it would have meant that Mrs. X was assuming an improper role, that Mr. X was being put down by her, and that his role as head of the household plus his *macho* role were being jeopardized.

The following day Mr. and Mrs. X came a little late to the meeting and were reluctant to talk about their conference with the probation officer. Mr. X just kept silent, looking down. Mrs. X, red-eyed, finally said, "I am very ashamed. You should have heard what the probation officer said about us. He blamed us for all the troubles with Freddy and said that if we were not able to speak English we should go back to Mexico. Perhaps worst of all, our daughter heard all of this because she had to translate for us."

It was suggested that they arrange to meet the probation officer the next time at the center; there the social worker could translate for them and make the necessary interpretations. Thus the harmful effect of the probation officer's prejudices against them would be minimized. Mr. and Mrs. X were assured that they had certain legal and moral rights that had to be respected—among them the right to be treated as human beings. Major differences between the systems of law in the United States and Mexico were explained, as were the functions of the probation department and the role of its officers.

Mr. and Mrs. X then seemed somewhat relieved and looked less tense and fearful. Mrs. X thanked the social worker and, looking at her husband, said: "We are not ignorant and dumb. We just did not understand anything about what was happening."

This family is not unusual. Nor are its problems. Many families in minority communities are facing problems like these every day. The situations can be far more critical when compounded by illness and poverty. Preparing the social worker in advance to serve such families effectively—rather than leaving it up to him to learn on the job from the community—offers a challenge to the schools of social work.

Cross-Cultural Rehabilitation

D. Corydon Hammond

The Vocational Rehabilitation Act of 1965 extended rehabilitation services to the socially and culturally handicapped. Up to the present time, however, little more than lip service has been given to providing rehabilitation and helping services to a forgotten population, the American Indian. With conditions of extreme poverty, unemployment rates often reaching forty percent on reservations, a frequent inadequacy of educational and employment skills, a considerable lack of awareness of employment opportunities, alcoholism, and cultural, language and experiential barriers, probably no other group in America could profit more from or has a more pressing need for the services provided by rehabilitation agencies. This article will examine problems which have contributed to this void in assistance to the native Americans and make some recommendations for the future of rehabilitation with this population.

Difficulties in Rehabilitation

The remoteness of many Indian reservations from urban areas and existing facilities and the low population density of rural reservations discourages rehabilitation efforts. The very magnitude of such problems as poverty, unemployment and educational deficiencies may also have been disheartening. These factors and the isolation of reservation living have contributed to a reluctance of professional workers to enter reservation rehabilitation.

Cultural difference is the label I would attach to the other broad problem area which has hindered rehabilitation efforts.

The modern Anglo-American, as Ruth Benedict has pointed out, knows little of ways of life except his own. He has been protected because of the wide diffusion of western civilization and has been led by this to accept a belief in the uniformity of human behavior. He has been culturally conditioned, and he often projects his own absolutes to all other men.[2]

Research reveals that the majority of psychotherapists in our society come from middle class backgrounds,[8,9,16] and I suspect most rehabilitation workers also come from these circumstances. Having developed in this environment, helping services have clustered in metropolitan areas, and both psychotherapeutic approaches and rehabilitation agencies have become oriented to the dominant culture and race. It is possible that some therapeutic principles we take for

JOURNAL OF REHABILITATION, Sept/Oct 1971, Vol. 37, No. 5, pp. 34-36 ff.

granted may even be culture specific and inappropriate for use with other populations.

Lending support to this possibility is evidence that the majority of the clients our middle class counselors see also come from the middle and upper classes [3,4,17] and that duration of stay in psychotherapy has likewise been found to favor clients from these socioeconomic strata.[1,6,10,12,19] It seems likely that these relationships also apply to rehabilitation counseling.

Culturally biased samples have typically made up treatment and research groups, and from these limited samples, unjustified overgeneralizations have been drawn about helping principles and services. Therapeutic formulations derived from such narrow samples are of dubious reliability in rehabilitation and therapy with divergent populations.

A statement by Devereux two decades ago about the cultural relativity of our helping professions seems relevant to rehabilitation services today:

> "Unfortunately, in the formulation of the techniques and goals of therapy, ethnocentrism still plays a preponderant role, and psychotherapy is still inspired by the motto, 'How to be more like *me*—or at least more like *us*.' " [5]

Value Differences

It should be remembered that the value system of Anglo-America is based on Judeo-Christian philosophy, whereas Indian traditional values generally contrast with such tenets as original sin, blind faith in a heaven after death and a reward for righteous living, proselyting, the death of a man atoning for sins and a Sunday religion.[14]

In the dominant culture, time is like a flowing river coming out of the past into the present and the future. We are tied to schedules, and indeed, often the present hardly exists. To the Indian, time tends to be a relative thing. In fact, among the Hopi Indians there is not a three tense language system; there is only the present tense.

Typically, tribal views of nature and concepts of life-space also differ from Anglo orientations. Instead of seeing nature as something to be mastered, most Indians believe man must live in harmony with nature. Where the white man views nature as something to be controlled and prevented from destroying, the Indian feels nature will take care of him if he lives as he should.

In the United States, "youth" is glamorized. Millions of dollars are spent annually for makeup and hair dyes. Indian cultures tend to have more respect for "the elders" and their wisdom, and to stress following the old ways and de-emphasize innovation and change. Attempts to hide white hair or conceal signs of age are not as often seen.

The middle class American believes in the prime importance of the biological family. However, in Indian cultures the extended family assumes more importance, and a large number of relatives may effect the socialization of the children, live together, and be referred to by biological family names, such as "father."

In our society, men should strive to be "the best," the "first" and climb toward success. Indian cultures, on the other hand, usually stress cooperation instead of competition, and anonymity rather than individuality.

"A penny saved is a penny earned," expresses a prominent value most counselors hold. Saving is not seen as a virtue in native American societies, however, and respected men are men who share their wealth and possessions.

Cross-Cultural Counseling

Perhaps these few generalizations have served to illustrate the problem: we see the world not as it is but as we are. In rehabilitation across cultures, where a client views the world from an unfamiliar and different frame of reference, the counselor will find communication and empathy difficult, and the interview may be frustrating and threatening for both participants.

From 1963 through 1966, a special Navajo Rehabilitation Project was funded at Flagstaff, Arizona. The technical reports indicate the magnitude of the problems of isolation, poverty and cultural-linguistic differences in rehabilitation counseling with members of the nations' largest Indian tribe. The project staff noted seven particular difficulties in the establishment of a counseling relationship.[7]

1. There was a high rate of unkept appointments, and when the client returned, it was often for assistance with something unrelated to the original contact problem.

2. Navajo clients perceived the counselor as a solver of immediate practical problems and not as an agent of psychological or interpersonal change.

3. Navajos viewed the counselor as an authority figure and seemed to expect him to be much like other Anglo authorities they had known.

4. Rehabilitation counselors found the language barrier insurmountable with most of the Navajo Indians. The staff did use interpreters, but they felt it made the establishment of rapport almost impossible.

5. More time was needed to acquire rapport, and they found that "Navajos generally withdraw psychologically when they are anxious rather than covering up the anxiety by talking."[7] The clients were more withdrawn than Euro-American clients in the early interviews.

6. The counselors seemed disturbed because their Indian clients did not disclose their inner thoughts or portray their behavior in psychologically meaningful terms. They did not perceive the counselor's role as that of an insight facilitator.

7. Navajo Rehabilitation Project counselors found educational, economic and social disadvantages frustrating for both them and their clients.

Osborn,[13] in evaluating his counseling experience with Paiute Indians, commented on the infrequency of self-analysis and self-inspection by his trade school clients. He found that they were present oriented, wanted help with immediate problems, did not anticipate the future or show concern with making long range plans, distrusted federal programs and were willing to try to manipulate authority figures. He interestingly observed that he saw the situation of some of the Indians as a problem, but because they did not recognize the circumstances as a problem it might be said that for them, no problem existed.

Despite the obstacles to Indian rehabilitation, the Navajo Rehabilitation Project staff at the conclusion of three years of reservation rehabilitation sounded an optimistic note:

> "If the cultural-personality differences are anticipated and accepted, and if stereotyping is avoided, constructive, warm and satisfying counseling relationships develop." [7]

Recommendations and Observations

My personal experiences on Indian reservations also indicate that very gratifying and productive relationships may be established with Indian clients. However, my own experience and that of others would prompt me to make the following recommendations which should assist in facilitating successful counseling among American Indians.

1. It is very difficult to talk about "the Indian." I believe one of the primary causes of failure among Anglo innovators on the reservation has been stereotyping. There are over two hundred and fifty Indian tribes in the

country, each with its own culture and background. Tribes, even when separated by only a few miles geographically, may have cultural differences as great as between Anglo and Indian. Therefore—and this should be taken as a qualification of this article also—anyone speaking about "the Indian," is speaking with questionable generality in many cases.

2. Become familiar with the local tribal culture and history. Understanding cultural values may often aid in understanding and communicating with the individual. But, again, beware of stereotyping the Indian or the culture concept will work against you and mask clients instead of promoting the understanding of unique individuals.[11]

Particularly recommended are home visits, attendance at local functions and knowledge of common phrases in the native language. This communicates respect and interest. If possible, the counselor should live on the reservation.

3. Analyze your own attitudes, values and background. What are your emotional reactions to their culture and traditional, native religion? What are your reactions to setting "dirty," perhaps ill clad, runny-nosed Indian children on your lap? How comfortable do you feel in an Indian home; eating Indian food? Do you feel superior to the Indian adults?

At the Pine Ridge Sioux reservation, Wax, in describing teachers, described (in my experience) most white men on the reservation when he noted that "very few of the Day School teachers actively dislike their pupils; quite a few seem fond of them; very few respect them. . . . The most common attitude is condescension, sometimes kindly, often well-meant, but always critical." [20]

I have seen many Indians who have grown tired of hearing sonorous rhetoric from white people about their "love" for the Indians as they condescendingly look down their noses at them. I'll pass on the advice an Indian friend once gave a missionary: "Don't love us, respect us!"

4. I believe informality and personal contact are required. The Flagstaff study has also recommended providing a sustained relationship, using the same counselor for intake interviewing and counseling. This seems essential if a longer time is needed to establish rapport.

5. In my experience, a lot of communication takes place nonverbally with some Indians. The reservation counselor will need to increase his sensitivity to these cues and learn to discriminate their nonverbal communications. If they do not develop ability in this, middle class counselors who are verbally oriented may miss a lot of what is going on, especially with clients who do not seem talkative.

The counselor will also need to take care that Indian clients are not telling him what they think he wants to hear. Also, superficially, some Indian clients may seem to share your values, but this may be illusory. The client may be trying to please you and to fulfill your expectations, or perhaps he is ashamed or reluctant to admit his true feelings.

Care should also be taken to differentiate between actual problems and what may appear to be difficulties because of cultural bias and comparisons to Anglo, middle class culture.

6. Become aware of opportunities and services available to Indians. For example, I understand that a university in Pennsylvania has had a nursing scholarship for Indian students for a couple hundred years which has seldom been used. Rehabilitation personnel will also need to become acquainted with Public Health Service facilities, the Bureau of Indian Affairs Branch of Welfare and their Branch

of Employment Assistance, tribal agencies, scholarships, money available for Indians through foundations, university Indian education programs and programs such as the Thiokol Chemical Roswell (New Mexico) Indian Employment Training Project.

7. A counselor working on the reservation will no doubt meet Indians who will stereotype him. Their reactions to you may have little to do with you as a real person. If you experience hostility, cool receptions or suspicions which seem unwarranted, try not to take it personally. Years of experience with "white men" and Anglo authorities are bound to have their carry-overs. It may take time to establish yourself as being different from those who have gone for decades before you.

8. Rehabilitation and counseling services may be entirely new to many reservation residents. The problem of role expectations has already been mentioned. There will probably be a need for community education about your program, precounseling orientations and structuring. Indian case aids may be almost essential, and certainly more Indians should be encouraged to enter rehabilitation counselor training programs.

Remember on the reservation that you are an alien. Just because you have a degree or title does not make you an "expert." Listen to and seek out local advice; they have learned something about their own people in a lifetime on the reservation.

9. My experience would recommend an active orientation toward casefinding. Do not expect clients to flock to you because you have established an office, or you may end up sitting in that office alone a mighty long time. You will probably need to "beat the bushes" and engage in an active outreach program. Hospitals may be an excellent place for establishing contact.

The responsibility for establishing contact and a relationship should be placed on the counselor rather than the client. The counselor should show an active caring by trying to meet the client's immediate needs (such as for transportation) and by activity on his behalf. Care should also be taken to set up short-range goals besides your long-range planning.

10. I view role-playing as a potentially very useful technique with Indians in developing assertive behaviors and building new behavioral repertoires, such as in social interactions and for job interviews.

11. Frank Riessman has made the following recommendations about counseling with the "culturally deprived":

> "Psychotherapeutic methods that stress authority, directiveness, the physical aspect, the group and the family, action rather than talk alone, are likely to be far more successful than introspective depth orientations. The educationally deprived person in therapy is more likely to see his problems as externally-caused, to want a doctor's prescription, to prefer action to words, and to want his "symptoms" cured rather than to submit to a complete overhauling of his personality." [15]

I partially agree and partially disagree with Riessman. A more active and behavioral approach seems to have merit to me. However, we must be careful to affirm the self-determination of Indian clients. This may be very difficult for the counselor when, from the frame of reference of his middle class values, the client seems to be making wrong choices.

I would warn the behaviorally oriented counselor not to manipulate clients into behaviors and goals in accordance with his frame of reference which may be unacceptable to the clients and their culture. It may be useful to present the client with alternatives from which to choose, but remember that different ways of life may lead to constructive goals and happiness. Don't be just another white man condemning the Indians' way and telling them yours is the only way.

In accordance with Riessman, however, I would caution the insight oriented rehabilitation worker that many Indians are not concerned with introspection and self-examination. They will probably want to concentrate on behavior and actual experiences rather than vicarious experiences.

But whether or not you use behavioral methods, I believe a relationship with the Indian client is very important. I believe skill in establishing a relationship with empathic understanding, acceptance of the client where he is and unconditional positive regard are almost essential to success with the Indian client. My experience also testifies to the importance of counselor genuiness. I have found that if you play a role and are not real, most Indians will see through it.

My recommendation would be to remain flexible in your therapeutic approaches and be willing to innovate. Consider the needs of the client first and not your own. If your therapeutic model is rigid, ask yourself if it is meeting your needs or those of your client.

Conclusion

Probably no other population in the United States has such a desperate need for rehabilitation services as the American Indian. The magnitude of the poverty-related problems which exist on the reservations, the isolation of reservation residents and cultural-linguistic differences may have accounted for the paucity of services. However, with the aid of staff recruitment incentives and the recommendations cited, it is the author's conviction that profitable and fulfilling cross-cultural rehabilitation can be carried out in the virtually untouched area of Indian reservations.

References

1. Bailey, M. A.; Warshaw, L.; and Eichler, R. M. "A Study of Factors Related to Length of Stay in Psychotherapy." *Archives of Neurology and Psychiatry* 15(1959): 442-444.
2. Benedict, Ruth. *Patterns of Culture.* Boston: Houghton Mifflin, 1934.
3. Brill, N., and Storrow, Hugh. "Social Class and Psychiatric Treatment." *Archives of General Psychiatry* 3(1960): 340-344.
4. Cole, N.; Branch, C. H. Hardin; and Allison R. "Some Relationships Between Social Class and the Practice of Dynamic Psychotherapy." *American Journal of Psychiatry* 118 (1962): 1004-1012.
5. Devereux, G. "Three Technical Problems in the Psychotherapy of Plains Indian Patients." *American Journal of Psychotherapy* 5(1951): 420.
6. Frank, J. D.; Gliedman, L. H.; Imber, S. D.; Nash, E. D.; and Stone, A. R. "Why Patients Leave Psychotherapy." *Archives of Neurology and Psychiatry* 77(1957): 283-299.
7. Henderson, N. B., and Avallone, V. L. "Problems in Counseling Navajo Rehabilitation Clients." *Navajo Rehabilitation Project Technical Report No. 4.* Flagstaff: Northern Arizona University, 1967.
8. Hollingshead, A. B., and Redlich, R. C. *Social Class and Mental Illness.* New York: John Wiley and Sons, 1958.
9. Holt, R. R. and Luborsky, L. *Personality Patterns of Psychiatrists,* Vol. 1, New York: Basic Books, 1958.
10. Imber, S. D.; Nash, E. H.; and Stone, A. R. "Social Class and Duration of Psychotherapy." *Journal of Clinical Psychology* 11 (1955): 281-284.
11. Leacock, E. "The Concept of Culture and Its Significance for School Counselors." *Personnel and Guidance Journal,* May, 1968, pp. 844-851.
12. Lorr, M.; Katz, M. M.; and Rubinstein, E. A. "The Prediction of Length of Stay in Psychotherapy." *Journal of Consulting Psychology* 22(1958): 321-327.
13. Osborn, Jr., H. B. "Evaluation of Counseling with a Group of Southern Paiute Indians." Unpublished doctoral dissertation, University of Utah, 1959.
14. Reichard, G. "The Navajo and Christianity."

American Anthropologist 51(1949): 66-71.
15. Riessman, Frank. *The Culturally Deprived Child.* New York: Harper and Row, 1962, p. 24.
16. Roe, Ann. *The Psychology of Occupations.* New York: John Wiley and Sons, 1956.
17. Schaffer, L., and Meyers, J. K. "Psychotherapy and Social Stratification." *Psychiatry* 17(1954): 277-292.
18. Wax, M., et al. *Formal Education in an American Indian Community.* Kalamazoo, Michigan: Society for the Study of Social Problems, 1964, p. 73.
19. Winder, A. E., and Hersko, M. "The Effect of Social Class on the Length and Type of Psychotherapy in a Veterans Administration Mental Hygiene Clinic." *Journal of Clinical Psychology* 11(1955): 77-79. ■

The Group: In Life and in Social Work

EMANUEL TROPP

THERE IS a gnawing dissatisfaction among young people today with the directions that modern life is taking, and this dissatisfaction has burst forth vividly in the phenomenon known as the happening. Originally taking the shape of bizarre occurrences among the most avant-garde segments of the up-coming generation, the happening has been settling more widely into a pattern that has more far-flung significance, becoming a direct form of free human communication in a group. Young people have been saying that all the natural juices have been drained out of living —which has become packaged, planned, synthesized, controlled, and just plain dull. In their desire to be truly alive, our successors in the human enterprise are informing us that we have been guilty of, or accomplices to, the act of removing those precious ingredients in human relationships that make them spontaneous, natural, relaxed, unpredictable, and, therefore, exciting. The generation now in the saddle, which has prided itself on doing so much for mental health, has been accused of turning health into sheer, unrelieved boredom.

It is not surprising, then, that we find young people desperately seeking to find intimate groups in which they can share spontaneity, intimacy, dialogue, existential encounter—in other words, something that is really and truly happening, not the counterfeit they see all around them. They see their elders acting out community patterns with less and less conviction, in organizational forms that are shallow and futile and in a manner increasingly resigned and cynical. They sense a kind of giving-up by the older generation of any hope for satisfying and productive human relations. For themselves, however, they refuse to give up. They insist on the search for interpersonal and group relations that will combine meaning, vitality, and effectiveness.

The relevance of the seemingly far-out concept of the happening to the values and purposes of social work can be quickly seen. For the social work profession is committed to a central role of helping people cope more effectively with their interpersonal relations. And effective coping today emerges as a problem not only for sick or maladjusted or deviant people, but for just about everyone. Now, to help people cope, those close on our heels in the rush of time are saying: "Let us stop talking about it. Let us do it. Let us make it happen."

The Meaning of the Happening for Social Work

There is something special about a happening that has a most important message, if one will only listen and hear. It is not a party, with scheduled games, prizes, and all the predictable niceties. It is a spontaneous set-to that gives people the chance to be authentically themselves, with all their strengths and their weaknesses, all their groping and their idiosyncracies, all their sense of wonder, and all their remarkable capacity to change and to grow and to contribute to one another—without Big Brother's having mapped it out fully in a master plan, in advance. To translate the message into social work terms: If one would help people in their social functioning, what better way to do it than to give them the opportunity to *make it happen,* not after they leave the agency, but while they

SOCIAL CASEWORK, May 1968, Vol. 49, No. 5, pp. 267-274.

are enjoying its hospitality, with the worker as part of the common enterprise, in groups in which they share with others some common concern.

Now what does this mean for the social worker's professional role? Does he take on the title of group therapist, with all the legerdemain, the mystique, and the glamour that supposedly accrue to this high position—a rôle that strikes fear into the hearts of many who contemplate it and yet has great appeal to others who see assuming it as an entry to a new secret order? What is the mysterious phrase *group therapy* all about after all? As we examine the current use of the term, it turns out to mean just about everything—and therefore nothing. To many, unfortunately, this thing called group therapy constitutes a strange process whereby a group leader arranges people in some complex preplanned pattern, puts them through their paces, and then proceeds to make the most miraculous things happen. Since everyone would like to be thought to have such magical powers, it has come to pass that all the uses of groups in social work today are being stirred and blended into some sort of representation of this one giddy alchemy, euphemistically called group therapy.

In the very act of looking at this "group therapy," one senses a sudden switch from the atmosphere of the happening—the freshness, the excitement, the drama of real life—to the atmosphere of the laboratory and the clinic. And though it may be valid to hold on to a somewhat clinical stance in a one-to-one relationship (though some are beginning to question this too), it should be clear now that to maintain this stance in the setting of the group is to destroy the essential value of the real-life event.

Carol Meyer recently asked why it was that audiences laughed at the social worker in the film "A Thousand Clowns." [1] At the risk of answering the obvious, it could be said today that the leading character in the film, in his off-beat way, represents the vibrant, alive qualities of the young generation and that any attempts by the social worker to deal with this lifelike quality by "interpreting" it as projection, displacement, and all the rest appear absurd. And such attempts will no doubt eventually be laughed into oblivion. An individual person facing a social worker's awesome arsenal of interpretations may be at a loss to cope with it or may learn, as Thomas Szasz says, to play the worker's peculiar game; but, in a group, real life had better be turned on if the *worker* wants to retain his mental balance.

The analyst Hyman Spotnitz describes his sense of wonder at the change that took place in him as he began to conduct group sessions. He says: ". . . the brighter atmosphere and more spontaneous emotional processes were at one and the same time more relaxing and more invigorating. The dramatic spirit of the interaction, the repartee and the intensity of the feelings coming to the fore made more of me come alive. . . ." [2] Marjorie Montelius also discusses how the group experience is a humanizing one for both the client *and* the worker.[3] Ludwig Binswanger refers to the same sort of experience when he speaks of the need of the analyst to become an "existential partner" of the patient, on a common plane of human existence—two human beings trying to accomplish something together.[4]

Styles and Values in Social Group Work

Today, in the arena of social group work theory, there are two polar views, and various people take stands at stages in between. There is Robert Vinter, at one end, who sees the group as the means by which the worker can meet individual treatment goals—carefully studied, diagnosed, and prescribed for each individual in the group—by unashamedly manipulating the group and its members to achieve these highly particularistic and differentiated goals. In 1959 Vinter honestly faced a dilemma that he was unable to re-

[1] Carol H. Meyer, "Casework in a Changing Society," *Social Work Practice, 1966,* Columbia University Press, New York, 1966, p. 11.

[2] Hyman Spotnitz, *The Couch and the Circle,* Alfred A. Knopf, New York, 1961, p. 19.

[3] Marjorie Montelius, *Working with Groups: A Guide for Administration of Group Services in Public Welfare,* U.S. Department of Health, Education and Welfare, Washington, D.C., 1966, pp. 9–10.

[4] See Floyd W. Matson, *The Broken Image,* George Braziller, New York, 1964, p. 238.

solve: If the natural forces of group life are the most potent means for effecting individual change in the group, how can the worker justify becoming deeply involved in controlling and fragmenting the group process?[5] The truth is that this dilemma is probably unresolvable. The manipulative clinical stance seriously weakens or destroys the very group forces that are so potent. Such practice is not only self-defeating, because it violates the nature of the medium, but also, understandably, productive of undue anxieties among social workers who contemplate the possibility of leading a group. To be able to juggle the complexities of many individual variables simultaneously with the complexities of group relationships is indeed a superhuman undertaking—and it is really not even a desirable one.

At the other pole is William Schwartz, who has developed the concept of the group as a system of mutual aid and who sees the group and its living experiences as the crucial focus for the worker.[6] He sees the worker and the members as engaged in a common enterprise, that of carrying out the group's purpose. He sees the individual members as growing essentially through their group-oriented efforts. Now, Schwartz's position, vis-à-vis Vinter's, holds within it something far more important than a technical difference. It is a philosophical difference—the value orientation—that is strikingly at issue. To Schwartz, the group is not a mélange of wholes and parts to be arranged, taken apart, put back together, and generally manipulated by a social worker in accordance with his own goals for different individuals; to him, the group is an organic whole that develops a life of its own and an integrity of its own, which the worker had better respect if he is to be useful.

[5] Robert D. Vinter, "Small-Group Theory and Research: Implications for Group Work Practice Theory and Research," in *Social Science Theory and Social Work Research*, Leonard S. Kogan (ed.), National Association of Social Workers, New York, 1960, pp. 123–34.

[6] William Schwartz, "The Social Worker in the Group," in *New Perspectives on Services to Groups: Theory, Organization, Practice*, National Association of Social Workers (for National Conference on Social Welfare), New York, 1961, pp. 7–17.

Have social workers not always said that their fundamental tenet was respect for the dignity and integrity of the individual? When dealing with a group, should they not embrace an analogous tenet, respect for the integrity of the group? The group is not an inanimate collection of nuts and bolts to be treated like a tinkertoy. There are very real group feelings, group attitudes, and group beliefs to which members develop deep ties, and, in fact, it is these very ties that make the group such a strong helping agent. Thus, respect for the integrity of the group is a *sine qua non* in social group work, and we must keep this kind of respect alive if we are to keep in mind what social work is all about. Is such respect not very much in keeping with the renewed respect for the balance of nature and the "wisdom of the body," for which we owe so much to Rachel Carson and Walter Cannon. Just as modern science is learning once again to help the body to mobilize its natural forces to heal itself, so we are again learning that the natural forces of the group hold the key to individual growth and that the worker's main role is to help the group use these natural forces.

Given these perspectives, can social workers still view a group approach mainly as a means of reaching more people at one time? If this were so, a group would be merely a kind of multiplication table. The real point is not that a group approach serves more people, but that it serves them in a very different way from an individual approach—and that is the root of what it is all about. Only in an orientation or information group meeting, where the same facts can be given at the same time to more than one person, can a group approach be seen as an economy measure. In most other groups, economy is an illusion, because group service is not of the same genre as individual service—and it is most often provided in addition to individual service, not in place of it.

Another view of groups is that they offer convenient stage settings in which one can watch the actors move around and thus learn more about them. While this may be so, it is hardly a valid reason for the use of the group method; it is an auxiliary gain, a lever to help, not the help itself.

When one gets down to the central core of what really happens that makes the group experience so meaningful and so useful, one discovers the simple truth that people with similar interests, similar concerns, or similar problems can help each other in ways that are significantly different from the ways in which a worker can help them in a one-to-one relationship. This is not to say that the group method is better—simply that it is different; and because it is different, it may be more effective for certain purposes. The key difference is that the members of the group take help from one another. And this is the way it has always happened in life: people have, from time immemorial, helped each other, sans benefit of therapy. Just as people do not have to be taught to breathe, so they move to help each other.

The Gifts of the Group and Their Meaning for the Worker

To be in a group means to have the resources available to satisfy some of the most fundamental human needs. It means, first of all, belonging, which itself says a great deal, because all human beings have a deep need to belong, to others and with others. Belonging implies acceptance by others, and that acceptance is a basic kind of affection from one's fellow human beings. To be in a group also means having opportunities for self-expression under circumstances in which others can appreciate it, so that it becomes achievement and brings recognition—and these are great supporters and strengtheners of that precious feeling of self-worth so necessary for mental health. Finally, to be in a group means having the opportunity to experience that important communal balance of freedom and limitation, which is at the root of social responsibility, one of the hallmarks of social maturity.

The group is not only an alliance through which normal needs can be met; it can also be a natural healer of hurts, a supporter of strengths, and a clarifier of problems. A group may serve as a source of strength and support for those whose inner strengths have been weakened. It may serve as a sounding board for expressions of anxiety, hostility, or guilt. It often turns out that group members learn that others in the group have similar feelings weighing them down in their aloneness, that they are not so different or so alone—and learning this in live confrontation with one's peers is a most powerful change-inducing experience. In fact, one of the key virtues of the group method is that people are indeed readier to take help from one another than from a worker.

Further, in a group, one may discover that one does have differences from others and that one must contend with these differences in the process of group conflict and group criticism. As this is discovered, one may either affirm one's differences or see a necessity for changing. Thus, the give-and-take of group life can deeply affect one's attitude toward oneself and toward others. It leads to an increased capacity for objective judgment, increased self-control, clearer perspectives on one's own needs, greater acceptance and understanding of the situation in which one finds oneself, more effective use of the services being offered, and, finally, increased social responsibility and preparation for more effective living in the larger society.

Thus, if groups have the capacity, as systems of mutual aid, to help people in such fundamental and powerful ways, it behooves a social worker who wants to lead a group to view this phenomenon with the respect it deserves—not with fear or trembling as if faced with some mystique, but with a healthy appreciation of the central fact that people can and do help each other in vital ways through group experience, and that, if he wants to help people through the group method, he must learn how to help *groups* to be effective.

As the potential leader begins to see the real meaning of group life, it comes to him that his place in it is quite different from what he had imagined. He is not an observer, watching guinea pigs in an experimental cubicle. He is not a puppeteer pulling the strings of responsive but lifeless dolls to produce whatever motions he has deemed best for them. He is not a master planner feeding large masses of complex data about the group members into a computer that will inform him just what each member should do to solve his problem.

If he really knows and respects what a group is all about, he will see that *real* life is *really* happening and that he is *really* a part of it and that it is exciting and dramatic and unpredictable and wonderfully human in the ways in which spontaneous human beings can be when they are sparked by some common concern. Most stimulating of all, he will discover that he is, willy-nilly, a part of this real human drama and that he is not separated as a worker, but suddenly quite humanly alive in the group, in the spirit of the common undertaking. And then his role in this vital atmosphere becomes clearly that of helping the group as best he can to use its natural qualities of mutual aid to help its members.

In this very natural, very alive context of a genuine happening, the worker further discovers, much to his relief, that he need not quake in awe of his own amazing powers, that the group finds its own ways to make its life proceed, sometimes with him, sometimes against him, often despite him, and sometimes even to help *him* do his job. The group does not wait breathlessly for his every move. This does not mean that he is expendable, or unimportant: it simply means he is not a god. His skill will be most effectively used in helping the group to be strong and to achieve its purpose and in helping individuals to play significant and satisfying roles in the process.

The Keys to Clarity: Purpose, Function, and Structure

All that has been said thus far may hold true generically with regard to most group approaches, but there are distinct and crucially important differences in basic group approaches that must be understood in order to know when to use which approach and when not to, and when one may blend approaches and when this is not feasible. To achieve such an understanding, one must look at the group's purpose, function, and structure.

The *purpose* of a group—why it is formed—is the principal element to be defined. It may be that the agency's idea of the group's purpose and the group's idea are not identical; but at the point at which they meet, an effective definition of the group's operational purpose can be found. If a group leader has not thought clearly about purpose, he will find himself drifting with the group into irrelevant, unproductive, and meaningless areas, into confusing situations and shaky operational patterns. Everything must start from the question that Schwartz keeps asking: "Why are we here?" And it is sound practice for the worker to keep checking himself against that question and to confront the group with it from time to time.

Having determined the purpose for which the group has been organized, the worker can clarify its *function*—what the group members are supposed to do to carry out that purpose. Are they gathered to discuss personal problems, or is it permissible for them to spend the sessions playing poker? Are they to be trained as homemakers, or can they change themselves into a wine-tasting club? Does anything go, or is there flexibility only within the bounds of purpose and function? If the worker is not clear about function, he will not be able to help the group conduct meaningful activities; for there is a world of possible group activities, but only some are relevant to any given group function.

Once the worker knows what a group is supposed to be doing, he can think clearly about *structure*—how the group will do it. If it is to be a training group, then someone has to be a teacher. If it is to be a social action group, then some form of self-government should be planned. If it is to be a counseling group, then a skilled professional discussion leader (of a special type) must be in charge. In each instance, the worker's role is different. A group can be effectively related to the realities of its existence only when it knows what its powers are and to what extent and in what ways they are limited by the leader. The group may be virtually self-directing, or the leader may exercise almost total control of its activities, or the group may operate in a realm between the two extremes. Too often group members are allowed to float in a sort of limbo, never certain whether the leader's assurances that it is really *their* group are true—and the leader, in fact, becomes uncertain after a while whether he really means what he says or not. The suppressed resentment of such a group at being either misled or confused or toyed with then becomes a new problem that the group *and* the leader could very well have done without. The worker may eventually have to spend several sessions clarifying the issue for the group, and thus the group and leader are both kept busy with an issue that is really not getting them anywhere except back to a better start.

Five Group Approaches

The *why* and the *what* and the *how* can be used for screening the five group approaches in common practice today. First, and perhaps simplest, is the *group education* approach. In its most rudimentary form, it may be a one-time assemblage of a group of people who all need the same information about an agency or institution, for example, at the beginning of their contact with it. We need not look condescendingly at work with such a group. A group of patients entering a hospital can gain much more than information from such a meeting. They learn that they are not alone. They see others like themselves. They experience the bond of physical closeness, of eye-to-eye contact, of sharing an experience. They gain some sense of security and identification and belonging and a sense of completion in that they have been told the terms of their contract. Even with an insensitive leader, there is something of value to be gained. But a sensitive leader who knows both the potential and the limits of such a group meeting can make the experience a truly helpful one to the patients by his way of handling the subject matter and by his expressions of empathy.

Such a one-time orientation program is not, of course, the only kind of group education. One of the most common forms, and distinctly more complex in regard to technique, is what has come to be known in family service agencies as family life education, which should not be confused with group counseling. A typical family life education program is made up of a relatively short series of lecture-discussions for a limited number of parents on a relatively specific subject, such as "How To Handle Your Adolescent Child." In such a program each session is usually started by a speech, a film, a playlet, a panel discussion, or some other device, after which there is discussion, conducted by the worker as group leader. The focus of the discussion is usually limited by the worker to a particular topic or closely related matters—"Should teen-agers be required to help with work around the house?" for example. Thus, the discussion is subject-oriented, not person-oriented. Group members who seek answers to private problems are appropriately directed to other resources, for it is not the function of the group to discuss intimate problems; the participants did not assemble for that purpose, and the leader is not prepared to work at that level. Still, in a family life education group there is considerably more interaction and involvement than in a group gathered for purely informational purposes, and so greater scope and depth.

The second group approach is known as *group counseling*. Firmly established today in family service agencies, child guidance clinics, residential treatment centers, public welfare agencies, and elsewhere, this approach is more individualized than group education. In the family agency, for example —by way of interesting comparison with the family life education model described earlier—a group of parents may be assembled to discuss the particular problems they are having as parents of adolescents. Usually these parents are selected for such a group from the caseload, whereas no problems are required as the ticket of admission to the education group and the members may not have had any connection with the caseload. And it is in this connection that the elusive distinction between purpose and function stands out most clearly. Whereas the parents in both groups would have the same general purpose (to discuss relationships between parents and adolescents), it would be the function of the educational group to discuss broad issues and the function of the counseling group to discuss the members' own very individual problems. In group counseling, a meeting does not start with a lecture, like an entertaining cultural night out; the point is to get right down to the specifics of the personal problems that brought the participants together. Discussion of broad issues may possibly become an evasion of the group's true function, whereas raising questions about one's own child is exactly in keeping with it—the reverse of the situation in the family life education meeting. In this context, it can be easily seen how the function of the group determines the role of the leader and the nature of the skills he needs. In the education group, he is conducting a general mental-health-oriented discussion, whereas in the counseling group he must be alert to the needs of the individual members and to the possibilities at hand for using their interaction helpfully.

The third approach, called *group psychotherapy,* is attended by the most confusion of all. In its essential form, as stated by its main proponents, it is a group method for the treatment of individuals with psychiatric disorders, and it aims at achieving basic personality change, which none of the other group approaches attempts. Whereas other group methods may seek to change behavior patterns, they make no claims to changing the basic personality structure. In group psychotherapy such change is accomplished through group discussion geared to the development of insight into the unconscious causes of behavior, the resolution of internal conflicts, and the modification of defense patterns. It is based on skilled handling of transference in depth, involving the use of fantasy, free association, and dreams and other unconscious material. It is a method that is generally used by professional people who are qualified, to begin with, to undertake individual psychotherapy—usually psychiatrists, sometimes clinical psychologists, and sometimes specially qualified social workers. What has created so much confusion is that some psychotherapists have conducted group sessions that have been no more than group education or group counseling and have labeled them group psychotherapy. To avoid such misconceptions, one must look at what is actually taking place—and use the phrase *group psychotherapy* most cautiously. Moreover, it should be remembered that group psychotherapy, whatever its advantages, also has its limitations; it is not appropriate for all occasions. And it should not be automatically considered the most advanced group method simply because it digs deeper into the psyche (or claims to do so).

Group recreation is the fourth approach. To many people, this seems to be the same as group work, simply because group work has unfortunately been associated by the public in the past with just playing games. However, the resemblance is really quite vague. In group recreation, participants engage in various play activities, under the direction of a leader. Group recreation tends to produce a relaxed kind of informal interaction; it stimulates interests; and it provides outlets for nonverbal expression and for the channeling of feelings. In some agencies a recreation approach is used with latency-age boys and called activity group therapy (although that may be conducted in the style of social group work).

Finally, there is *social group work,* one of the three basic methods of social work. In the course of applying this method, all the other approaches (except group psychotherapy) come into play as part of the total process. The social group work method aims at the full utilization of forces in group life to bring about social growth in the individual members. It is in the process known as group-goal-achieving that these forces are at their maximum, the members being most fully engaged with each other and with the group as a whole.[7] This process involves common decision and common action toward the accomplishment of common goals, shared by the members for the group as a whole. In the course of guiding this process, the group worker uses a variety of group experiences and program media, including social action, community service, and cultural, educational, social, and athletic activities. The group is involved in discussion and decision-making about the specific goals it wishes to achieve. It may also find itself, in the course of its life, discussing general matters of concern to its members or specific

[7] For a more detailed treatment of this position, see Emanuel Tropp, "The Further Development of Group Work as a Separate Method," *Social Work Practice, 1966,* Columbia University Press, New York, 1966, pp. 44–53.

matters dealing with the problems of individuals, but these discussions will have arisen naturally out of the work the group has cut out for itself and the relationships that ensue. An example of the group work process in action is a ward council of patients in a hospital who meet to discuss the conditions in which they are living and to make recommendations to the hospital for specific improvements in policies and programs. The group work method thus includes, in addition to goal-achieving by the group, the dimensions of group recreation, group education, and group counseling, but any of these methods can be used separately.

Summary

This survey of the group, in life and in social work, has viewed it in a variety of contexts —the contemporary world of the happening; the innermost meaning of the group experience; the reasons for using groups in social work; the common human needs that are met in groups; the place of the leader in the group; the importance of purpose, function, and structure; and finally the diversity of group approaches. It started with a statement of basic conviction that *people can be helped to help each other*: this is the heart of the matter, and all else is commentary.

ASSESSING THEORETICAL MODELS OF COMMUNITY ORGANIZATION PRACTICE: ALINSKY AS A CASE IN POINT

ROBERT PRUGER AND HARRY SPECHT

The uneven growth of community organization theory is attributed to the absence of an analytic framework for comparing and evaluating existing practice models. A paradigm potentially useful to this end is offered. The practice variations and rationales associated with Saul Alinsky are used to illustrate the organized statements made possible by the paradigm.

Any method of community organization is based on some type of theory about planned change. Frequently the theory which the practitioner uses is implicit and unstated. Regardless of the extent to which their theories are articulated, all practitioners formulate hypotheses about the nature and origin of problems and the institutionalized procedures for bringing about change.[1] They all choose, consciously or not, to take account of certain variables and not others, to consider certain behavior significant and to ignore other behavior.

The elucidation of theory has great value to the practitioner who wants to improve his practice, because it provides a coherent way to organize the factors that have a bearing on his work. To develop sounder systems of practice requires study of the specific conditions under which specific behaviors will change in specific directions. Without such a systematic approach, the practitioner's methods are likely to be inefficient, even haphazard or destructive.

The intention in this paper is to present one means of analyzing theories of community organization in a systematic way. Such an analysis[2] allows for a practical way of inspecting a number of theoretical approaches simultaneously, but does not attempt to defend any

[1] The general approach used in this paper is based on the framework described by Ford and Urban (6:3–106).

[2] The approach used here is frequently referred to as an "analytic paradigm"; the varied uses and values of formal paradigms are discussed in detail by Merton (11:13–16).

SOCIAL SERVICE REVIEW, June 1969, Vol. 43, No. 2, pp. 123-135.

particular theory as more effective than another. Rather, its purpose is to spell out the assumptions and hypotheses underlying methods of practice in order to answer the essential question: What methods produce what changes in what situations?

A brief comment on the present state of theory for community organization practice is necessary lest our title and introductory comments suggest that we believe a genuine theory for community organization practice is imminent. Ideally, a theory of community organization practice would be capable of ordering the vast array of discrete data available about communities, community problems, and methods of intervention. At present, however, there are available only orientations or frameworks which suggest the critical nature of certain variables affecting the behavior of various community systems. In a recent assessment of community organization theory, Kramer and Specht (10) have stated:

> There is no community organization theory in the sense of a series of interrelated propositions that explains and predicts community behavior. Indeed, as Warner Bloomberg, Jr., has declared, "there can no more be a 'theory of communities' any more than there can be a 'theory of rocks and stones.' " What are found in innumerable community case studies and surveys are various substitutes or facsimilies for a theory such as typologies, ideologies, metaphors, and hypotheses. Most of the descriptive studies have focused on the ecological or demographic character of a community, its institutions and values or its power structure. If the findings do not yield a coherent picture of community life, they at least suggest "sensitizing" concepts or analytic categories that direct attention to the horizontal (local) and vertical (extracommunity) axes of a community, reference groups, monolithic or pluralistic decision-making structures, community influentials, social stratification, status, norms, values, and so forth.

The purpose of this paper is to present an analytic scheme designed to make some order out of the rather fragmented and disparate knowledge used in community organization practice. Four major categories of questions should be included in such an analysis. The first three categories include hypotheses about the causes of the problem, the methods of action planned, and the probable outcomes. The fourth category is an examination of the empirical evidence relating to the first three sections. The remainder of this paper will be a discussion of these categories and their application in an examination of Saul Alinsky's organizing methods.[3]

PROPOSITIONS ABOUT PROBLEMS

The first category of questions deals with how the particular community organization method defines the problems to be dealt with. These definitions are based on assumptions about the structure and function of the social system. We will examine Alinsky's propositions[4] to see how he deals with the following questions: (*a*) What are the problems

[3] This is, of course, only one of several systems by which to assess theory. Here we are using a common set of issues and questions which would be applied to any theory. One alternative approach would be to take a single theory (such as that suggested by Ross [18]) and compare others to it. In all cases, the system must provide some stable reference point for the analysis.

Readers unfamiliar with the work of Saul Alinsky may wish to refer to his major work (1).

[4] The term "proposition" includes both assumptions and hypotheses. While the distinction between the two is not of great importance in this paper, it becomes important as this kind of analysis becomes more refined. Essentially, propositions relate variables to one another (26:12). Generally speaking, an assumption is a statement that one accepts as true, while a hypothesis is a conjecture regarding the relationship between variables of a phenomenon which is not asserted to be true. The purpose of scientific research is to determine the credibility of a hypothesis (17:37).

to be dealt with? How are they identified and selected? What problems are excluded or treated as marginal? (*b*) Who is the client, and how is this unit of attention selected?

What problems are selected? Alinsky is concerned about changing those conditions of modern life which alienate men from society, making them—particularly the poor—nonparticipants in the social order. His view is that our societal arrangements not only determine the differential distribution of socially esteemed rewards but also encourage the poor to social adaptations whereby they come to act as if those rewards were not esteemed enough to pursue, and to behave in ways (e.g., with apathy and intraclass hostility) that contribute to the stability of the very social arrangements that victimize them. In their numbers the poor have an option on power, but to become powerful they must organize. Thus Alinsky puts his major focus on the tactics and strategies relevant to the acquisition, elaboration, and use of power. Furthermore, as the poor become oriented to the uses of their own power it is expected that they will effect the structural reform they seek and develop the sense of self-worth that goes with full participation in society.

Alinsky does not often specify his meanings, and the concept of "alienation" as a condition of life among the poor has achieved a central place in his work more by virtue of its frequent repetition than by its controlled usage (21). Most frequently, his uses of the concept seem to be to connote (*a*) powerlessness (i.e., both the belief among the poor that they cannot influence the outcomes of their lives, and the objective fact of their powerlessness) and (*b*) the lack of understanding the poor have of the events in which they are caught up.[5] The first definition clearly commits him to the problems of creating and wielding political power; the second probably underlies his concern for popular education.[6]

He does not, however, consider a third possible meaning of alienation, namely, the alienation of the self or the "inability of the individual to find self-rewarding activities that engage him" (21:790). This condition probably has a more even distribution in modern technological society than that suggested by the other two definitions; and a program to attack it would have to go well beyond the mere redistribution of power in society. Alinsky is in the noble tradition of those who have sought a more humane, less brutal materialism; those seeking a more fundamental social reconstruction, however, would have to go well beyond his prescriptions and perspectives (e.g., 14).

Probably the major contribution Alinsky and his associates have made here is in the detailed descriptions of the sequential, strategic phases of organizing instrumental groups in the low-income community—i.e., they have clearly identified the problems to be solved to be the problems of political, rather than social, organization. It is from this insight that the single most important programmatic feature, the management of conflict, derives.

[5] "Social objectives, social welfare, the good of the nation, the democratic way of life—all these have become nebulous, meaningless, sterile phrases" (1:67).

[6] "In the last analysis the objective for which any democratic movement must strive is the ultimate objective within democracy—popular education. . . . The very purpose and character of a People's Organization is educational" (1:174).

A variety of other problems are given a more peripheral place. While popular education is identified as the ultimate objective of what Alinsky calls "People's Organizations," it seems to have a lower claim on organizational resources than does conflict management. Education seems to serve the organizational need to follow conflict strategies rather than the need to develop personal skills which, if possessed, might reduce the readiness to support conflict action. Thus, though the poor are pictured as being oppressed and intimidated by the urban environment, personal skills to manage that environment (from ability to negotiate the subway to making full use of the established social services) are hardly considered. Whatever the defects of the poor (and qualities such as avarice, brutality, malice, and selfishness are mentioned) and whatever the defects of the system, all will be made right by the successful exercise of power.

There is one class of problem Alinsky more than overlooks; he simply denies its existence. This is the problem of the degree and direction of influence exerted on the People's Organization by its own process over time. The following passage provides one entry into the problem:

> The substance of a democracy is its people, and if that substance is good—if the people are healthy, interested, informed, participating, filled with a faith in themselves and others—then the structure will inevitably reflect its substance. The very organization of a people so that they become active and aware of their potentialities is a tremendous program in itself. It is the ultimate people's program [1:20].

The minor flaw here is its circuitous reasoning, i.e., if the participants have certain qualities, the organization can only be democratic. However, they must first acquire these qualities from the organization. Far more serious is the fact that it dismisses a subtle, inconvenient reality that all organizations struggle with, but never overcome, and even less resolve as a matter of "inevitable" process—the tendency of structure to powerfully shape substance. Stated in its more familiar form, the larger an institution becomes and the longer it exists, the greater will be the tendency for the program or service of the organization to serve its own needs rather than those of its constituents.

It is not Alinsky's confidence in democracy that is questioned here; as an item of personal faith it is easy to commend it. But to posit the moral justification for waging war, pursuing power, manipulating friend and foe, and doing whatever else is necessary within the law to build a People's Organization, on the belief that the democratic ethic is the inevitable property of People's Organizations is another matter. Michels, in a classic of political sociology, has offered a powerful argument to demonstrate the inevitably undemocratic or oligarchic nature of such organizations (12). Many more recent writers have explicated the role of structural forces in effecting a transfer of sentiment from organizational ends to organizational means.

Alinsky assumes that the People's Organization must, with computerlike precision, make consistently correct moves (at least insofar as the elaboration of its democratic substance is concerned) at each of the many crossroads it comes to. While this is a remarkable faith for someone so critical of ivory towers, it is not sufficient to guarantee the democratic character of People's Organizations. His proud claim, for example, that the "expansion of [native] leadership from a partial role to a more complete one is a natural development that goes hand in hand with the growth of the People's Organization" (1:96), is embarrassed by the finding of political science that identifies specialization of leadership (i.e., leadership limited to one sphere of activity) as a circumstance under which individuals who have the greatest power in a political system do not become a ruling elite.

Who is the client? Organizations of the poor are to have the dual role of rehabilitating society as well as the poor themselves. The commitment to conflict as a means of solving problems is implemented by a People's Organization. Alinsky works with a neighborhood or community group, almost exclusively of an urban character. A model statement of bylaws for a People's Organization asserts that the client on whose behalf work is to be done is any organization representative of the people or any portion thereof in that area which participates in the life of the community. An "organization" refers to an officially organized group which has a minimum of ten members (1:222). Writing almost twenty years after Alinsky, Haggstrom says the organization "may be a direct membership neighborhood council or an organization of previously existing organizations" (8:6–7).

Almost all of the material available describes organizational efforts to activate and insure the continuing participation of the poor. While there is little empirical evidence that the organizations include a wide range of religious and class differences, there is, in theory, a vision of all elements of the community united in some shared concern for community improvement. In addition, whereas other theoretical frameworks view social and governmental agencies as potential allies, in Alinsky's scheme they are considered untrustworthy because they cannot be counted on to keep the people's interests paramount. Unaffiliated individuals in poverty neighborhoods and expressive organizations of low-income persons are treated as either nonexistent or irrelevant.

PROPOSITIONS ABOUT METHODS OF ACTION

The second major category of questions is directed at an analysis of the specific ways in which systems are to be changed. These propositions aim at answering questions about how the overall goals are interpreted by the agent of intervention, how the change is to be effected, what is expected of the community for change to occur, and what is expected of the change agent.

What are the goals of intervention and who determines them? A distinction must immediately be made between the general organizational ends identified as appropriate by Alinsky and the ends actually pursued by the specific organizations. Only the former can be stated without regard for the resources and strategies available; the latter are inevitably shaped by considerations of strategy and resources, even if they do not always come as a result of deliberate planning.

The three major goals of People's Organizations seem to be:

1. to alter environmental conditions, identified at various places as economic injustice, unequal opportunities, prejudice, unemployment, disease, etc.
2. to alter men's beliefs about them-

selves, variously identified as feelings of hopelessness, apathy, anonymity, etc.

3. to educate the people, primarily so that they learn more about one another as a basis for greater cooperation and, secondarily, so that they can manage their affairs better.

The hierarchy of these goals is very unclear, especially in regard to the role of education. Within the framework of Alinsky's view of society's shortcomings and his firm moral commitment to brotherhood and equality, he seems to believe that everything is subject to change, and, presumably, that whatever can be changed should be changed. He writes: "A people's program is limited only by the horizon of humanity itself" (1:80). Given the well-known fact that horizons (especially the "horizon of humanity itself") are ever receding before us, it should not be surprising that Alinsky forgives himself the task of ordering its elements.

However, if nowhere else, Alinsky is unmistakably clear about who should be the authors of organizational goals:

> In the last analysis of our democratic faith, the answer to all of the issues facing us will be found in the masses of the people themselves, and *nowhere else.*
>
> The substance of a democracy is its people and if that substance is good—if the people are healthy, interested, participating, filled with a faith in themselves and others—then the structure will inevitably reflect its substance. The very organization of a people so that they become active and aware of their potentialities is a tremendous program in itself. It is the ultimate people's program [1:20, 64].

It is, then, the "people" who should define the goals of the People's Organization. Taken as an article of faith or as an alarm to warn against those who would intentionally and with malice aforethought have it otherwise, Alinsky's statements give little reason to doubt his fervid sincerity or praiseworthy values. Fault with his discussion of goals, however, can be found in at least three ways.

First, there is a substantial literature to suggest the complex array of forces that come into play as organizations go about settling on their goals. Wishing, even fervid wishing with all fingers crossed, cannot reduce that complexity; the belief that the people should set the goals, even if poetically expressed, has little bearing on the facts of the case.

Second, a growing number of thinkers and planners concerned with the elaboration of a community development technology, though sympathetic to the notion that the people should be defining organizational goals, doubt the value of treating that ideological point as a fixed limitation on the organizer's (i.e., the outsider's) role. Miller put it as follows:

> Many social action programs (e.g., Alinsky, Wilcox, Murrow) emphasize that they do not have a program nor provide a direction of action: the people in a neighborhood should decide what they want to do; the task of the action programs is to help in the program that is developed by the neighborhood and to encourage a frame of mind of doing things for oneself, insisting on being heard by the powers-that-be, etc. Obviously, this approach has much to recommend it. . . . But isn't it also a limited approach emphasizing "spontaneity" and "localness"? Are "grass-roots," knowledgeability, and wisdom enough to handle and solve problems? . . . Consequently, the social actionist needs an ideology . . . if that is a disturbing word, then a goal . . . and the willingness to be involved at many levels, not only as a starter or choke but perhaps even at times as a map-reader [13: 1–3].

Third, though not substantial enough a flaw to cast serious doubt on his belief in his own testimony, Alinsky does make one curious remark:

There should not be too much concern with specifics or details of a people's program. The program items are not too significant when one considers the enormous importance of getting people interested and participating in a democratic way [1:79].

The point here is that program goals (with the possible exception of that one elusive, semi-mythical goal that all organizational activity theoretically serves) are themselves also always program means. It seems reasonable, therefore, to consider program goals as being among "the program items [that] are not too significant when one considers the enormous importance of getting people interested and participating in a democratic way." Thus it is possible to conclude that Alinsky leaves goal-setting to the people, not because of some compelling article of the democratic faith, nor even because of the practical argument that only the people are sufficiently wise to perform the task, but simply because it makes no difference what the goals are; they are unimportant. Moreover, in assigning this unimportant task to the people, the organization gains the advantage of high claim to a generally highly esteemed moral point (i.e., being democratic). The crucial activity, however, really is initiating and sustaining a process, and that responsibility is safely in the hands of the Alinsky organizer.

While still avoiding a clear statement of the appropriateness of the organizer as a conscious influence on organizational goals, a recent associate of Alinsky has prescribed a more active role for the organizer than did Alinsky:

An organizer may find it necessary to disagree aggressively with the members, not to convince people of his own point of view on issues, but rather to make it possible to organize, to build effective organization. The people provide the content of action. The organizer has the responsibility to create and maintain the effective democratic structure of action. . . . The organizer, thus, must sometimes assert vigorous, aggressive leadership, even though he is not a member of the organization, and although such leadership should never include projecting his own substantive orientations upon the neighborhood [8:4].

How is change effected? The tactics through which change is achieved can be grouped under two major headings: (*a*) those tactics that contribute to the creation of a group whose major property is power, but which is also presumed to be efficiently and permanently representative of the larger immediate community; and (*b*) those tactics that bespeak the most effective use of the organization's power, understood always as the management of conflict situations so that favorable resolution of the conflict is the most likely outcome. The first set of tactics is largely stated as a series of prescriptive, preferred, and proscriptive guides for the organizer's behavior; the second set of tactics has a similar relationship to the organization's behavior.

In reality, of course, the division is not so neat; nor can it even be allowed to appear as such, since a key assumption of Alinsky's scheme is that the proper curve of the organizer's activity is roughly parabolic, i.e., the organizer more or less quickly rises to a point of his maximum influence only more or less quickly to return this power to the organization itself. Thus the organizer always recruits the original group membership, then turns future recruitment over to those already recruited (a prescribed tactic). Sooner or later the organization must maintain its own strength by winning conflicts, securing high levels of participation, and co-opting or outlasting potential competitors to its local power monopoly.

The list of specific tactics is, of course, never complete. The following tactics, drawn from the writings of Alinsky and his associates (1:99–173), are therefore only a sample:

1. Tactics to build the People's Organization (instructions to the organizer):

   a) Become thoroughly familiar with the traditions, conditions, attitudes of the community through informal, low-keyed movement in the community. Identify the specific problems of concern to the people. Do not rely on the organizer's own judgment of the people's problem, nor turn to agency boards or administrators whose leadership is not based on a local constituency.

   b) Bring the people (or more exactly, their leaders) together. Perform a variety of discrete maneuvers so that the coming together is most likely to result in a commitment either to establish a formal organization or effect some easily consummated social action. Among these discrete maneuvers are included the articulation of general issues of concern to the people, avoidance of supplying program specifics, awakening of emotional support for the organization, making arrangements to facilitate attendance (car pools, baby sitting, etc.), asking action-oriented questions, use of the "program ballot," describing what other organizations in similar circumstances have done, and providing alternative courses of action as content for discussion. Once a decision to act has been made, employ other tactics to make sure that the people's intent is carried out.

2. Tactics for the use of power (instructions to the organization):

   Over time, continuously deepen the commitment to an ever enlarged scope of group action, with special reference to the requirements of a conflict strategy. Some specific recommended tactics are refusing cooperation with the enemy, "having a fight in the bank," "making positives out of negatives" (e.g., Negroes eating watermelon while staging mass protest marches through white residential areas); carrying out a continuous series of campaigns to keep the opposition off balance; and planning campaigns that tap the skills and interests of the widest possible number of persons in the area, etc.

There is no need in Alinsky's scheme for means or techniques to extinguish the immorality, greediness, or other "bad" behaviors of the people. (The technique known as "creating a new social situation," however, might be considered one.) But this is not oversight on Alinsky's part; rather, it is a reflection of his oft-stated belief that, once the people have found their head, things can only, and inevitably do, get better. This inevitability guarantees personal transformations (i.e., malevolent, selfish individuals become benevolent cooperators in waging the good war) as well as group transformations (i.e., narrow, reactionary groups or organizations become progressive, militant bastions of democracy).[7]

[7] "The organizer need not be too concerned at the start about the reactionary policies of individual community agencies. He will find that a mixture of the progressive policies of a progressive People's Organization with the individual con-

How is the community involved in the change process? In Alinsky's scheme, some element in the community must invite Alinsky in and must offer some assurance of community support for the enterprise and provide finances to cover the work to be done for some specified period of time. A group such as a local church may have, in addition, primary connections with other elements beyond the community, but those community groups who enroll in the People's Organization must be willing to give up that part of their sovereignty which overlaps with the program of the People's Organization. A constitution binding all parties to democratic procedures must be drafted and agreed to; it is the social contract that establishes the organization's legitimacy, and its specific items define the eligibility, obligations, limits, and prerogatives of members. The organization's purpose is therein defined as the instrument through which all the people will be united. While not specifically mentioned in the constitution, it is nevertheless clear that affiliation commits the membership to the view that the major strategy to be pursued is to make latent conflicts between the community and its oppressors manifest; the willingness to accept the People's Organization as setting the discipline for managing conflict is implicit and absolutely essential.

An important feature of this "discipline of conflict" strategy is the refusal to enter into alliances. Alinsky's attack on those most likely to be considered as allies has included special classes of persons, such as liberals or intellectuals, and potentially influential programs, such as the war on poverty. Indeed, this is one of the few elements in Alinsky's scheme that he has vociferously kept up to date. His diligence can be likened to that of Madame DeFarge, whose woolly inventory was necessary to insure an absentminded people against a tendency to forget just who their enemies were. An alternate meaning to the purity Alinsky insists upon was provided by Michels in 1915:

> Thus the hatred of the party is directed, not in the first place against the opponents of its own view of the world order, but against the dreaded rivals in the political field, against those who are competing for the same end—power. It is obvious that these are no more than the means vulgarly employed by competitors who wish to steal one another's customers [12:375–76].

Writing as an activist involved in the current scene, Rustin gives still another name to Alinsky's "no-alliance" strategy:

> It is precisely this sense of isolation that gives rise to . . . the tendency within the civil rights movements which, despite its militancy, pursues what I call a "no-win" policy. . . . Spokesmen for this tendency survey the American scene and find no forces prepared to move toward radical solutions. From this they conclude that the only viable strategy is shock; above all, the hypocrisy of white liberals must be exposed. These spokesmen are often described as the radicals of the movement, but they are really its moralists. They seek to change white hearts—by traumatizing them [19:28].

What is required of the change agent? Alinsky organizers need not have any academic preparation, and in practice they have been drawn from all walks of life. Requirements of the organizer are of two dimensions: (*a*) what he must

---

servative policies of a conservative neighborhood agency will result in a progressive product. Experience has shown this to be true no matter how wide a gap previously existed between the two agencies" (1:110–11).

be or believe and (*b*) what he must do. The beliefs that Alinsky delineates for helping the organizer achieve his goals are little more than sentimental absurdities. Thus the organizer "constantly finds his faith in man fortified" (1:114), and he "does what he does because of his love of his fellow men" (1:113); moreover, "frequent demonstrations of brutality, selfishness, hate, greed, avarice, and disloyalty among masses of people do not harden the Radical nor lessen his affection for the people" (1:113), and, as icing for this somewhat silly cake, "the Radical cannot suffer personal defeat because in a sense he is selfless" (1:113).

In the practical realm of action, there are major events for which the organizer is responsible and which, presumably, do hasten the group's process as it moves to a self-controlled and sustained readiness to act on its own behalf. Haggstrom defines the realistic but nevertheless immense demands made for skill as the organizer goes about intervening in the life of the group:

> To build organization in low-income areas is something like playing a long game of blindfold chess in which no player is sure of the rules. The chess pieces move themselves; skillful players help get this movement channeled into planned patterns, strategies, and tactics. There are standard beginning lines (e.g., house meetings versus dramatic large public meetings), and some established principles of play ("rub raw the sores of discontent," "the social situation sets the limits for moves"), but much depends on attention to detail, immense energy, and an individual brilliance in capitalizing on whatever happens. Finally, these chess pieces can throw an ineffective player right out of the game [8:1].

Thus, Alinsky's requirement that the organizer be a saint is modified so that it seems more like the kind of work any immensely skilled, finely tuned artist could perform.

ASSESSMENT OF OUTCOMES

There is little in the literature of community organization which can explain how the benefits of intervention are realized in the larger system with which the worker is concerned. With the exception of sociological analyses like those of Warren, Dahl, and Rossi and Dentler (4, 20, 25), there has been a lack of theoretical propositions about how to assess the results of community organization.

How is outcome assessed? What is success? When does intervention end? Success is assessed subjectively by Alinsky, i.e., someone defines the organization as strong and self-directed enough. While Alinsky does not actually state it this way, it seems to be the most likely deduction possible. The primary concern in Alinsky's work is with the condition of the organization rather than the state of the environmental conditions presumed to have required the creation of the organization. And, of course, change that has occurred without benefit of a People's Organization or without the careful cultivation of conflict is ignored and thus is no embarrassment.

One might also judge success, not on the condition of the group or the external world, but on whether the organizer has performed as well as possible under the circumstances. This would be the case if the group dismissed the organizer or took positive steps that violated the moral or other conditions defined in the written and unwritten contract between Alinsky and the organization, or if the organizer himself judged the situation to have reached a point of intractability. On still other grounds, intervention presumably might end simply because the term of the contract had been reached.

EMPIRICAL VALIDATION

The last category of the paradigm calls for an examination of the empirical status of the theoretical assumptions included in the other three categories. By this is meant the extent to which the propositions used have been verified by the facts of experience.

In Alinsky's case there is only scanty literature on the changes effected by the People's Organizations. However, if one may define "empirical validation" somewhat loosely, the following observations can be made:

1. Both Alinsky critics and Alinsky sympathizers, though in varying degrees, point to local changes that have been effected:

> [Alinsky] organizations have enabled areas to decrease or end exploitation by some absentee landlords and unethical businesses. They have also ended police brutality and secured police protection, street cleaning, and other services which low-income neighborhoods had not previously received at a level equivalent to that of the remainder of the community [9: 222].

2. Alinsky does cite one study to support his claim that People's Organizations produce higher degrees of participation in low-income communities than more traditional organizational forms (1:188–89). In addition, by shifting emphasis, one can claim effect on even greater numbers, as does Haggstrom:

> Many people are swept into action, not by direct active membership in the organization, but through identification with an acting neighborhood-based mass organization. The organizer has succeeded when he has ensured the creation of such a structure which expands the area of freedom for persons in the action area [8: 20].

3. Alinsky's great emphasis on the irreplaceability of indigenous leadership in activating and shaping community effort has found varying degrees of confirmation, or at least support, in the work of organizations committed to community change, such as Mobilization for Youth and the Community Action Program of the War on Poverty. In the case of Mobilization for Youth, which made use of persons representative (in the sense of typical) of the community, problems have developed about maintaining the representative qualities of these persons once they have been made conscious of their leadership positions (7). This outcome suggests a limited viability to the assumption that a single organization or type of organization can plan and engineer a continuing process of community change while maintaining a continuing responsiveness to community residents.

4. Several empirical studies confirm the theory that functional social learning in individuals tends to occur more readily when those individuals have confidence in their capacity to determine the outcome of their lives (e.g., 5). These studies clearly affirm the soundness of Alinsky's major emphasis on participation in the action of a People's Organization as a way of restoring a sense of power to people socially fixed and disabled by their sense of powerlessness. The relationship of powerlessness and social learning, stated so sharply by Alinsky in 1946, has only grown in importance since then. His critics, however, claim that these benefits are only ephemeral because of the failure to change the outside environment, and

thus may lead a more profound sense of the people's pathetic condition.[8]

In summary, one must note that, in spite of the more than two decades of experience in a large number of American cities, Alinsky-style organizations have not brought any results to bear out his faith that low-income groups easily move from expressive to instrumental concerns. Nor is there evidence that the successful consummation of instrumental activities on one level conditions the readiness of low-income groups to move on to higher levels of instrumental action (3). As yet Alinsky's assumption that these things will occur remains only an article of faith.

It is somewhat ironic that, although we have chosen Saul Alinsky's work to illustrate the use of such an analysis, Alinsky himself would probably deny the value of the effort, inasmuch as it is not based on intimate association with him or any of the activities generated by his Industrial Areas Foundation (16). One who leans so heavily on direct observation and "inside" experience is likely to view the theorist as one who sits down at the typewriter to commit an act of foul play.

Another difficulty lies in the nature of Alinsky's material, particularly his major work, *Reveille for Radicals.* It smacks of distortions which reflect, at best, an ingenuousness of monumental proportions or, at worst, a belief that fraud, if it serve the cause, is less than fraud. In a word, the results claimed for Alinsky organizers are often unbelievable, and there is often the imputation of a high degree of effectiveness to his techniques and strategies which is based largely on the loud squeals arising from the "power structure" he has threatened to dethrone. Thus, beliefs that Alinsky has a significant contribution to make to the development of an applied theory of community change are often based on the familiar but flimsy notion that where there is smoke there must be fire.

Although the literature by and about Alinsky and his methods is quite meager, the social unrest of the past decade has given him a new relevance. Some of this is reflected in an accelerated writing program among his followers and other writers in the professional literature (e.g., 8, 9, 22, 23, 24), although the largest supply of descriptive material is still randomly distributed among popular magazines and occasional newspaper accounts.[9]

We have selected Alinsky's work for this analysis because, in spite of the negative aspects stated above, few community organization writers have described their methods and techniques in such particularity and color, or revealed them with such frankness. While glorifying irreverence, Alinsky delights in telling us of his hidden motives. While he is often contradictory and inconsistent, his methods and techniques in community organization are described in a detail which can be matched by very few.

The analytic scheme we have used points up many inconsistencies, ambiguities, and contradictions in Alinsky's method of organizing. It also makes clear that Alinsky has developed many ideas and techniques which are of enor-

[8] "Alinsky-organized movements are bound to lead to frustration because they cannot transcend the immediate object of oppression" (2:104; see also 15:35).

[9] Over the years articles about Saul Alinsky have appeared in *Look, The New Republic, Harper's, Fortune, Saturday Evening Post, National Observer, The Reporter, Commentary,* and elsewhere.

mous utility to community organization practitioners. Most important, a systematic assessment of the theory used in this particular model of practice reveals these strengths and weaknesses. Parallel assessments of other models of community organization practice would, we believe, yield analytic statements that are more comparable than heretofore. An inventory of such statements would constitute a first significant step in the codification of knowledge for community organization practice.

REFERENCES

1. Alinsky, Saul. *Reveille for Radicals*. Chicago: University of Chicago Press, 1946.
2. Aronowitz, Stanley. "Poverty, Politics, and Community Organization." *Studies on the Left* 4, no. 3 (1964): 103–12.
3. Brager, George, and Specht, Harry. "Mobilizing the Poor for Social Action." In *Social Welfare Forum, 1965*. New York: Columbia University Press, 1965.
4. Dahl, Robert A. *Who Governs?* New Haven, Conn.: Yale University Press, 1961.
5. Evans, John W., and Seeman, Melvin. "Alienation and Learning in a Hospital Setting." *American Sociological Review* 27 (December 1962): 772–82.
6. Ford, Donald H., and Urban, Hugh B. *Systems of Psychotherapy: A Comparative Study*. New York: John Wiley & Sons, 1963.
7. Grosser, Charles F. "Local Residents as Mediators between Middle-Class Professional Workers and Lower-Class Clients." *Social Service Review* 40 (March 1966): 56–63.
8. Haggstrom, Warren. "The Organizer." Paper read at the Annual Conference of the Greater Washington Chapter of Americans for Democratic Action, Georgetown University, September 18, 1965.
9. ———. "The Power of the Poor." In *Mental Health of the Poor,* edited by Frank Riessman, Jerome Cohen, and Arthur Pearl. New York: Free Press, 1964.
10. Kramer, Ralph M., and Specht, Harry, eds. *Readings in Community Organization Practice*. Englewood Cliffs, N.J.: Prentice-Hall, 1969.
11. Merton, Robert K. *Social Theory and Social Structure*. Glencoe, Ill.: Free Press, 1957.
12. Michels, Robert. *Political Parties*. New York: Dover Publications, 1959.
13. Miller, S. M. "Social Action Programs: Some Questions." April, 1963. Mimeographed.
14. Polanyi, Karl. "Our Obsolete Market Mentality." *Commentary* 3 (February 1947): 109–17.
15. Riessman, Frank. "Self-Help among the Poor: New Styles of Social Action." *Trans-Action* 2 (September-October 1965): 35.
16. Riessman, Frank, and Alinsky, Saul. Exchange of letters in "Feedback from Our Readers." *Trans-Action* 2 (September-October 1965): 2.
17. Ripple, Lilian. "Problem Identification and Formulation." In *Social Work Research,* edited by Norman A. Polansky. Chicago: University of Chicago Press, 1960.
18. Ross, Murray G. *Community Organization: Theory and Principles*. New York: Harper & Bros., 1955.
19. Rustin, Bayard. "From Protest to Politics." *Commentary* 39 (February 1965): 28.
20. Rossi, Peter H., and Dentler, Robert A. *The Politics of Urban Renewal: The Chicago Findings*. New York: Free Press of Glencoe, 1961.
21. Seeman, Melvin. "On the Meaning of Alienation." *American Sociological Review* 24 (December 1959): 783–91.
22. Sherrard, Thomas, and Murray, Richard. "The Church and Neighborhood Community Organization." *Social Work* 10 (July 1965): 3–14.
23. Silberman, Charles. *Crisis in Black and White*. New York: Random House, 1964.
24. Von Hoffman, Nicholas. "Finding and Making Leaders." New York: Students for a Democratic Society, n.d. Mimeographed.
25. Warren, Roland L. *The Community in America*. Chicago: Rand McNally & Co., 1963.
26. Zetterberg, Hans L. *On Theory and Verification in Sociology*. Totawa, N.J.: Bedminster Press, 1963.

GROUP ACTIVITIES AND ASSIGNMENTS

Building on a previous session of role playing with individual, group, or community problems: Discuss the nature of the problem presented by each member of the triads, formulate an analytic statement related to the individuals modes of communication, his role function, his attitudes about himself and significant others, his strength and weaknesses, the causes of the problem and how he is able to cope with them.

Discuss the problems presented by each individual in your group, formulate a tentative analytic statement related to the effect of the group on the individuals, the roles assumed in the group, the interaction, etc.

Discuss the problem presented by the community group and formulate an analytic statement based on your total impression of the problem and the community or neighborhood.

Write a summary recording of either the individual, group, or community session. Include an analytic statement.

SELECTED BIBLIOGRAPHY

Barnwell, J. E., "Group Methods in Public Welfare," International Journal of Group Psychotherapy, 15 (4), 1965, pp. 446-463.

Brager, George A., "Institutional Change: Perimeters of the Possible," Social Work, 12 (1), 1967, pp. 59-69.

Briar, Scott, "The Family As An Organization: An Approach to Family Diagnosis and Treatment," Social Service Review, 38 (3), 1964, pp. 247-255.

Churchill, S. R., "Social Group Work: A Diagnostic Tool in Child Guidance," American Journal of Orthopsychiatry, 35 (3), 1965, pp. 581-588.

Etzioni, Amitai, "Toward a Theory of Guided Societal Change," Social Casework, 49 (6), 1968, pp. 335-338.

Feldman, R. A., "Determinants and Objectives of Social Group Work Intervention," Social Work Practice, 1967, pp. 34-55.

Galper, J., "Non-Verbal Communication Exercises in Groups," Social Work, 15 (2), 1970, pp. 71-78.

Kramer, R. M., Denton, C., "Organization of a Community Action Program: A Comparative Case Study," Social Work, 12 (4), 1967, pp. 68-80.

Krill, D., "Family Interviewing As An Intake Diagnostic Method," Social Work, 13 (2), 1968, pp. 56-63.

Morris, R., and Randall, O.A., "Planning and Organization of Community Services for the Elderly," Social Work, 10 (1), 1965, pp. 96-102.

Mullen, E. J., "The Relation Between Diagnosis and Treatment in Casework," Social Casework, 50 (4), 1969, pp. 218-226.

Perlman, H. H., "Freud's Contribution to Social Welfare," Social Service Review, 31 (2), 1957, pp. 192-202.

Pruger, Robert and Sprecht, Harry, "Assessing Theoretical Models of Community Organization Practice: Alinsky as a Case in Point," Social Service Review, 43 (2), 1969, pp. 123-135.

Riessman, R., "The Myth of Saul Alinsky," Dissent, July-August, 1967, pp. 469-478.

Solomon, B. B., "Social Group Work in the Adult Outpatient Clinic," Social Work, 13 (4), pp. 55-61.

Vinter, R. D., and Sarri, R. C., "Malperformance in the Public School: A Group Work Approach," Social Work, 10 (1), 1965, pp. 3-13.

INTERVENTION

Data collection and analysis are justifiable only insofar as they contribute to the effectiveness of intervention. No matter how effective a practitioner is at obtaining pertinent information related to the problem and the appropriate systems, and understanding that data through the analytic process, these skills remain academic for the client system unless conscious choices of action are selected and tested for their validity.

Depending on the system with which you are dealing, intervention can begin informally at the data collection stage. The very fact that a worker is forming a relationship with an individual or group by his positive interaction can relieve some of the pressures that an intolerable situation might have precipitated. However the formal intervention occurs only after the data have been collected and analyzed. It is at this point that he is able to identify with more precision, the client system, the action system, and the target system and choose the appropriate level of intervention, his own role and activities. For example, a number of mothers in a neighborhood organization might have expressed concern over their pre-teenaged children sniffing paint in the local park. Presume that after collecting data about the problem the worker finds that the children in the neighborhood do not have opportunities for socialization and developmental type programs and are involved with the paint sniffing more out of boredom and lack of anything positive to do, rather than any severe pathological reason. The client system is the families who have engaged the worker's services and who are the expected beneficiaries of his services. The action system, that is, the system the change agent works with and through to influence the target system, might be the local schools which might initiate some community school projects, the local youth programs which extend their services to make them more accessible to this particular neighborhood. The target system and action system might be a combination of the parents and children, as well as the school system and the youth agency system which are not meeting the needs of the neighborhood.

A number of different roles are suggested as the change agent relates to the different systems. He might assume the role of facilitator as he helps the parents and children express their feelings about the problem; educator as he imparts necessary information to the client system; advocate as he approaches the target system, etc.

Admittedly there are other possible systems that are perhaps more indirectly contributory to this problem, such as the housing system, the welfare system, and the employment system, but it is necessary for the change agent to choose those action and target systems which are immediate and amenable to change efforts.

"Use of Group Techniques with Unwed Mothers and Their Families" by Marguerite Papademetriou, combines crisis intervention theory and family group work techniques to facilitate meaningful communication between unwed mothers and their parents. The techniques are generic, although applied to a particular situation, and the two case histories illustrate the approach very well.

"Group Work with Welfare Recipients" is a brief account of a small group of Black welfare fathers who benefitted from describing their problems in finding employment. The case history is a good example of an action system, i.e., the group being used to effect change in a client system which also happens to be the target system, and changes being made in another target system, the employment service, to accommodate its services to the needs of the welfare client.

"The Use and Misuse of Groups" by Helen Levinson, although primarily a research report on a number of articles that have appeared on groups in social work journals, offers a framework that should be useful for collecting data with a task oriented or developmental group.

The article by Harry Specht and F.P. Purcell, "House on 6th Street," fits very well into the framework and approach of this reader. Their basic thesis is that the social worker should fulfill his professional function and agency responsibility by seeking solutions to social problems through system changes that are not confined to the individual's problems in social functioning. They suggest a generalist's knowledge and skills applied to a number of systems. A case history of a client with a housing problem illustrates the shift in focus from the individual to the group of co-tenants experiencing the same problem, to the housing system which was responsible for the problem.

BY MARGUERITE PAPADEMETRIOU

Use of a Group Technique with Unwed Mothers and Their Families

▪ ***When an illegitimate pregnancy occurs in a middle-class family, it represents an acute crisis situation. The Representative Family Interaction Group, which combines crisis theory and family and group work techniques, has been used in a maternity care agency to facilitate meaningful communication between unwed mothers and their parents. In group discussions involving several families, the therapists attempt to clarify defective communication patterns that exist in these families and to help them develop more effective communication as a means of restoring family equilibrium.*** ▪

FOR ALL FAMILIES an illegitimate pregnancy represents a crisis that disrupts the family structure. When illegitimate pregnancy occurs in middle-class families, however, it is regarded as a symptom of family pathology.[1] A group that combines elements of crisis theory and family and group work techniques is one good way of dealing with these two aspects of the situation. The Representative Family Interaction Group—first tested at Florence Crittenton Services in Houston, Texas—has been used successfully to help unwed mothers and their families gain a more constructive and meaningful intimacy.

Florence Crittenton Services is a multiservice agency that provides outpatient and residential medical care, casework, group discussion, and educational facilities to unmarried parents and their families. It maintains a staff of ten full-time social caseworkers, a psychiatric consultant, and a part-time pastoral counselor. All members of the casework staff have been trained in individual insight-oriented casework. The agency's clientele includes girls who generally range in age from 14 to 21 and come from all socioeconomic levels. Each client and her family is assigned to an individual caseworker and a discussion group. Parents are strongly encouraged to attend weekly parent group meetings, led by a caseworker and a pastoral counselor who function as co-therapists.

MARGUERITE PAPADEMETRIOU, MSW, *is a caseworker at Florence Crittenton Services in Houston, Texas.* *The author wishes to thank Frank Sargent and Lucy Borders for their assistance in preparing this article and Mrs. Marie Jacobson for her help with the dynamics of group process.*

GROUP PROGRAM

Originally, agency staff conceived of the girls' group as a way of supplementing individual casework. The dynamics of group process would offer each member an opportunity for mutual support and provide a situation in which problems that were generic to her situation might be explored. On this basis the "personal growth" discussion group was originated. Each group consisted of eight girls who lived in the maternity residence and a male and a female co-therapist. Girls were recommended for group membership by their caseworkers on the basis of their need for a group experience. Most of the girls were from

[1] Leontine Young, *Out of Wedlock* (New York: McGraw-Hill Book Co., 1954).

Reprinted with permission of the National Association of Social Workers, from SOCIAL WORK, Vol. 16, No. 4, (October 1971), pp. 85-90.

middle-class families, although a few from lower- or upper-class families attended as well. The group met in the residential setting for an hour and a half each week, and the membership was kept open ended because of relatively rapid client turnover.

The group sessions were oriented primarily toward discussion, and the girls were free to bring up any material they wished. The only restriction was that they not discuss content outside the group. The co-therapists functioned as guides, providing insight and understanding whenever possible. Occasionally, role-playing and psychodrama were used when the therapists felt that these tools might help to clarify feelings in a particular situation.[2]

Because the staff wanted to involve parents in the agency's program, they decided to organize a parents' group. It was hoped that the group would offer the parents an opportunity to share honest feelings about their daughters' pregnancies with one another. The aim of the group discussions was to enable the parents to develop heightened self-awareness with regard to their roles, recognize the disruptive effect of their daughters' pregnancies on the family system, and acquire a feeling of solidarity through mutual interaction with other parents who were experiencing the same crisis.

The parents' group met once a week for two hours and a caseworker and a pastoral counselor functioned as co-therapists. The number of sessions was limited to four. Open discussion was the primary technique, but role-playing was also used occasionally. Referrals were made by caseworkers on the basis of the parents' expressed interest in the group, and it was recommended that both parents participate whenever possible.

The therapists noted several recurring themes in both the girls' and parents' groups. Feelings of frustration, isolation, and guilt were expressed frequently and blame and anger often were directed toward various family members. In the opinion of the therapists, one source of these feelings was faulty communication among family members at a time when meaningful communication was necessary. The problem seemed to be caused by lack of knowledge about the essential process of effective communication rather than lack of motivation. For example, comments such as the following were heard frequently: "I want to discuss this with my parents but I can't. They get angry and ask me why it happened" or "I have tried to reach my daughter, but she draws into her shell."

When this information was shared among the therapists, they decided that joint meetings between the girls' and the parents' groups might be helpful. The group situation apparently provided the members with the support they needed to express feelings that might go unsaid in the more traditional forms of family therapy, and it was felt that interaction between the two groups would be beneficial in resolving some of the recurrent themes that could be handled only tangentially in either group alone.

CONJOINT GROUPS

Subsequently, conjoint meetings between the girls' and parents' groups were held weekly for two hours. The number of sessions was limited to four, with an option to continue for two additional sessions if the group desired. Three therapists assisted with the combined group because as many as thirty people frequently attended. In order to acquaint the members with group process, each group met separately at least twice with the coleaders before they were combined. The discussion technique was used and the therapists' role was to clarify and facilitate communication as well as provide insight. It was assumed that girls whose parents were not present could also benefit from the group experience; thus they were allowed to join the conjoint group. For this reason, the group was

[2] William C. Schutz, *Joy* (New York: Grove Press, 1967), pp. 80–90.

named the Representative Family Interaction Group.

The Representative Family Interaction Group has been in existence since November 1969, and the pattern of the meetings has been fairly predictable. During early meetings, the anxiety level of the members is quite high. Although material about the illegitimate pregnancy is shared, it is often heavily veiled and ambiguous. There are frequent discussions about the generation gap and the sexual revolution—led primarily by the parents—and the therapists try to clarify real meaning by bringing out underlying feelings. In essence, the therapists' role is to decontaminate communication so that the group members' words reflect their real attitudes. The girls are encouraged to share their ideas, and the presence of other girls enables them to do so. During later meetings, a noticeable change takes place. A sense of group solidarity has formed and there is a feeling of excitement in the air. Statements are clearer and more direct. Individual family problems are often brought out and sometimes resolved. The quality of communication is generally more appropriate and positive. For example, real feelings are expressed and responses to them are increasingly appropriate. The group experience is intense and rewarding, judging by membership feedback. It is common for those girls whose parents are absent to call their parents after group meetings for the express purpose of making a breakthrough in communication. The members often encourage the sessions to go overtime, and the option of two extra sessions is almost always exercised.

DEFECTIVE COMMUNICATION

The two aspects of an illegitimate pregnancy in a middle-class family—that pregnancy represents a family crisis and is a symptom of family pathology—apparently account for the success of the Representative Family Interaction Group. Ackerman has indicated that a middle-class teen-age girl's sexual delinquency is often symptomatic of family pathology that remains undetected until the crisis of a pregnancy occurs.[3] He suggests that one form this pathology takes is defective communication at home. Based on casework experience, the author assumed that for many families the problem is not a lack of communication as such. Often there is a great deal of communication, but it is defective and distorted. Thus the term "weather family" was coined by the author to describe what takes place in some families. In the weather family there is an unspoken consensus that communication will never go beyond a certain level of intensity. Topics such as fashion, sports, or the weather are safe, but other topics are considered unsafe, e.g., honest feelings of love, anger, happiness, and grief are either heavily veiled or are not expressed at all. This pattern of communication is incorporated into the family structure and often remains consciously undetected by family members unless the family system is disrupted. A family crisis, such as an illegitimate pregnancy, may bring defective communication patterns into sharp painful focus. Although a crisis brings some families closer, the weather family's pattern of communication often is too firmly entrenched to be disrupted.

Crisis has been defined as a stressful event that the individual feels unable to handle on an emotional level.[4] In the Representative Family Interaction Group, the pregnancy is seen as a crisis in which the family communication system is not functional, that is, it does not enable family members to become emotionally accessible to one another. If the family's communication

[3] Nathan W. Ackerman, "Sexual Delinquency Among Middle Class Girls," in Otto Pollack and Alfred S. Friedman, eds., *Family Dynamics and Female Sexual Delinquency* (Palo Alto, Calif.: Science & Behavior Books, 1969).

[4] Martin Strickler and Jean Allgeyer, "The Crisis Group: A New Application of Crisis Theory," *Social Work*, Vol. 12, No. 3 (July 1967), pp. 28–32.

pattern is not altered, the results are frustration and a sense of loneliness for the family's members.

With this view of illegitimate pregnancy, the function of the conjoint group becomes clear. It provides the means whereby families may learn new, more appropriate communication behavior. Hallowitz indicates that focusing on solving real problems is an effective means of helping a family through a crisis.[5] Thus the Representative Family Interaction Group serves to focus on the defective communication process as a real problem that can be handled successfully by a family if its members have an opportunity to learn better ways of communicating. In some instances, family members learn how to communicate better when the therapists and the group decode messages that are sent and inappropriately received in a family system. In other instances, good communication among the therapists in the group's presence serves as a positive model.

Once the group has pointed out the problem of communication, family members can act to bring about communication that results in the kind of familial intimacy necessary for dealing with a crisis. Two cases serve to illustrate the impact this experience has on families in crisis.

JANE X

Jane X, an 18-year-old college student, became pregnant by a young man she barely knew. Although her rather conservative middle-class parents were aghast at her pregnancy, they wished to help her and agreed to pay for her maternity care. Jane expressed pronounced feelings of inferiority and inadequacy in the girls' group. She often expressed anger at her parents, saying that her pregnancy was their fault. Mr. and Mrs. X came to the parents' group in the hope of reaching Jane. It was difficult for them to break through their natural reserve, but their concern for Jane was genuine, although heavily disguised, in references to "the illegitimacy problem."

During the first conjoint meeting, the X family was noticeably hostile. Although most girls sat near their families, Jane chose a seat on the opposite side of the room. At one point, Mrs. X admitted that she was quite angry at Jane because of her pregnancy. When the group pushed Mrs. X to explain what she meant, she expressed her disappointment in Jane and said that the father of the child was the exact opposite of everything she and her husband wanted for their daughter. Jane had been silent up to this point. After hearing her mother's remarks, however, she quietly but bitterly remarked that she had become pregnant because of all the loving attention she had received from her "dear mother." The first attempt at real communication had been made and the therapists tried to define the feeling behind Jane's remark. Although Jane tried to pass over it, the therapists would not allow her to do so. By the second session—with the encouragement of the group—Jane began to describe how lonely she had felt as the middle child. Her sister was the "pretty one" and her brother was the "smart one," but "What am I?" she asked. She had always thought of herself as the odd one in the family, the member who did not belong. Jane's parents were surprised; they had no idea Jane felt that way. Mrs. X said that Jane had seemed embarrassed by affection when she was a child so she had assumed Jane did not want it. Because her other children were more demanding, she had decided that Jane would have to "make it on her own."

During the second and third sessions the exchanges between Jane and her parents were sometimes heated and often painful. For the first time the family members were telling each other honestly how they felt. The other group members and the thera-

[5] David Hallowitz, "The Problem Solving Component in Family Therapy," *Social Casework*, Vol. 51, No. 2 (February 1970), pp. 67–75.

pists encouraged them to express these feelings, and often helped Jane or her parents clarify what they were trying to say. There was a strong current of excitement in the air as the families began to understand what was happening.

By the fourth session the quality of communication in the X family had improved dramatically. They expressed affection for one another, and warm feelings of mutual acceptance were shared by the Xs and other group members. These feelings were genuine because they arose during a meaningful shared experience. The group members felt they had witnessed and participated in something beautiful. During the last session, Jane sat between her parents and looked happy.

What happened to the X family was quite simple. Formerly, the Xs had a set of false assumptions about one another. Jane had assumed that her parents loved her siblings more than they loved her because she had nothing special to offer. Mr. and Mrs. X had been unaware of how desperately she wanted their love and closeness and, assuming that Jane's seeming lack of interest in them was genuine, had tried to respect her wish to be left alone. The group was supportive of the X family's efforts to reach out to one another, and, with the group's help and encouragement, their communication became increasingly direct and distortions in communication were clarified. The result for the Xs was positive acceptance of one another, and they helped some of the other members by example.

ANN Y

Ann Y, whose parents were not present at the meetings, is the second case illustration. Ann was 16 years old and pregnant by a boy she had been dating for two years. Her family situation was a difficult one in which both parents were verbally angry and attacking. When Ann described their vicious fights in detail to the girls' group, the therapists expressed surprise that she could describe such painful material in a detached manner. "Listen," Ann said, "I have been on my own [emotionally] for the last five years. It has not been easy, but I made it by being tough. I never cry—there's no point to it." When Ann expressed her wish to attend the conjoint sessions, the therapists were surprised but were happy to allow her to do so. Ann was the most verbal member of the group and directed many questions to the parents who were present. She was especially interested in their feelings about their daughters' pregnancies. The parents enjoyed Ann and were able to express many feelings to her honestly. Her directness was disarming and they genuinely liked her. Their feelings for her were openly expressed several times. Ann enjoyed the sessions and felt that she had learned a great deal. The therapists did not realize how much Ann had learned until she returned to the residence later for a visit. She told one of the therapists that after her group experience, she wanted "something better" with her parents. When she returned home after the birth of her baby, she made a concerted effort to communicate with them. At first they were resistant, but she kept at it and they began to communicate a little better. "The first time it happened," she said, "I almost cried."

The experiences of the X family and of Ann have not been unique. From questionnaires circulated after each series of meetings, the therapists found that most members thought the group was extremely helpful in providing new insights and they expressed their desire to continue. Caseworkers on the staff have indicated that a large amount of material has carried over from the group to individual casework sessions. The therapists have observed that by the final sessions, communication and familial solidarity have improved, positive and loving feelings are shared among family members (often for the first time), and parents and girls commonly remain after the meeting "just to talk." Parents have indicated that they are able to use what they learned with their other children. Girls whose parents have not been present often take the initiative in improving communication with their own parents. The therapists' general impression is that the Representative Family Interaction Group is a highly useful tool to help families gain a more meaningful family intimacy.

SOME TECHNICAL CONSIDERATIONS

Because the Representative Family Interaction Group technique is still in the experimental stage, several limitations must be recognized: (1) It is not intense family therapy. It is designed to help identify certain family problems, provide new ideas about how a family can communicate more effectively, and offer new insights into the dynamics of illegitimate pregnancy—in a sense, to open certain doors—but it cannot deal with deeply rooted family pathology. It is a crisis-oriented technique that can help to support a family for a brief period of time. For this reason, follow-up counseling and psychiatric referrals must be made available to each family. (2) Communication among the therapists must be of prime importance. Because the group situation emphasizes communication, there must be as little ambiguity as possible among the therapists. Thus regularly scheduled meetings for the group therapists are necessary to analyze transference patterns among themselves and countertransferences to various family members. Of course, group content and group goals also should be discussed and analyzed. (3) Because the group is designed to complement casework, data about group content must be made available to staff members on a weekly basis. Frequent individual discussions between therapists and caseworkers should be held, especially with regard to psychiatric or counseling referrals for families who are in serious difficulty.

Group Work with Welfare Recipients

PHILLIP S. GREEN

The Los Angeles County Department of Public Social Services set up a group work program whose main goals were to increase the effectiveness of social worker and agency intervention, to test the feasibility of using groups as an adjunct to agency services, and to discover additional individual problems that might be dealt with more directly. Desired outcomes for group members —unemployed fathers receiving Aid to Families with Dependent Children (AFDC-UP)—included increased self-esteem, motivation to seek employment, and insight into behavior and attitudes that inhibit effective functioning. The group was viewed as a potential vehicle for gaining additional social skills as well as group feedback and support. Ventilating feelings, trying new roles, and time-limited problem-solving were the methods that were emphasized.

Group members were selected by two methods: (1) submission of the names of two prospective members by each AFDC-UP supervisor and (2) direct contact by the group worker with intake- and AFDC-UP-approved social workers. The first method provided too few prospective members but the second method was effective; it increased direct communication of goals and results to workers and produced a larger list of prospective participants.

The client population—unemployed fathers —was chosen because it was viewed by the agency as one of the most resistant and difficult to help. All the men resided in the Los Angeles Negro ghetto. They ranged in age from 22 to 52, and their problems ranged from lack of skills to police records that inhibited employment prospects.

The eight-member group was heterogeneous in age, police records, family size, and length of status as welfare recipients. However, care was taken to assure common interests and problems, such as feeling unable to find work and being under family pressure to do so, so that the group could quickly assume a purpose and direction. Ten sessions (meeting twice weekly for two hours per session) were established as a maximum. Attendance was regular, with only three absences in the entire period.

As a means of creating an informal and comfortable environment, a small agency conference room was colorfully decorated with posters and pictures. Coffee and cookies were served during each session. The group members reported that they felt welcome, that they were "talking over a cup of coffee," and had never experienced this feeling before in the agency.

The two group leaders began by assuring the members of confidentiality since some stated their fear that what was discussed in the group might affect their eligibility for welfare and their relationship with the agency. In the first session members expressed their negative feelings about the agency. When the leaders accepted these feelings (the men paused after their initial comments to see how the leaders would react), the men relaxed and began to speak openly about their problems and feelings. The group members also expressed distrust of each other. However, after a testing-out period, the group assumed a degree of trust that increased steadily with each meeting.

At the leaders' suggestion, the group decided to adopt two standards—there would be no violence and members would be honest with themselves and each other. Because a democratic framework was established by the leaders (and later rigorously enforced by the entire group), all members began to challenge each other and the leaders. After the first two or three meetings the rules were established and the members' and leaders' roles were clearly defined; then the group was able to establish its purpose and begin the process of problem-solving.

Perhaps one of the most surprising phenomena was the members' enthusiastic discussion of their problems. During the initial and early middle phases of the group the members expressed much anger and despair. However, they also stated they did not realize that anyone else (including the agency) was interested in their feelings or difficulties. By the fifth meet-

Reprinted with permission of the National Association of Social Workers, from SOCIAL WORK, Vol. 15, No. 4, (October 1970), pp. 3-4 ff.

ing they began to verbalize their identification with the group and soon used the group as a place to try out new behavior and social skills.

One of the most important dynamics of the group was the attempt of each member to obtain, retain, and offer acceptance. It was during the middle phase that the members' behavior and perspective began to change. They became more oriented toward planning and appeared more patient. Many moved from an outlook of pessimism and depression to one of optimism, which the leaders continually reinforced.

The leaders' role was complex. They attempted to keep the group moving at a pace comfortable for the majority but also kept the group within the established limits and focus. Many times they would intervene to protect an individual from being unduly or too harshly attacked. Furthermore they acted as facilitators and catalysts. For example, one of the leaders was identified as an expert on employment, the other as a resource for information about community services.

Support of individual effort and change became the most important aspect of the group process. Its effectiveness originated in the cohesiveness, identity, and importance of the group to its members. Group support changed dysfunctional attitudes and values and perpetuated newly gained social skills.

The major themes discussed in the group were as follows:

1. All the group members expressed feelings of racial discrimination during employment interviews. They later became more able to distinguish between actual discrimination and other forms of rejection and when they were using the label "prejudice" as an excuse or crutch.

2. The group discussed the agency's positive and negative features. Some felt they were being dealt with in a demeaning fashion. However, all expressed their understanding of the pressures placed on the agency and its workers.

3. Many expressed discouragement and frustration (which at first results from unsuccessful experiences and later aids in creating them). Group support and ventilation helped to relieve these feelings.

4. The members discussed what changes occurred in their roles as fathers and husbands as a result of their being unemployed. These changes lowered their self-esteem and therefore their motivation. Many felt like "just another child" in their home. Their wives, on the whole, were more suspicious than supportive. When husbands returned from a day of unsuccessful job-hunting, wives often said: "Are you sure you were looking for a job?"

5. Individual problems, such as being over age 45, lacking skills and education, having a police record or physical handicap, served to impede their finding employment and increased feelings of helplessness. In the course of group discussion the members began to increase their self-esteem and find methods, courses, and programs for educational advancement that would change their present situation.

6. Means of interacting and communication of attitudes were other areas discussed. Many members found they were angry with themselves and learned that their anger was often defensively projected onto others. Thus many of the men appeared to have a "chip on their shoulders."

7. Employment-seeking skills were discussed. The employment interview, employment agencies that specialize in assisting men to find jobs, and job training programs were emphasized. The leaders created role-playing situations in which group members played both employers and employees during a structured interview. This technique was particularly useful for practicing new skills in interviewing and in creating a new understanding of role expectations and the problems of the employer as well as the prospective employee. Part of this discussion centered around keeping jobs once they had been obtained.

The following dialogue from the sixth session may further illustrate the group's functioning. Mr. F, a 38-year-old man with a tenth-grade education and a police record, had much difficulty in retaining jobs because of frequent altercations with his supervisors. When he began to discuss his problem in dealing with foremen on the job, the leader placed two chairs in the center of the group and asked if he would like to role-play a discussion about his work with a volunteer from the group playing his foreman. Mr. F agreed and Mr. A volunteered to play the foreman. As soon as the role playing began, Mr. F became caustic and hostile. After the two men finished, the following discussion ensued:

LEADER: Mr. F., is that the way your usual encounters with foremen go?

MR. F: Yea, pretty much that way.

MR. A: No wonder you get into fights and lose jobs! You come on like a mad bull. [The other members agreed.]

MR. F: I don't like nobody to tell me what to do. Everywhere I go there's always somebody telling me to do this or that.

LEADER: Mr. A, how did it feel to be his employer?

MR. A: Scary. [Now looking at Mr. F] You looked like you were going to explode or something. Everytime I tried to say something, you cut me down. Let me tell you, brother, I wouldn't hire you. If you worked for me and acted that way, I would fire you too!

MR. C: You are walking around with a tree-sized chip on you shoulder. [Other members made similar comments.]

MR. F: Are you guys saying that I scare people away? [At this time each member was asked to discuss his feelings toward Mr. F during the role-playing sequence and to suggest other ways he might deal with similar situations.]

LEADER: Mr. F, you said earlier that there's always someone telling you what to do. Is there anyone in particular in your life who does this?

MR. F: Yea, my wife. Especially when I'm not working.

The group then began to discuss the changes unemployment had brought to their roles as fathers and husbands.

Both the leaders and agency staff considered the group project successful. The members gained not only employment-oriented skills, but also more useful attitudes and perspectives. The increase in self-esteem and confidence (resulting from group support) produced higher levels of motivation and persistence. The public assistance workers reported that men who in the past were resistant began calling them for assistance and services.

All group members entered job training programs or found employment. Perhaps the major goal achieved by the group was providing members with new value inputs and significant others in a primary group. Because the group project was considered successful, the agency began to use the group process as a regular modality in its social services program.

BY DANIEL THURSZ

The Arsenal of Social Action Strategies: Options for Social Workers

■ ***According to the author, the desire for social change is not sufficient. Irrationality in social action must be replaced by careful planning as to which strategies are selected to attain specific goals. This paper discusses various social action strategies and suggests significant ethical boundaries. Administrative rule-making and the election process are highlighted as priorities to be considered by social workers.*** ■

VETERAN SOCIAL ACTION leaders in social work have had a somewhat startling experience during the past few years. They have been accustomed to exhorting their fellow professionals, reminding them of the historic antecedents of social work in social reform and the ethical codes they as professional social workers are pledged to support. This effort has met with only partial success over the years, but these veterans have persevered. In most recent times they have had a different experience. They have been confronted by both students and young militants who have been critical of what they regard as the "system." Not satisfied to challenge apathetic social workers to participate in social action, these students and young militants have denounced the veteran group for trying to cope with the problems of the profession and society by fairly traditional and, in their view, unsuccessful means.

According to many of these new critics, there is only one establishment, and the differences that separate many NASW members are blurred, incidental, and not too relevant. As DeMott has pointed out, this is the age of overkill, in which a strange affliction has overcome nearly all forms of verbal expression—a hardening of epithets:

> By the end of the 1960's, the entire articulate Anglo-American community—young, middle-aged, and aged alike—was transformed into a monster chorus of damnation-dealers, its single voice pitched ever at hysterical level, its prime aim to transform every form of discourse into a blast.[1]

The overkill aphorisms stand as shocking evidence of the irrational character of the debates:

> Theodore Roszak proclaims: The world belongs to politics, which is to say the world belongs to death. Robert Welch asserts: The whole country is one vast insane asylum and they're letting the worst patients run the place. Jacques Brel denounces: The middle class are just like pigs, the middle class are just

[1] Benjamin DeMott, "The Age of Overkill," *New York Times Magazine*, May 19, 1968, p. 104.

Reprinted with permission of the National Association of Social Workers, from SOCIAL WORK, Vol. 16, No. 1, January 1971, pp. 27-34.

like pigs. H. Rap Brown accuses: You call yourselves revolutionaries? How many white folks you killed today? And Susan Sontag declares: The white race is the cancer of history. It alone now threatens the very existence of life itself.[2]

In this sort of atmosphere it is difficult to try to cope with the subject of social action strategies without encountering attacks from all sides and risking the possibility of being left without allies. This is especially true when the writer finds himself disagreeing with old-time as well as young professionals. The fact is that one can be disturbed by *both* the apathy toward social action evident in the large part of our profession and by the rash, simple, and at times irrational suggestions from young colleagues.

The purpose of this paper is to discuss the arsenal of social action strategies and the options for social welfare agencies and personnel from two basic points of view: the strategic and the ideological. During the past few years, many social workers have realized that social action is not the antithesis of professionalism and that they and the groups to which they belong must engage in social reform. However, motivation is not sufficient. How a commitment is transformed into an effective program of social action activities depends on an understanding of the process of social action and a careful consideration of the possible boundaries that exist for professional social workers. On examination, some of the boundaries may turn out to be myths. Others may force social workers to reject the options supported by some elements in our society today.

STRATEGIC CONSIDERATIONS

Social action requires a rational, planned approach based on an identification of specific objectives and an analysis of the options available for reaching such objectives. As part of that analysis, the planner needs to examine carefully all the obstacles that conceivably may stand in the way of success and match the specific mechanism contemplated for the social action operation with the area to be tackled.

In a sense the basic method of social action planning does not differ from that required by a military operation. In a military offensive it is fatal to use inadequate or inappropriate weapons or deployment of troops to reach a military objective. It is just as fatal to base a social action operational plan on a commitment to a specific strategy without relating it to its efficacy in achieving the goal. At a now-famous NASW social action workshop, held April 25–27, 1968, a group of members were dissatisfied with a lecture that had repeated many views already stated. During the question period, one person took the microphone and proclaimed: "I didn't come all the way here to sit . . . and listen to speeches. I came here to act. I think we ought to march—I don't care for what—but we should march somewhere for something."

It is this sort of irrational approach to social action that should be deplored. It may provide psychic satisfaction to the persons involved, but it does not contribute at all to the achievement of a goal. One can find faddism in the social action arena as well as in most other fields. At one point it is the "in" thing to march or to sit in; at other points, it is some other technique that wins the enthusiastic approval of the cult. A desire to relate proposed acts to goals does not necessarily mean opposition to militancy.

The criteria needed in examining strategies are clear:

1. What is the goal we have set for ourselves?

2. What are the forces that must be conquered or neutralized before we can reach the objective?

3. What other forces can be brought into a coalition to accomplish our goal?

4. What type of strategy will be most

---

[2] Ibid.

effective in overcoming the opposition? What power can offset the power mobilized against the achievement of the goal?

5. What risks are involved if we are not able to complete the operation as planned?

6. What will be the aftermath of this operation—whether it be successful or unsuccessful?

The criteria ought *not* to be as follows:

1. What will give us the greatest "kick"?

2. How can we get the most publicity (unless this is a specific goal of the operation)?

3. What methodology is "in" today?

Banfield has indicated that every actor—or every system—has a limited stock of power that he gives up piecemeal or spends. He points out that power is like capital; it can either be consumed or invested, and states the following:

> Every actor seeks to maintain or increase his stock of power. . . . An actor exercises power only when he thinks doing so will improve his net power position. When there are alternative investment possibilities, he always chooses the one he thinks will be most profitable. These are the processes by which a good politician decides on his moves. Actions are investments that use up capital. Once used up, that capital cannot be used again.[3]

These are the ways a social action strategist must think. Timing is as important as the appropriate selection of a specific strategy. For instance, a massive march on Washington at a time when Congress and the President are on vacation is hardly an effective plan if the goal is to support a piece of legislation. It is equally absurd to invest in efforts to convince a state senator to support a bill that he has already publicly supported. And it is political suicide to picket or attack friends and neglect enemies. In social action it is important to weigh carefully the ability of the group to carry out a threat or promise made to a local official. Cahn and Cahn stress this need as follows:

> The question of rendering bureaucracy accountable is usually approached as a matter of raw power. This approach simply inquires: what are the sources of pressure that can be brought to bear upon an official or an agency? The traditional answers include direct political pressure, legal pressure, mass demonstrations, public censure—but range to more subtle and sophisticated methods.
>
> Although escalation of a conflict into the bureaucratic equivalent of nuclear warfare may on occasion be necessary, it is rarely, if ever, sufficient. The capacity to escalate is more important than the exercise. A direct power confrontation rapidly depletes the available sources of power. And those reserves, once used, are not readily replenished.[4]

There are many who view mass demonstrations not just as fads or methods for ventilation, but as symbolic rallying tools. One would have no hesitation in supporting such steps if those who planned them were clear about their objective and assessed their cost in terms of power. For example, the writer was a strong supporter of the Poor People's March when it was first announced because of its symbolic value. Yet many supporters wished desperately that the organizers could have been clearer as to the goals and strategies to be used. The obvious lack of rational planning and the absence of any sort of tough analytical appraisal of options lessened the effectiveness of the operation and ultimately destroyed most of its intended mission.

Although a call for reason—for scientific method—may be ignored or regarded as a "cop-out," there may be some comfort in the knowledge that the problem is not limited to those of us who examine options

[3] Edward C. Banfield, *Political Influence: A New Theory of Urban Politics* (New York: Free Press, 1961), p. 312.

[4] Edgar S. Cahn and Jean Camper Cahn, "The New Sovereign Immunity," *Harvard Law Review*, Vol. 81, No. 5 (March 1968), p. 24.

for social action, but extends into other areas—including the arts.[5]

IDEOLOGICAL CONSIDERATIONS

There are certain ideological limits that exist for social workers engaged in social action. Even if a method is certain to bring about the desired goal, it still may not be used. The bases for rejecting a social action method are not the myths that have plagued social action supporters, such as the limits of the Hatch Act or the false issues of the profession's expertise, professional status, or dignity. The decision to participate should be made on more substantial grounds and involves such issues as civil disobedience, the use of violence, and the worker's alliance with clients who may choose more violent actions than he would.[6]

The Hatch Act permits far more political activity by social workers than those who hide behind it have ever realized. Furthermore, social workers need not worry about their professional image if they participate in marches, picket lines, and sit-ins. In most cases, the professional image would be enhanced. Social workers should be aware that the concept of the professional has an important element of individual autonomy. Agency policies cannot control all aspects of a professional's conduct. In brief, whenever appropriate to an objective, the professional social worker ought to use all means at his disposal—including the most militant action. If these means are used to achieve a goal, they become an integral part of his professional role and cannot be seen as separate or in contradiction to it.

Keniston has identified a series of major value changes resulting from World War II. He writes that the impact on young people and our society can be summarized in the names Auschwitz, Hiroshima, and Nuremberg:

> Auschwitz points to the possibility of a civilized nation embarking on a systematized, well organized, and scientific plan of exterminating an entire people. Hiroshima demonstrates how "clean," easy, and impersonal cataclysm could be to those who perpetrate it—and how demonic, sadistic, and brutal to those who experience it. And Nuremberg summarizes the principle that men have an accountability above obedience to national policy, a responsibility to conscience more primary even than fidelity to national law.[7]

It is the Nuremberg lesson that, in this writer's opinion, has unleashed the great force that is causing such deep concern throughout this country as well as the rest of the world. If all men are to behave *not* according to national law, but according to the dictates of their own consciences, then they do not have to cope with the disparity between their views of right and that of the rest of society. The struggle between an individual's perception of justice and the decision of his fellow men does not have to take place. It is an invitation to anarchy.

CIVIL DISOBEDIENCE

There are times when a man is forced to participate in civil disobedience. According to Bay, the term "civil disobedience" refers to any act or process of public defiance of a law or policy enforced by established governmental authorities, insofar as the action is premeditated, understood by the actor to be illegal or of contested legality, and carried out and persisted in for

---

5 For example, when Stanley Kramer met with students and student film makers to discuss his film *Guess Who Is Coming to Dinner?* he found them hostile. *See* Stanley Kramer, "Guess Who Didn't Dig 'Dinner,'" *New York Times,* May 26, 1968, p. D. 21.

6 *See* Daniel Thursz, "Social Action As a Professional Responsibility," *Social Work,* Vol. 11, No. 3 (July 1966), pp. 12–21.

7 Kenneth Keniston, "Youth, Change, and Violence," *American Scholar,* Vol. 37, No. 2 (Spring 1968), pp. 227–245.

limited public ends by way of carefully chosen and limited means.[8]

> The ends of civil disobedience must be public and limited. . . . The ostensible aim cannot be a private or business advantage; it must have some reference to a conception of justice or the common good. The proclaimed ends must be limited too. They must fall short of seeking the complete abolition of the existing legal system. Those who want a non-violent revolution may engage in civil disobedience, but they, too, proclaim *specific limited ends* each time. [Italics added.] [9]

The important aspect of this definition is that civil disobedience is a social action methodology for persons who are willing to accept the system as a whole. It is not a revolutionary methodology. In a classic document, former Supreme Court Justice Fortas stated:

> Civil disobedience, even in its broadest sense, does not apply to efforts to overthrow the Government or to seize control of areas or parts of it by force, or by the use of violence to compel the Government to grant a measure of autonomy to part of its population. These are the programs of revolution.[10]

There are many situations in which social workers may decide consciously to violate laws—because they find the laws to be either immoral or unconstitutional. Laws need to be defied if they are to be tested in the courts on the basis of their constitutionality. But the social worker who participates in civil disobedience—no matter what his motive—needs to be ready to pay the price imposed by society. He cannot request amnesty or claim that his arrest is a violation of his rights as a citizen. Fortas made this point abundantly clear:

> The motive of civil disobedience, whatever its type, does not confer immunity for law violation. Especially if the civil disobedience involves violence or a breach of public order prohibited by statute or ordinance, it is the State's duty to arrest the dissident. If he is properly arrested, charged, and convicted, he should be punished in accordance with the provisions of law, unless the law is invalid in general or as applied.
>
> He may be motivated by the highest moral principles. He may be passionately inspired. He may, indeed, be right in the eyes of history or morality or philosophy. These are not controlling. It is the State's duty to arrest and punish those who violate the laws designed to protect private safety and public order.
>
> . . . . .
>
> The rule of law is the essential condition of individual liberty as it is of the existence of the State.[11]

The phraseology of our day is such that it is easy to confuse concepts. One can be a militant in social action without participating in civil disobedience. One can participate in civil disobedience without engaging in violence. One can support civil disobedience and yet totally reject revolution and violence.

VIOLENCE AND DISRUPTION

The crux of the matter is that a professional social worker cannot and must not condone violence. The destruction of human life as well as the destruction of the ordered democratic society cannot receive his support. Violent activities must be regarded as intolerable regardless of the race, creed, or status of the perpetrators or the justice of their objective.

Perhaps the time has come to proclaim a belief in the "system," imperfect as it may

[8] Christian Bay, "Civil Disobedience, Pre-requisite for Democracy in Mass Society," in David Spitz, ed., *Political Theory and Social Change* (New York: Atherton Press, 1967), p. 166.

[9] Ibid., p. 168.

[10] Abe Fortas, "The Limits of Civil Disobedience," *New York Times Magazine,* May 12, 1968, p. 92.

[11] Ibid., p. 94.

be. That system is the ordered society—a democratic society with established procedures for changing the ways of doing things—one that guarantees to every individual the protection of the state, regardless of his beliefs or actions. It is not a perfect mechanism and the author is willing to struggle through a whole variety of acts to improve it—but he is wedded to it.

There are some today who not only see imperfections, but are convinced that the system is obsolete and cannot work. They wish to punish individuals or groups of people by violence and by usurping their rights. The element of nihilism is found on every campus in this country. There is no substitute system suggested; instead there is a single purpose—the destruction of institutions and the community. This the author rejects—not with blind hatred —but with the clarity of conscience implicit in the following statement:

> Violence is immoral, because it thrives on hatred, rather than love. It destroys community and makes brotherhood impossible. It leaves society in monologue, rather than dialogue. Violence ends by defeating itself. It creates bitterness in the survivors and brutality in the destroyers.[12]

There is another social action technique that has come into vogue. It is not violence and ought not to be confused with it. It is disruption. Again, its efficacy must be determined on the basis of the success it brings to the specific campaign. It often serves to call public attention to a cause and may on some occasions serve as a prelude to new negotiations and advances in the relationship between an institution—public or private—and the population it is expected to serve. Obviously, one cannot generalize about its use. There are some who support disruption for disruption's sake—those whose goal is chaos. Such persons have no interest in the resolution of issues, but only in the destruction of the target institution. Some institutions deserve such treatment—including some social agencies —but escalation of a conflict to the level of a death struggle ought not to be decided glibly and must be clear to all who participate. While there are some who favor conflict for conflict's sake or hold to a revolutionary ethos rejecting the overall "system," Alinsky has pointed out that in a democratic system, conflict must be seen as an essential prelude to consensus.[13]

FADDISM

There was a time when the thing to do was to write letters or send telegrams to congressmen. Then the petition-signing process became the way to try to effect change. Today the arsenal of social action strategies has broadened considerably. Many of the more recent techniques depend for their success on their newness and innovative features. As the methodology is used over and over again, it begins to lose its strength.

In part, this stems from the fact that the countermeasures used by opponents are perfected. In addition, support from the public media is lost when the "happening" ceases to be news. Finally, the public that initially supported the cause and reacted with admiration and surprise at the boldness of the strategy becomes annoyed by either the dullness of the approach or the repetitive barrage. Thus suburban housewives eventually refuse to sign petitions if asked each day and congressmen cease to count them as meaningful; poor people in ghettos get tired of rallies, soundtrucks, and pickets; and, as has been evident in recent conferences, constant interruptions of speakers by a dedicated vociferous group can alienate the audience from the cause and give the speaker who is being attacked far more sympathy than he deservies.

12 Lottie Hoskins, *I Have a Dream: The Quotations of Martin Luther King, Jr.* (New York: Grosset & Dunlap, 1968), p. 147.

13 Stephen C. Rose, "Saul Alinsky and His Critics," *Christianity and Crisis*, Vol. 24, No. 13 (July 20, 1964), pp. 143–152.

To spread garbage on the mayor's lawn to protest the inadequacy of garbage collection in the inner city may dramatize the need to rectify the situation. The question is whether there is any gain to the group involved in seeking change if it constantly resorts to the same technique. There is a need today to find some newer and less traditional ways of expressing militancy and seeking social change.

There are literally hundreds of techniques and strategies that can be used. The arsenal is full. Yet there are two areas in which social workers can be especially helpful. One is a relatively new and virtually ignored area for social action—the administrative watchdog role or "keeping the institution faithful to its mission."[14] The other is old—and yet for a whole host of reasons social workers are still reluctant to enter it in full force—that is, the political arena where votes have the power to change drastically the pattern of life in a community.

WATCHDOG ROLE

Increasingly, the role of the federal government and many state and city agencies is the distribution of funds to achieve a national goal. As Cahn and Cahn indicate, there are many steps in the process: establishing criteria, determining eligibility, assessing capability, evaluating past performance, setting the range of permissible experimentation. By these means, broad legislative mandates are given concreteness; the ambiguous, often contradictory desires of Congress are given content when national goals are translated into specific programs with specific price tags.

> Administrators, in making these complex determinations, have the power to advance or to thwart social goals, to benefit or not to benefit the intended beneficiaries, to realize or to subvert the democratic will as expressed, however imperfectly, in legislative programs.[15]

One of the major problems confronting those who are concerned with social welfare is that major decisions affecting programs and people at the local level are made by inexperienced and often incompetent bureaucrats on the basis of gut reactions. Appeal procedures are not established, rarely discussed, and handled by the officials as if this route constituted high treason to the government as well as to the program in question. Similar concern must be expressed with the rule-writing that follows every piece of legislation at the national, state, or local level.

Keeping the institution faithful to its mission is a task for social welfare professionals. At the least, social action concerns should include the demand that

> . . . every funding agency establish the appeal routes, promulgate procedures to ensure fairness to adjudication and adequacy of review, articulate the grounds for a decision or order to compel consistency with officially stated agency policy, and establish procedures whereby adversely affected parties are afforded opportunity to intervene and present their case.[16]

The Cahns are essentially correct in pointing out that congressmen and senators are subject to pressures from their constituencies while most administrators work in the shadowy never-never lands and are rarely held accountable. The administrators of social programs are excellent targets for those who are concerned with social justice. Their power to impede progress is much greater than most assume.

POLITICAL ARENA

Whether or not social workers agree about specific details, there is consensus that to win the War on Poverty, we need job programs, individual improvement programs,

[14] Cahn and Cahn, op. cit., p. 27.

[15] Ibid.

[16] Ibid.

community betterment programs, and income maintenance. This will require national legislation. Our social action agendas at the state and local levels give a high priority to legislative action and appropriation of funds.

It is the writer's contention that by and large Congress represents the will of the people. This may not be true in the power given to an individual senator regarding a specific piece of legislation, but the mood of Congress parallels closely the mood of the nation. In its value orientation it is for better or worse representative of the people.

If this is the case, then for those of us who are committed to government by the will of the majority—to the essential democratic process—there is no alternative to accepting the challenge of changing the attitudes of the majority. Our black colleagues are correct in suggesting that the task is to confront and deal effectively with white racism. It is not a question of the establishment, a minority that has kept power and dominates the majority. It is much easier to plan a militant strategy to combat bank presidents who will not hire blacks or specific wine companies who exploit migrant workers than to convince the majority of the people to support specific programs. It is, then, not the establishment that must be fought, but the masses of citizens that must be scared, cajoled, convinced, and reformed.

For example, in Maryland liberal forces worked for several years to develop a new constitution. It had the support of influential persons on the Right and the Left and was supported by both political parties. The governor and the Chamber of Commerce, as well as every liberal and radical organization, expressed confidence in the new document. Yet it was defeated at the polls by a 2 to 1 margin.

The common man is common. Democratic rule does not mean wise decisions. This represents the greatest challenge to all who are involved in social action, especially professional social workers who know a good deal about human behavior, social systems, reference groups, and so forth. Can we win the battle at the polls? Can we, through coalitions, hard bargaining, data, policy formulation, courageous leadership, and experimentation, convince the people that our cause is right and that they must elect and support representatives who will vote for what we think this country deserves?

The support of the majority cannot be won by insulting it. Strategies to convince people to reduce prejudice and irrationality must be put to work. The difference between victory and loss at the polls is often counted in terms of minute percentages. Perhaps for all of us it is the polling booth that represents the ultimate test not only of our convictions and our value system, but of our ability to organize effectively for social action.

BY FRANCIS P. PURCELL AND HARRY SPECHT

The House on Sixth Street

THE EXTENT TO WHICH social work can affect the course of social problems has not received the full consideration it deserves.[1] For some time the social work profession has taken account of social problems only as they have become manifest in behavioral pathology. Yet it is becoming increasingly apparent that, even allowing for this limitation, it is often necessary for the same agency or worker to intervene by various methods at various points.

In this paper, the case history of a tenement house in New York City is used to illustrate some of the factors that should be considered in selecting intervention methods. Like all first attempts, the approach described can be found wanting in conceptual clarity and systematization. Yet the vital quality of the effort and its implications for social work practice seem clear.

The case of "The House on Sixth Street" is taken from the files of Mobilization For Youth (MFY), an action-research project that has been in operation since 1962 on New York's Lower East Side.[2] MFY's programs are financed by grants from several public and private sources. The central theoretical contention of MFY is that a major proportion of juvenile delinquency occurs when adolescents from low-income families do not have access to legitimate opportunities by which they can fulfill the aspirations for success they share with all American youth. The action programs of MFY are designed to offer these youths concrete opportunities to offset the debilitating effects of poverty. For example, the employment program helps youngsters ob-

FRANCIS P. PURCELL, MSW, *is now Professor of Social Work, Rutgers University, Graduate School of Social Work, New Brunswick, New Jersey. He was formerly Chief, Training and Personnel, Mobilization For Youth, New York, New York.* **HARRY SPECHT, Ph.D.,** *now Assistant Executive Director, Research Projects, Contra Costa Council of Community Services, Walnut Creek, California, was formerly Assistant Chief, Community Development, Mobilization For Youth.*

[1] Social work practitioners sometimes use the term "social problem" to mean "environmental problem." The sense in which it is used here corresponds to the definition developed by the social sciences. That is, a social problem is a disturbance, deviation, or breakdown in social behavior that (1) involves a considerable number of people and (2) is of serious concern to many in the society. It is social in origin and effect, and is a social responsibility. It represents a discrepancy between social standards and social reality. Also, such socially perceived variations must be viewed as corrigible. *See* Robert K. Merton and Robert A. Nisbet, eds., *Contemporary Social Problems* (New York: Harcourt, Brace, and World, 1961), pp. 6, 701.

[2] A complete case record of the Sixth Street house will be included in a forthcoming publication of Mobilization For Youth.

Reprinted with permission of the National Association of Social Workers, from SOCIAL WORK, Vol. 10, No. 4 (October 1965), pp. 69-75.

tain jobs; other programs attempt to increase opportunities in public schools. In addition, there are group work and recreation programs. A wide variety of services to individuals and families is offered through Neighborhood Service Centers: a homemaking program, a program for released offenders, and a narcotics information center. Legal services, a housing services unit, a special referral unit, and a community development program are among other services that have been developed or made available. Thus, MFY has an unusually wide range of resources for dealing with social problems.

THE PROBLEM

"The House on Sixth Street" became a case when Mrs. Smith came to an MFY Neighborhood Service Center to complain that there had been no gas, electricity, heat, or hot water in her apartment house for more than four weeks. She asked the agency for help. Mrs. Smith was 23 years old, Negro, and the mother of four children, three of whom had been born out of wedlock. At the time she was unmarried and receiving Aid to Families with Dependent Children. She came to the center in desperation because she was unable to run her household without utilities. Her financial resources were exhausted—but not her courage. The Neighborhood Service Center worker decided that in this case the building—the tenants, the landlord, and circumstances affecting their relationships—was of central concern.

A social worker then visited the Sixth Street building with Mrs. Smith and a community worker. Community workers are members of the community organization staff in a program that attempts to encourage residents to take independent social action. Like many members in other MFY programs, community workers are residents of the particular neighborhood. Most of them have little formal education, their special contribution being their ability to relate to and communicate with other residents. Because some of the tenants were Puerto Rican, a Spanish-speaking community worker was chosen to accompany the social worker. His easy manner and knowledge of the neighborhood enabled him and the worker to become involved quickly with the tenants.

Their first visits confirmed Mrs. Smith's charge that the house had been without utilities for more than four weeks. Several months before, the city Rent and Rehabilitation Administration had reduced the rent for each apartment to one dollar a month because the landlord was not providing services. However, this agency was slow to take further action. Eleven families were still living in the building, which had twenty-eight apartments. The landlord owed the electric company several thousand dollars. Therefore, the meters had been removed from the house. Because most of the tenants were welfare clients, the Department of Welfare had "reimbursed" the landlord directly for much of the unpaid electric bill and refused to pay any more money to the electric company. The Department of Welfare was slow in meeting the emergency needs of the tenants. Most of the children (forty-eight from the eleven families in the building) had not been to school for a month because they were ill or lacked proper clothing.

The mothers were tired and demoralized. Dirt and disorganization were increasing daily. The tenants were afraid to sleep at night because the building was infested with rats. There was danger of fire because the tenants had to use candles for light. The seventeen abandoned apartments had been invaded by homeless men and drug addicts. Petty thievery is common in such situations. However, the mothers did not want to seek protection from the police for fear that they would chase away all men who were not part of the families in the building (some of the unmarried mothers had men living with them—one of the few means of protection from physical danger available to these women—even though mothers on public assistance are threatened with loss of income if they are not legally married). The anxiety created by these conditions was intense and disabling.

The workers noted that the mothers were not only anxious but "fighting mad"; not only did they seek immediate relief from their physical dangers and discomforts but they were eager to express their fury at the landlord and the public agencies, which they felt had let them down.

The circumstances described are by no means uncommon, at least not in New York City. Twenty percent of all housing in the city is still unfit, despite all the public and private residential building completed since World War II. At least 277,500 dwellings in New York City need major repairs if they are to become safe and adequate shelters. This means that approximately 500,000 people in the city live in inferior dwelling units and as many as 825,000 people in buildings that are considered unsafe.[3] In 1962 the New York City Bureau of Sanitary Inspections reported that 530 children were bitten by rats in their homes and 198 children were poisoned (nine of them fatally) by nibbling at peeling lead paint, even though the use of lead paint has been illegal in the city for more than ten years. Given the difficulties involved in lodging formal complaints with city agencies, it is safe to assume that unreported incidents of rat bites and lead poisoning far exceed these figures.

The effect of such hardships on children is obvious. Of even greater significance is the sense of powerlessness generated when families go into these struggles barehanded. It is this sense of helplessness in the face of adversity that induces pathological anxiety, intergenerational alienation, and social retreatism. Actual physical impoverishment alone is not nearly so debilitating as poverty attended by a sense of unrelieved impotence that becomes generalized and internalized. The poor then regard much social learning as irrelevant, since they do not believe it can effect any environmental change.[4]

INTERVENTION AND THE SOCIAL SYSTEMS

Selecting a point of intervention in dealing with this problem would have been simpler if the target of change were Mrs. Smith alone, or Mrs. Smith and her co-tenants, the clients in whose behalf intervention was planned. Too often, the client system presenting the problem becomes the major target for intervention, and the intervention method is limited to the one most suitable for that client system. However, Mrs. Smith and the other tenants had a multitude of problems emanating from many sources, any one of which would have warranted the attention of a social agency. The circumstantial fact that in individual contacts an agency that offers services to individuals and families should not be a major factor in determining the method of intervention. Identification of the client merely helps the agency to define goals; other variables are involved in the selection of method. As Burns and Glasser have suggested:

> It may be helpful to consider the primary target of change as distinct from the persons who may be the primary clients. . . . The primary target of change then becomes the human or physical environment toward which professional efforts via direct intervention are aimed in order to facilitate change.[5]

The three major factors that determined

[3] *Facts About Low Income Housing* (New York: Emergency Committee For More Low Income Housing, 1963).

[4] Francis P. Purcell, "The Helping Professions and Problems of the Brief Contact," in Frank Riessman, Jerome Cohen, and Arthur Pearl, eds., *Mental Health of the Poor* (New York: Free Press of Glencoe, 1964), p. 432.

[5] Mary E. Burns and Paul H. Glasser, "Similarities and Differences in Casework and Group Work Practice," *Social Service Review*, Vol. 37, No. 4 (December 1963), p. 423.

MFY's approach to the problem were (1) knowledge of the various social systems within which the social problem was located (i.e., social systems assessment), (2) knowledge of the various methods (including non-social work methods) appropriate for intervention in these different social systems, and (3) the resources available to the agency.[6]

The difficulties of the families in the building were intricately connected with other elements of the social system related to the housing problem. For example, seven different public agencies were involved in maintenance of building services. Later other agencies were involved in relocating the tenants. There is no one agency in New York City that handles all housing problems. Therefore, tenants have little hope of getting help on their own. In order to redress a grievance relating to water supply (which was only one of the building's many problems) it is necessary to know precisely which city department to contact. The following is only a partial listing:

No water—Health Department
Not enough water—Department of Water Supply
No hot water—Buildings Department
Water leaks—Buildings Department
Large water leaks—Department of Water Supply
Water overflowing from apartment above —Police Department
Water sewage in the cellar—Sanitation Department

The task of determining which agencies are responsible for code enforcement in various areas is not simple, and in addition one must know that the benefits and services available for tenants and for the community vary with the course of action chosen. For example, if the building were taken over by the Rent and Rehabilitation Administration under the receivership law, it would be several weeks before services would be re-established, and the tenants would have to remain in the building during its rehabilitation. There would be, however, some compensations: tenants could remain in the neighborhood—indeed, in the same building—and their children would not have to change schools. If, on the other hand, the house were condemned by the Buildings Department, the tenants would have to move, but they would be moved quickly and would receive top relocation priorities and maximum relocation benefits. But once the tenants had been relocated—at city expense—the building could be renovated by the landlord as middle-income housing. In the Sixth Street house, it was suspected that this was the motivation behind the landlord's actions. If the building were condemned and renovated, there would be twenty-eight fewer low-income housing units in the neighborhood.

This is the fate of scores of tenements on the Lower East Side because much new middle-income housing is being built there. Basic services are withheld and tenants are forced to move so that buildings may be renovated for middle-income tenants. Still other buildings are allowed to deteriorate with the expectation that they will be bought by urban renewal agencies.

It is obvious, even limiting analysis to the social systems of one tenement, that the problem is enormous. Although the tenants were the clients in this case, Mrs. Smith, the tenant group, and other community groups were all served at one point or another. It is even conceivable that the landlord might have been selected as the most appropriate recipient of service. Rehabilitation of many slum tenements is at present nearly impossible. Many landlords regard such property purely as an investment. With profit the prime motive, needs of low-income tenants are often overlooked. Under present conditions it is financially impossible for many landlords to correct all the violations in their buildings even

[6] Harry Specht and Frank Riessman, "Some Notes on a Model for an Integrated Social Work Approach to Social Problems" (New York: Mobilization For Youth, June 1963). (Mimeographed.)

if they wanted to. If the social worker chose to intervene at this level of the problem, he might apply to the Municipal Loan Fund, make arrangements with unions for the use of non-union labor in limited rehabilitation projects, or provide expert consultants on reconstruction. These tasks would require social workers to have knowledge similar to that of city planners. If the problems of landlords were not selected as a major point of intervention, they would still have to be considered at some time since they are an integral part of the social context within which this problem exists.

A correct definition of interacting social systems or of the social worker's choice of methods and points of intervention is not the prime concern here. What is to be emphasized is what this case so clearly demonstrates: that although the needs of the client system enable the agency to define its goals, the points and methods of intervention cannot be selected properly without an awareness and substantial knowledge of the social systems within which the problem is rooted.

DEALING WITH THE PROBLEM

The social worker remained with the building throughout a four-month period. In order to deal effectively with the problem, he had to make use of all the social work methods as well as the special talents of a community worker, lawyer, city planner, and various civil rights organizations. The social worker and the community worker functioned as generalists with both individuals and families calling on caseworkers as needed for specialized services or at especially trying times, such as during the first week and when the families were relocated. Because of the division of labor in the agency, much of the social work with individuals was done with the help of a caseworker. Group work, administration, and community organization were handled by the social worker, who had been trained in community organization. In many instances he also dealt with the mothers as individuals, as they encountered one stressful situation after another. Agency caseworkers also provided immediate and concrete assistance to individual families, such as small financial grants, medical care, homemaking services, baby-sitting services, and transportation. This reduced the intensity of pressures on these families. Caseworkers were especially helpful in dealing with some of the knotty and highly technical problems connected with public agencies.

With a caseworker and a lawyer experienced in handling tenement cases, the social worker began to help the families organize their demands for the services and utilities to which they were legally entitled but which the public agencies had consistently failed to provide for them.

The ability of the mothers to take concerted group action was evident from the beginning, and Mrs. Smith proved to be a natural and competent leader. With support, encouragement, and assistance from the staff, the mothers became articulate and effective in negotiating with the various agencies involved. In turn, the interest and concern of the agencies increased markedly when the mothers began to visit them, make frequent telephone calls, and send letters and telegrams to them and to politicians demanding action.

With the lawyer and a city planner (an agency consultant), the mothers and staff members explored various possible solutions to the housing problem. For example, the Department of Welfare had offered to move the families to shelters or hotels. Neither alternative was acceptable to the mothers. Shelters were ruled out because they would not consider splitting up their families, and they rejected hotels because they had discovered from previous experience that many of the "hotels" selected were flop-houses or were inhabited by prostitutes.

The following is taken from the social worker's record during the first week:

Met with the remaining tenants, several

Negro men from the block, and [the city planner]. . . . Three of the mothers said that they would sooner sleep out on the street than go to the Welfare shelter. If nothing else, they felt that this would be a way of protesting their plight . . . One of the mothers said that they couldn't very well do this with most of the children having colds. Mrs. Brown thought that they might do better to ask Reverend Jones if they could move into the cellar of his church temporarily. . . . The other mothers got quite excited about this idea because they thought that the church basement would make excellent living quarters.

After a discussion as to whether the mothers would benefit from embarrassing the public agencies by dramatically exposing their inadequacies, the mothers decided to move into the nearby church. They asked the worker to attempt to have their building condemned. At another meeting, attended by tenants from neighboring buildings and representatives of other local groups, it was concluded that what had happened to the Sixth Street building was a result of discrimination against the tenants as Puerto Ricans and Negroes. The group—which had now become an organization—sent the following telegram to city, state, and federal officials:

> We are voters and Puerto Rican and Negro mothers asking for equal rights, for decent housing and enough room. Building has broken windows, no gas or electricity for four weeks, no heat or hot water, holes in floors, loose wiring. Twelve of forty-eight children in building sick. Welfare doctors refuse to walk up dark stairs. Are we human or what? Should innocent children suffer for landlords' brutality and city and state neglect? We are tired of being told to wait with children ill and unable to attend school. Negro and Puerto Rican tenants are forced out while buildings next door are renovated at high rents. We are not being treated as human beings.

For the most part, the lawyer and city planner stayed in the background, acting only as consultants. But as the tenants and worker became more involved with the courts and as other organizations entered the fight, the lawyer and city planner played a more active and direct role.

RESULTANT SIDE-EFFECTS

During this process, tenants in other buildings on the block became more alert to similar problems in their buildings. With the help of the community development staff and the housing consultant, local groups and organizations such as tenants' councils and the local chapter of the Congress of Racial Equality were enlisted to support and work with the mothers.

Some of the city agencies behaved as though MFY had engineered the entire scheme to embarrass them—steadfastly disregarding the fact that the building had been unlivable for many months. Needless to say, the public agencies are overloaded and have inadequate resources. As has been documented, many such bureaucracies develop an amazing insensitivity to the needs of their clients.[7] In this case, the MFY social worker believed that the tenants—and other people in their plight—should make their needs known to the agencies and to the public at large. He knew that when these expressions of need are backed by power—either in numbers or in political knowledge—they are far more likely to have some effect.

Other movements in the city at this time gave encouragement and direction to the people in the community. The March on Washington and the Harlem rent strike are two such actions.

By the time the families had been relocated, several things had been accomplished. Some of the public agencies had

---

[7] *See,* for example, Reinhard Bendix, "Bureaucracy and the Problem of Power," in Robert K. Merton, Alisa Gray, Barbara Hockey, and Horan C. Sebrin, eds., *Reader in Bureaucracy* (Glencoe, Ill.: Free Press, 1952), pp. 114–134.

been sufficiently moved by the actions of the families and the local organizations to provide better services for them. When the families refused to relocate in a shelter and moved into a neighborhood church instead, one of the television networks picked up their story. Officials in the housing agencies came to investigate and several local politicians lent the tenants their support. Most important, several weeks after the tenants moved into the church, a bill was passed by the city council designed to prevent some of the abuses that the landlord had practiced with impunity. The councilman who sponsored the new law referred to the house on Sixth Street to support his argument.

Nevertheless, the problems that remain far outweigh the accomplishments. A disappointing epilogue to the story is that in court, two months later, the tenants' case against the landlord was dismissed by the judge on a legal technicality. The judge ruled that because the electric company had removed the meters from the building it was impossible for the landlord to provide services.

Some of the tenants were relocated out of the neighborhood and some in housing almost as poor as that they had left. The organization that began to develop in the neighborhood has continued to grow, but it is a painstaking job. The fact that the poor have the strength to continue to struggle for better living conditions is something to wonder at and admire.

IMPLICATIONS FOR PRACTICE

Social work helping methods as currently classified are so inextricably interwoven in practice that it no longer seems valid to think of a generic practice as consisting of the application of casework, group work, or community organization skills as the nature of the problem demands. Nor does it seem feasible to adapt group methods for traditional casework problems or to use group work skills in community organization or community organization method in casework. Such suggestions—when they appear in the literature—either reflect confusion or, what is worse, suggest that no clearcut method exists apart from the auspices that support it.

In this case it is a manifestation of a social problem—housing—that was the major point around which social services were organized. The social worker's major intellectual task was to select the points at which the agency could intervene in the problem and the appropriate methods to use. It seems abundantly clear that in order to select appropriate points of intervention the social worker need not only understand individual patterns of response, but the nature of the social conditions that are the context in which behavior occurs. As this case makes evident, the social system that might be called the "poverty system" is enduring and persistent. Its parts intermesh with precision and disturbing complementarity. Intentionally or not, a function is thereby maintained that produces severe social and economic deprivation. Certain groups profit enormously from the maintenance of this system, but larger groups suffer. Social welfare—and, in particular, its central profession, social work—must examine the part it plays in either maintaining or undermining this socially pernicious poverty system. It is important that the social work profession no longer regard social conditions as immutable and a social reality to be accommodated as service is provided to deprived persons with an ever increasing refinement of technique. Means should be developed whereby agencies can affect social problems more directly, especially through institutional (organizational) change.

The idea advanced by MFY is that the social worker should fulfill his professional function and agency responsibility by seeking a solution to social problems through institutional change rather than by focusing on individual problems in social functioning. This is not to say that individual expressions of a given social problem should be left unattended. On the contrary, this approach is predicated on the belief that individual problems in social functioning are to varying degrees both cause and effect. It rejects the notion that individuals are afflicted with social pathologies, holding, rather, that the same social environment that generates conformity makes payment by the deviance that emerges. As Nisbet points out ". . . socially prized arrangements and values in society can produce socially condemned results." [8] This should direct social work's attention to institutional arrangements and their consequences. This approach does not lose sight of the individual or group, since the social system is composed of various statuses, roles, and classes. It takes cognizance of the systemic relationship of the various parts of the social system, including the client. It recognizes that efforts to deal with one social problem frequently generate others with debilitating results.

Thus it is that such institutional arrangements as public assistance, state prisons, and state mental hospitals, or slum schools are regarded by many as social problems in their own right. The social problems of poverty, criminality, mental illness, and failure to learn that were to be solved or relieved remain, and the proposed solutions pose almost equally egregious problems.

This paper has presented a new approach to social work practice. The knowledge, values, attitudes, and skills were derived from a generalist approach to social work. Agencies that direct their energies to social problems by effecting institutional change will need professional workers whose skills cut across the broad spectrum of social work knowledge.

[8] Merton and Nisbet, *op. cit.*, p. 7.

GROUP ACTIVITIES AND ASSIGNMENTS

Role play the following situations and choose the appropriate level or levels of intervention:

> As a community worker for a poverty agency in the inner city, you discover through a number of door-to-door interviews that welfare recipients are having a difficult time paying their utility bills.
>
> As a service worker for the Welfare Department a number of mothers on your "caseload" have expressed anxieties about their pre-teenage children who are sniffing paint in a park in the area to which you are assigned.
>
> As a juvenile probation officer a number of mothers whose teenagers you are responsible for, have expressed fears because of harassment from their former husbands, and unresponsiveness from the police when called to protect their safety.

Write a plan for intervention based on the data you have collected and analyzed in one of the above situations.

SELECTED BIBLIOGRAPHY

Aronson, H., and Overall, B., "Treatment Expectations of Patients in Two Social Classes," Social Work, 11 (1), 1966, pp. 35-41.

Baldin, K., "Crisis Focused Casework in a Child Guidance Clinic," Social Casework, 49 (1), 1968, pp. 28-34.

Boehm, Werner, "Toward New Models of Social Work Practice," Social Work Practice, 1967, pp. 3-18.

Brager, G. A. and Jorrin, V., "Bargaining: A Method in Community Change," Social Work, 14 (4), 1969, pp. 73-83.

DePalma, Donald, "A Work Group Model for Social Work Intervention," Social Casework, 51 (2), 1970, pp. 91-94.

Erlich, John, "The Turned-On Generation: New Antiestablishment Action Roles," Social Work, 16 (4), 1971, pp. 22-27.

Feldman, R. A., "The World of Social Group Work," Social Work Practice, 1968, pp. 77-93.

Frey, L. A., "A Social Groupwork Approach to Socially Disadvantaged Girls in a School," Child Welfare, 44 (10), 1965, pp. 563-569.

Garvin, Charles, and Glasser, Paul, "The Bases of Social Treatment," Social Work Practice, 1970, pp. 149-177.

Gottlieb, W. and Stanley, J., "Mutual Goals and Goal Setting in Casework," Social Casework, 48 (8), 1967, pp. 471-481.

MacRae, R. H., "Social Work and Social Action," Social Service Review, 40 (1), 1966, pp. 1-7.

Oppenheimer, J. R., "Use of Crisis Intervention in Casework with the Cancer Patient and His Family," Social Work, 12 (2), 1967, pp. 44-52.

Parad, H. J., "The Use of Time Limited Crisis Intervention in Community Mental Health Programming," Social Service Review, 40 (3), 1966, pp. 275-282.

Radin, Norma, "Preventive Intervention with Low Income Families Through the School," Social Work Practice, 1970, pp. 183-197.

Selby, Lola, "Supportive Treatment: The Development of a Concept and a Helping Method," Social Service Review, 30 (4), 1956, pp. 400-414.

Strauss, E. T., "The Caseworker Deals with Employment Problems," Social Casework, 32 (11), 1951, pp. 388-392.

Sunley, Robert, "Family Advocacy: From Case to Cause," Social Casework, 44 (2), 1970, pp. 347-357.

Taylor, Robert, "The Social Control Function in Casework," Social Casework, 39 (1), 1958, pp. 17-21.

Thomas, Edwin, "Selected Sociobehavioral Techniques and Principles: An Approach to Interpersonal Help," Social Work, 13 (1), 1968, pp. 12-26.

Thursz, Daniel, "The Arsenal of Social Action Strategies: Option for Social Workers," Social Work, 16 (1), 1971, pp. 27-34.

Turner, John, "In Response to Change: Social Work at the Crossroad," Social Work, 13 (3), 1968, pp. 7-15.

Van Til, Jon, "Reconstruction and Redistribution: Which Way for Welfare Rights?," Social Work, 16 (4), 1971, pp. 58-62.

Warren, Roland, "Change By Conflict," Canadian Welfare, 44 (May-June), 1968, pp. 4-7.

Wineman, David and James, Adrienne, "The Advocacy Challenge to Schools of Social Work," Social Work, 13 (2), 1968, pp. 23-32.

Wyers, Norman, "Adaptations of the Social Group Work Method," Social Casework, 50 (10), 1969, pp. 513-518.